The Ancient Routes of the Deccan and the Southern Peninsula

Dilip K. Chakrabarti

The Ancient Routes of the Deccan and the Southern Peninsula

ARYAN BOOKS INTERNATIONAL
New Delhi

THE ANCIENT ROUTES OF THE DECCAN AND
THE SOUTHERN PENINSULA

ISBN: 978-81-7305-389-4

Published in **2010** by:
ARYAN BOOKS INTERNATIONAL
Pooja Apartments, 4B, Ansari Road, New Delhi - 110 002 (India)
Tel.: 23287589, 23255799; Fax: 91-11-23270385
E-mail: aryanbooks@vsnl.com, aryanbooks@gmail.com

Computer Typeset and Printed in India at
ABI Prints & Publishing Co., New Delhi

For

Brij Mohan Pande,

in acknowledgement of a friendship since 1964 and
his contribution to the Indus studies;

Rakesh Tewari,

in acknowledgement of our long field-association and
the significance of his excavations at
Raja Nal-ka-Tila, Malhar, Kalpi, Dadupur and Lohuradeva,
and explorations in the Sonabhadra plateau.

Preface

This volume is rooted in my field-study (1999-2002) of the ancient routes, which linked the Ganga plain with the Deccan. The result was published in 2005 as *The Archaeology of the Deccan Routes* (Delhi: Munshiram Manoharlal). In this volume, based on a field-study in 2004-2006, I have traced the web of routes which linked the Konkan coast and its Maharashtra hinterland with a vast region from the mouth of the Godavari to the tip of the southern peninsula. I have also noticed how the various parts of the southern peninsula were mutually connected. These two field-studies (1999-2002 and 2004-2006) thus demonstrate the way in which the whole of the region south of the Ganga plain was integrated into a communication network with the long arc of this plain.

The communication network is a major theme of my field-studies in the Ganga plain between the Bhagirathi delta in West Bengal to the foothills of Uttarakhand: *Archaeological Geography of the Ganga Plain: The Lower and the Middle Ganga* (Delhi 2001: Permanent Black) and *Archaeological Geography of the Ganga Plain: The Upper Ganga (Oudh, Rohilkhand and the Doab)* (Delhi 2007: Munshiram Manoharlal). In 2006-2008, the work was extended to the area between the Yamuna and the Ravi, i.e., Haryana and the Indian part of Panjab right up to the boundary with Pakistan (*The Problem of the Sarasvati River and Notes on the Archaeological Geography of Haryana and Indian Panjab*; with Sukhdev Saini; Delhi 2009: Aryan Books).

Some major regions still remain largely unstudied from this point of view, which include Rajasthan, Gujarat, Orissa and the whole of the northeastern region. Even in the areas which I have extensively studied in the field, what I have been able to achieve is only a scaffolding – hopefully a secure and dependable scaffolding, but still a scaffolding. One hopes that there will come a time when the communication network of ancient India can be spelled out in much greater detail on the ground than I have been able to achieve with my limited time and resources.

The financial grant to carry out the field-work came from the McDonald Institute for Archaeological Research, and the travel fund of Cambridge University. In 2004 we received logistical support in Mumbai from my brother Shri Ajay Kumar Chakrabarti of the Nuclear Power Corporation and his wife Prof. Mahua Chakrabarti of the Victoria Jubilee Training Institute. But for the support and guidance of Shri C.B. Patil of the Archaeological Survey of India, Bangalore, we would not have been able to study all the Asokan rock edict sites in Karnataka in 2004. We were helped in every possible way in 2005 by Prof. K. Rajan (currently at the Central University, Pondicherry; then at Thanjavur University), Dr. N. Athiyaman (Thanjavur University) and Dr. B. Sasisekeran (National Institute of Ocean Technology, Chennai). Prof. Rajan and Dr. Athiyaman were in the field with us, and Dr. B. Sasisekeran was singularly helpful in Chennai. Prof. K.P. Rao of the Central University, Hyderabad, was constantly in the field with us in 2006. Prof. Selvakumar (currently of Thanjavur University) took us to the site of Pattinam in Kerala.

I gratefully acknowledge the warm hospitality that we received from Prof. Rajan's friends at Thandikudi in Tamil Nadu, Shri C.B. Patil's family and friends at Kopbal in Karnataka, and Prof. K.P. Rao's family at Amalapuram in the Konasamudram delta of Andhra.

Dr. Rakesh Tewari (2004-2005), Director of the Uttar Pradesh State Archaeological Department, and Dr. R.N. Singh (2004-2006), Reader in the Department of Ancient Indian History, Culture and Archaeology of Banaras Hindu University kindly provided me with constant support in the field. My wife Sima and daughter Nayana were also with me in the field during all the three seasons. Nayana took down my field-dictations and was responsible for a lot of photography. Somewhere in the Rayalseema section of Andhra, she was thrilled to find a village called 'Nayanapalli'.

I am aware that there has been no uniformity in my rendering of place-names in this volume. The old names occur frequently alongside their modern versions.

Dilip K Chakrabarti

Contents

List of Illustrations

MAPS

PLATES

The Konkan Coast and the Related Areas

I. INTRODUCTION: THE KONKAN COAST, AND A NOTE ON ITS MARITIME HISTORY

The purpose of this chapter is two-fold: (1) to outline the geographical, historical and archaeological details of the coastal region from the Umbergaon - Sanjan section of the Valshad district of southern Gujarat to Mangalore in the South Kanara district of Karnataka, and (2) to examine how the passes across the Western Ghats, which link this coast with its hinterland, primarily in Maharashtra and Karnataka, form part of the historical network of routes of those regions.

In its section on the history of Konkan, the first volume of *The Gazetteer of the Bombay Presidency* defines Konkan as the coastal strip at the foot of the Western Ghats from Daman or the Damanganga River in the north to the Terekhol at the southern border of the Ratnagiri district of Maharashtra with Goa. Little more than 500 km long, this stretch of India's west coast varies in width from about 50 to 100 km. This gazetteer's description of north and south Konkan is brisk and pointed:

> North of Bombay the coast is low and sandy, containing in many places great expanses of salt swamp, the rivers few and shallow, and the harbours insignificant. South of Bombay the coast is bold with a line of hills often bordering the sea, never receding more than two or three miles from it; there are many navigable rivers and commodious harbours, and in most parts deep water near the shore. At various places along the coast are small rocky islands, generally within a quarter of a mile of the mainland, and which were in earlier times, and especially under the Marathas, fortified and highly valued.... Passing inland, the North Konkan is less

> rugged, and contains far more arable land though a thinner population than the South Konkan, which is, speaking generally, a rocky plateau slightly elevated, and from want of soil exceedingly sterile. But it is intersected by many great rivers and arms of the sea, and the valleys through which these and their tributary streams flow, partly make up by their fertility for the barrenness of the surrounding plateaux. The North Konkan is still in most parts well wooded, and in the coast districts the Palmyra and the date palm spring up spontaneously in every direction. Parts of the Southern Konkan are also well covered with trees, though, from the nature of the soil, many parts are bare. On this part of the coast neither Palmyra nor date tree is seen, but their place is better supplied by great groves of coconut trees planted all along the sandy parts of the coast and the banks of the creeks (*Gaz. Bomb. Presidency* [hereafter cited as *GZB*], vol. 1, section on the history of Konkan, pp. x-xi).

C.D. Despande, the author of *Geography of Maharashtra* (Deshpande 1971), takes his cue from the above-mentioned gazetteer and limits Konkan to the coastal stretch of only modern Maharashtra. From this point of view the British Indian districts of Thana, Kolaba and Ratnagiri and the Bombay metropolitan area constitute the Konkan coast.

In his chapter on political history in the *Gazetteer of the Bombay Presidency*, vol. 1, part 2, J.F. Fleet draws attention to the fact that the Aihole inscription (AD 634-635) of the Western Chalukyan king Pulakesin II refers to Konkan in plural – *Konkaneshu*, i.e., 'in the Konkanas' (*GZB*, vol. 1, part 2, pp. 282-283, note 5). His review of the relevant literary sources, which are not always properly dated or even unambiguous regarding their testimony, leads him to divide the Konkan area into the following segments: North Kanara, Goa, Ratnagiri-Sawantbadi, and Alibag to Thana. He goes on to add that the subject is capable of further elucidation, provided Konkan is held to extend up to Kerala or the former princely states of Travancore and Cochin. In that case the divisions of Konkan would correspond to Travancore and Cochin, Malabar, South Kanara, North Kanara, Goa, Ratnagiri and Kolaba, Thana and Surat, virtually the whole sweep of the west coast from Daman downward.

The Konkan Railway section of the Indian Railways covers the distance between Mumbai and Mangalore, and there are at least two justifications to extend the meaning of the term 'Konkan' to include Goa and the coastal stretch of Karnataka. First, the character of the coastline does not significantly change throughout this extended region. In the whole of the distance from the Umbergaon-Sanjan part of northern Maharashtra to Mangalore in Karnataka, the spine of the coastline is the Western Ghats which, either in the form of transverse ridges or in the form of lateritic table-lands, are never far from the sea-shore. Secondly, the Konkani language is widely spoken throughout the belt.

The main Konkan rivers in Maharashtra are the Vaitarna, Ulhas, Savitri and Vashishti. Goa has a coastline of about 100 km and is crossed by a number of rivers originating in the Western Ghats – Mandovi, Zuari, Terekhol, Chapora, Betul, and others. Up to Mangalore or a little further south, Karnataka has a coastline of about 320 km, with 48-64 km width. All of it falls in the two sections of North Kanara and South Kanara. In all, the length of the coastline from Umbergaon-Sanjan to Mangalore is about 900 km. The Western Ghats form its backdrop throughout, but around Mangalore it recedes somewhat from the coast and continues to join the Eastern Ghats near the Nilgiri hills further south.

H.C. Raychaudhuri (1960) points out the different contexts of the ancient references to the geographical term *Konkana* and the related *Aparanta*. The drift of his textual and epigraphic reference is that *Aparanta* denoted the present-day Thana district north of Mumbai but south of Daman. *Konkana* appears as the administrative unit of *Vishaya* in a grant of the king Mangalesa (AD 597-609) of the Chalukyan dynasty and has been identified as covering the present Ratnagiri district. However, in about AD 1112, another epigraphic record mentions the state of Konkana or *Konkana-Rashtra* in the geographical context of Gokarna, a place in the modern North Kanara district of Karnataka. Possibly a still later source includes even Kerala in Konkan. There is no doubt that in the ancient context *Konkana* has meant the better part of the western coastal rim of India.

Raychaudhuri also draws attention to the concept of 'greater Konkan', a concept which he seems to have derived from Fleet's discussion on Konkan on the basis of a pre-modern *Malayalam Dictionary*. Greater Konkan would mean not only Konkan proper but also Karad in Satara, Virata or Hangal in Dharwar, Maratha country or the area around Pune, Havyaga (probably North Kanara), Tauluva (South Kanara), Kerala, and Malabar. The collective epigraphic evidence points out, according to Raychaudhuri, the following divisions of Konkan:

1. *Payve, Hayve* or *Haive five hundred* (North Kanara)
2. *Konkana Nine hundred* or Goa
3. *Revatidvipa* or Redi, a fortified promontory 8 miles south of Vengurla in Ratnagiri
4. *Irridige country* or Sawantwadi-Ratnagiri
5. *Konkana fourteen hundred* with Puri as the chief city (including *Shatshashti Vishaya* or Salsette) – parts of Thana and Kolaba districts (including Sopara and Chaul)

6. *Kapardikadvipa* or *Karadidvipa,* which possibly means the same area as *Konkana fourteen hundred*
7. *Lata,* including *Variavi hundred and sixteen,* broadly Surat and Navsari.

It is well-known that this coastal rim has enjoyed a traditional importance in Indian history as one of the most important areas of maritime trade in the country from the Mauryan period in the third century BC to the domination of the Maratha power in the region, which ended only in the early nineteenth century. The historical dimension of this trade is no doubt vast and scattered in a variety of sources, but perhaps one of its important aspects was the chain of different historically recorded pre-industrial ports in the 900-odd km stretch from Umbergaon to Mangalore. An enumeration may be attempted with reference to their locations, historical character and the basic information available on them in the different relevant district gazetteers and other sources. The data, although uneven, can indicate both the richness and complexity of the maritime and inland trade of the entire region. Apart from the brief details and the limited amount of excavated data on only a handful of them, we shall focus on the related communication corridors through the Western Ghats and their links with the centres of economic and political powers in both inland Maharashtra and Karnataka.

An important feature of this coastline, apart from a profusion of pre-industrial ports, is the presence of numerous forts which were meant to control and protect these ports: "in some parts every rock and promontory, mountain and hill, were fortified" (*GZB*, vol. 1, p. xii). In their present ruinous states, they date mostly from the Maratha period, i.e., the first half of the 18th century AD, but are rooted quite clearly in the earlier Portuguese presence in the region. Many of the Portuguese forts fell to the Marathas. In some cases the Portuguese are likely to have taken over the Mughal or still earlier Muslim period forts, but whether there is a core of forts established by the different pre-Muslim dynasties of the region is uncertain. However, the way these forts have dotted the coastline and the routes to the interior is a sure indication of the traditional importance of maritime and inland trade of this region.

A number of political centres located beyond the coastal stretch of Konkan exerted influence on its history, and the distribution of these foci of power will give a general idea of the extent of Konkan's hinterland. The Mauryas, for instance, had a major centre at Sopara north of Mumbai but they were also strongly based in Gulbarga, Chitaldurg and Bellary in Karnataka. The Satavahana dynastic control of the Deccan and Konkan is well-known, and one of their major centres of power was Paithan or

Pratisthana on the Godavari. The Bijapur-Badami-Bidar sector, i.e., Karnataka from Gulbarga to Bellary, played an important role in Konkan's history virtually throughout, from the Mauryas in the third century BC to the period of the Bahmani, Adil Shahi and Vijayanagara rulers of the 14th-17th centuries AD. The rulers of Ahmednagar had also played a role during this period, and they were preceded in this by the Yadava power based in Devagiri near Aurangabad in the 13th century. This gives us a general idea of the outlying points of the hinterland with which Konkan was connected. This hinterland apparently incorporated a major chunk of the Deccan in Maharashtra and Karnataka. In Maharashtra, the interior areas which were directly connected historically with Konkan were Nasik, Aurangabad, Ahmednagar, Pune, Satara, Kolhapur and Osmanabad. In the case of Karnataka, the relevant non-Konkan territories are Belgaum, Dharwar, Shimoga, Chitradurg, Bellary, Badami, Bijapur, Gulbarga and Bidar. The network of routes over this whole territory is important, but perhaps the routes which linked the coast with the hinterland across the Western Ghats deserve some special notice.

The references to Konkan in the foreign textual sources (unless specified, this section is based on *GZB*, vol. 1, pp. 1-8), which date back to the *Periplus* of the mid-first century AD and Ptolemy of about a hundred years later, are remarkably diverse. North Gujarat and possibly parts of north Konkan are mentioned in Ptolemy as Larika and the rest of the Konkan as possibly Ariaka. The *Periplus* does not mention Larika, which is otherwise connoted by its reference to Barygaza, but it mentions Ariaka which is also given the reputation of having pirates. The gazetteer cites the opinion of James Rennell that "the multitude of shallow ports, an uninterrupted view along the shore, and an elevated coast favourable to distant vision, have always fitted this tract of the country for piracy". Among the ports mentioned in this stretch of the coast by Ptolemy and the *Periplus* – Broach, Sopara, Semulla, Mandagora, Palaipotomai/ Balapatna, Melizigara, and Toparan of the Byzantiuns (Byzantium) – the fixed points of identification are Sopara, Kaliena and possibly the Vengurla rocks. Ptolemy mentions the river Binda between Sopara and Semulla, Hippocura south of that, and the islands called Heptanesia. According to C. Lassen, these last-mentioned islands were Bombay and Salsette islands, and according to him, Bassein was Semulla and Balipatna was Chaul or Danda-Rajapur. Mandagora lay a little further south and he puts Melizigaris at Suvarnadurg. Some other scholar puts Melizigaris at Jaygad. Lassen thinks that Vijaydurg was Byzantium and Rennell identifies Nitrias mentioned by Pliny as the chief centre of the pirates with Nivti between

Malvan and Vengurla. The gazetteer occasionally offers its own opinion; regarding Melizigaris or Zizerus it thinks that the Arabic word *Janjira,* which is supposedly reminiscent of the term Melizigaris/Zizerus, "is still used not only for the rocky island off Danda-Rajpur, but also for the similar rocks at Suvarnadurg and Malvan, either of which places, with the towns on the mainland they protect, might then be identified with Melizigara or Zizerus" (*Ibid.*, p. 2). However, it adds that the possibility of identifying these places with accuracy is small.

The major Classical reference to the coast later in its history is Cosmas Indicopleustes of the 6th century, who refers to a king of Calliana, a major trade centre of the day which sent return cargoes of sesamum, brass, wood and articles of clothing to Sri Lanka. According to him, there was a Bishop's see along with a Christian community at Kalyan, subject to the Persian metropolitan. This possibly denotes the presence of Persian traders at Kalyan during this period. That Calliana of Cosmas may even be Quilon is another matter.

The Arabic geographers knew Konkan by various names: Kemkem, Komkam, Kankan, Konkan, and Konkan-Tana. The last term, mentioned by Ibn Batuta (1340), is also said to be known in other 14th century European sources. The term is also suggested for this coast by Marco Polo (1290) who writes that this was divided into the kingdoms of Lar and Tanna. Many ships and merchants frequented Tanna where leather, buckram and cotton were the exports. There is a Christian tradition dating from 1322 that the Friar Odoricus who visited Thana about this period mentioned the killing of four Christian friars by the Muslim *Kadi/Qazi* of the place. The Friar Odoricus reported the houses of 15 Nestorian Christians at the place. An early immigrant group to this coast could have been the Bene-Israel people who are found scattered in the northern parts of the Colaba collectorate and supposedly arrived from Yemen in the 6th century. The Parsis came after them.

In the post-Classical period, Konkan prominently figured in the network of Arab trade from the 7th century onward, and it is probable that the diplomatic contact of the Chalukyan king Pulakesin II (c.612-642 AD) with the Persian king was a result of this development. The first two Chinchani copper-plate inscriptions, both dating from the tenth century when the Rashtrakutas were ruling in this region, speak clearly of the Arab relationship of the Rashtrakutas, and even a later Chinchani grant, which dates from the Silahara period in the 11th century AD, refers to Muslim merchants. The significance of the maritime trade of the region is also highlighted by the Silahara records, which date from between c. AD 997 and c. AD 1144. In his analysis of these records, Ranavir

Chakravarti (1986) draws attention to the various types of merchants mentioned in these inscriptions and their significance and role in the royal administration. He also draws attention to the depiction of a naval battle scene in a Borivli cave, which has been interpreted as the scene of a naval battle between the Silaharas and the Kadambas of Goa. On the basis of the Kharepatan copper, plates of Anantadeva (c. AD 1084) and Rattaraja (c. AD 1008), he writes that the *Sresthis* of these records were rich and powerful merchants owning vessels and employing sailors for coastal trades and voyages, covering, among other places, Sopara, Nagar or Nagapura in Kolaba, Thana and Chaul. Kharepatan, or the port of Balipattana, was visited by at least two types of vessels – *Vahitra* and *Pravahana* – not only from Chaul or Chemuliya and Chandrapura south of Goa but also from *Dvipantara* or overseas. He also points out (Chakravarti 2000) that the Kharepatan record of c. AD 1084 refers to a person called Vasaida as a *Nauvittaka,* i.e., somebody whose wealth is associated with vessels. The correlation with the Islamic term *Nakhuda* or a shipowner is unmistakable.

The royal income from the sea-going trade is obvious from the Kharepatan record of Rattaraja of AD 1008. In the lines 56-61 of this copper-plate inscription, he assigns a *gadiyana* of gold from every vessel arriving from foreign lands (from *Vahitras* arrived from *Dvipantara*). This unit was certainly a small unit. Otherwise it could not have been imposed in gold. *Dharana,* another unit of gold, was levied on vessels arriving from near home – 'arriving from *Kandalamuliya,* excepting *Chemulya* and *Chandrapura*'. Chandrapura is Chandor in Goa whereas Chemulya is Chaul. Kandalamuliya remains unidentified (Kielhorn 1894-95).

It has further been pointed out that the Kadamba kings of Goa in about this period used to make regular pilgrimages in their own vessels up to Somanatha in Gujarat. The ship of one of these kings, Guhalladeva, sank near Goa and he was rescued by an Arab Muslim merchant bearing in the inscription the name *Aliya* or Ali. According to Chakravarti (1998), the maritime commercial significance of Konkan during this broad period is also seen in the letters of the India traders of the Geniza records. One such letter of AD 1145 was from Mahruz ben Jacob, a *Nakhuda* or ship-owner, to his brother-in-law Judah ben Jacob. Mahruz as a merchant often plied between Aden and India, and Judah was a representative of merchants in Cairo. At the time of writing this letter Mahruz was in Mangalore and Judah, after being attacked by pirates off the Konkan coast, was then in Thana. The letter was sent through Tinbu, an Indian ship-owner, who carried not merely the letter but also some money for Judah. In his letter Mahruz asks Judah that if he needed any gold, he should take it on his account from Tinbu with whom Mahruz claims "bonds of inseparable friendship and brotherhood". As Chakravarti (1998: 118) puts it, "The letter illustrates the linkages between a Jewish *Nakhuda*, operating between Aden and India, and his Indian counterpart, plying with his ships in the coastal network."

II. PRE-MODERN PORTS

II.1. From Umbergaon to Elephanta

Around Umbergaon

The northernmost pre-modern port in this sector seems to be *Nargol*, which lies about a mile north of Umbergaon. The Thana gazetteer specifically mentions it as a sea-port (*GZB, Thana District*, p. 291). A port also existed at Umbergaon, which in addition had a fort to protect it. A small sea-port has also been reported at *Maroli*, about 7 miles north of Umbergaon.

Sanjan

The major place of this sector is Sanjan (20-12 N/72-52 E), about 5 miles north-east of Umbergaon and located on the Varoli creek. According to the tradition of the Parsi community, this is the place where they came first to India.

The tradition of the arrival of the Parsi community at Sanjan has been discussed in a document of about AD 1600, i.e., several centuries after the time when the event was supposed to have occurred. The document, *Qissa-i-Sanjan*, is signed by a Parsi priest named Bahman Kaikobad, and has been available in English in a translation done by S.H. Hodivala (1920). The date of the arrival is disputed, and the choice is between AD 716 and AD 936. The Parsi community first shifted to Bushire on the Iranian coast of the Gulf and from there they moved first to Diu and then to Sanjan. The king who ruled in the area was known as Jadi Rana whom Hodivala interprets as a king of the Silahara dynasty. He allowed the Parsis to settle in his kingdom and they laid down the foundations of a new city which was given the name Sanjan. Subsequently, with the royal permission a Fire Temple was established, and the Fire came to be mentioned in the document as *Iranshah*. Some later sections of the document describe the Muslim invasion of Sanjan and it ends by pointing out that the fire from the temple at Sanjan was eventually taken to a new temple at Navsari in modern southern Gujarat.

Whatever might have been the date of the Parsi migration to Sanjan – AD 716 or AD 936 – the community was unlikely to have opted for an unknown place on the western Indian coast. That Sanjan was already a well-known settlement and a prosperous port even before the coming of the Parsi community has been highlighted both on the basis of textual and epigraphic sources by Ranabir Chakravarti (1990, 1996). He argues that its earliest textual mention as *Sazantion* is in Ptolemy around AD 150. D.C. Sircar (1963) further points out that the place is often identified with *Sanjayantinagari*, which has been mentioned in the *Mahabharata* in connection with Sahadeva's conquest of the south. The name *Sanjayapura* occurs in the Nagarjunakonda inscription of the time of Abhira Vasushena, year 30 (Sircar 1963). It has been identified with Sanjan, but the context in which the name occurs is important. The inscription records that an image of the eight-armed Narayana or Vishnu, which was possibly made of *Udumbara* wood, was installed on the *Seta-Giri* hill, the name of the general range of hills, of which the Siddhaldhari hill of Nagarjunakonda formed a part, by a number of royal personages including the *Yavana-rajas* or 'Yavana kings' of Sanjayapura. It should be fair to recall that the interpretation of the actual term *Yorajibhih* as *Yavanarajabhih* or *Yavanarajaih* is by no means a conclusive one. However, the idea that there were Yavana kings at Sanjan or in the Sanjan area around AD 278, the date of the inscription accepted by Sircar, is interesting in itself. That there was contact between ancient Andhra and the northern segment of the Konkan coast is also suggested by the reference to Dhenukataka or ancient Amaravati in an inscription from Kanheri (*GZB*, vol. 1, p. 11). More important from the point of view of the history of Sanjan is the set of five copper-plate records discovered in 1955 at Chinchani in the same region. The first of these inscriptions belongs to the Rashtrakuta king Indra III and is dated 17 April, AD 926. The relevant portion of the inscription may be summarized in Sircar's words:

> It is said that, when Indra III (AD 915-928) was reigning, there was a ruler named Madhumati who belonged to the Tajika (i.e. Arab) community, and that he had received the entire *mandala* or territorial division of *Samyana* from Krishnaraja (Krishna II, AD 878-915). Madhumati is no doubt the Sanskritised form of the Arabic name Muhammad. This Arab chief was thus appointed the governor of Samyana by Krishna II and was continuing in his post during the rule of Indra III. It is stated that Madhumati conquered the chiefs of all the harbours (*Velakula*) of the neighbourhood, apparently on behalf of his master, and placed his own officials in them (verse 18).... Verse 20 says how this Arab governor of Samyana established free ferry on two streams (near Samyana, apparently on the Sanjan river) and also a feeding house (at Samyana) where Sali rice, curries and ghee were catered free of cost (Sircar 1962a, p. 47).

The Tajik governor Madhumati also bore the epithet *Sugatipa,* and he had a minister called Puvvaiya who was a friend of Annaiya or Annammaiya, a Brahmin of Bharadvaja *gotra* and the son of Narayana Bhatta. The inscription mentions that Annammaiya established a Mathika, i.e., a monastery or temple at Samyana. The inscription goes on to state that at the request of Annammaiya and with the permission of *Paramabhattaraka Maharajadhiraja Paramesvara Indrarajadeva* (i.e., Indra III), Sugatipa or Madhumati made a grant of the village of *Kanaduka* situated in the *Kolimahara vishaya* within *Samyana-mandala* together with half a *Dhura* of land in the village of *Devihara*. The purpose of this endowment was to carry out, with the income accruing from it, repairs of this monastery/temple and also to offer *Naivedya* to the goddess *Dusumi* (i.e., *Durga*) and feed nine persons belonging to the *Pancha-Gaudiya-Mahaparshad* of Samyana. This would mean a community of *Gaudiya* or North Indian Brahmins settled at Samyana. The five classes of these Brahmins are known as *Sarasvata, Kanyakubja, Gauda, Maithila,* and *Utkala*.

The governor declared the creation of this endowment in an assemblage of the *Hamyamana-pauras, Dhruvas* and *Vishayik-adikarikas* of Samyana, the two last categories of people being administrative officials. Sircar takes *Hamyamana-pauras* to indicate that a Parsi community was settled in the area. The boundaries of the donated village have been described in detail.

The second Chinchani charter (Sircar 1962a), which offers no date but belongs to the reign of Krishna III (AD 939-967), has been given a tentative date of the middle of the 10th century AD. Verses 12-14 of this charter refer to the god *Bhillamaladeva,* also called *Madhusudana* (Vishnu), who was installed by the descendants of the merchants of Bhillamala (modern Bhinmal in the Jodhpur area of Rajasthan). Verses 15-19 refer to another temple/monastery devoted to the worship of a mother goddess at the same place. There is little doubt that this mother goddess temple was the one which found mention in the previously discussed charter of Indra III. There is also a reference to the *Anagha-parshad* or what was called *Pancha-Gaudiya-Mahaparshad* in the earlier inscription, in this charter and this *Parshad* was supposed to belong to the mother goddess temple. It appears from a later portion of the inscription that a piece of land owned by the Bhillamaladeva temple fell in the precincts of the mother goddess temple and was thus under an unlawful possession of the latter. The inscription declares an 'arrangement', which is said to emanate from the deity or Bhillamaladeva himself and was said to be binding on the temple authority of Bhillamaladeva and the *Maha-parshad* of the mother goddess temple. The terms of the arrangement were that the latter would pay the former 40 *drammas* annually at the end of the festival of lights or *Dipavali*. The *drammas* had to be paid in coins minted by a trader named Sresthin Gambhuvaka who apparently enjoyed a license to mint coins or *drammas* on behalf of the ruling authority.

The three other copper-plate grants from Chinchani were issued by the local ruling family of the *Modhas* who were under the overlordship of the Silahara kings (Sircar 1962b). The first of these three grants was made by Chamundaraja who was the governor of *Samyana-pattana* under the Silahara king Chhinturaja. This charter has been dated 15 September, AD 1034. Its purpose was to record the grant of a *Ghanaka* or oil-mill in favour of the mother goddess temple mentioned earlier with the aim of providing oil for the burning of a lamp in front of the goddess and for "besmirching oil" on the feet of the members of the *Maha-parshad* of her temple and the other Brahmin visitors to it. The second *Modha* family charter was issued by Vijjala and dated 22 January, AD 1048. According to this charter, a sort of tax or cess relating to the mother goddess temple was granted "in favour of the householders Bahudhara and Kankua as well as the scholars Mahadeva and Lakshmidhara ", all of them attached to the said temple. The grant was made by Vijjala on the occasion of *Magha-Samkranti* after having worshipped *Mayukhamalin* or Sun-god. The third *Modha* family charter was issued by Vijala or Vija/Vijja (the same person who issued the second *Modha* charter) and is dated 13 November, AD 1053. This grant basically states that the tax or cess of three *drammas* on account of the village of Kenasa-grama in the possession of the mother goddess temple was granted in favour of the said temple for the purpose of feeding 25 Brahmins (probably) per day. The grant was addressed, among others, to the *hamyamana* or Parsi community of *Sristhana* or modern Thana, who apparently were also settled at Sanjan, which was further referred to as "*Samyana-pattana 700* which was a *Mandala* or district consisting of 4000 *drangas*". Sircar (1962b: 73) comments the following on this:

> We know that expressions like 'Samyana-pattana 700' normally meant the 'Samyana-pattana division consisting of 700 villages or hamlets', although the number may have been conventional or exaggerated. But the word *dranga* generally means 'a town' and it is impossible to believe that a territorial division consisting only of 700 villages or hamlets contained as many as 4000 towns. It therefore seems that *dranga* in the inscription is a mistake for *dramma*. The intended meaning of the passage in question may therefore be that the annual revenue income of the territory under the rule of the Modha chief of the Samyana district consisting of 700 villages

or hamlets was 4000 *drammas* possibly meaning coins of silver. A locality called *Akasika* is stated to have stood on the borders of the said district.

The set of three post-Rashtrakuta grants specify a number of administrative officers of the district including a chief executive officer or *Mahamatya* and a minister in charge of war and peace (*Sandhivigrahika*). On the whole, the Chinchani copper-plate grants throw a flood of light on Sanjan of the early mediaeval period: a prosperous area which was a port and commercial centre with rice cultivation and at least two religious organizations and a well-organized administrative machinery under local chiefs and their suzerains. The presence of the Parsi community is also testified by D.C. Sircar's interpretation of the term *hamyamana*. If 'Sazantion' mentioned by Ptolemy stands for Sanjan – and the similarity between 'Sazantion' and 'Sanjayantinagari' of the *Mahabharata* is striking – the history of the importance of Sanjan as a major port on the north Konkan coast as early as the early historic period seems to be undeniable. However, the epigraphic evidence is well-focussed on the site only in the early mediaeval period.

Sanjan retained its importance in the mediaeval period as well, appearing in a variety of sources, some of which have been cited by H.M. Elliot and J. Dowson (1897). In the text of *Salsilatu-t Tawarikh of the Merchant Sulaiman with Additions by Abu Zaidu-l Hasan, of Siraf* (c. AD 851-916), the Balhara or the Rashtrakutas were said to be the most eminent of the princes of India. Konkan or *Komkam* is specifically mentioned as falling in the Balhara territory (Elliot and Dawson 1897, p. 4). Sindan is placed among the 'countries of Sind' in the 9th-early 10th century text of Ibn Khurdadba, according to which the teak tree and canes grew in Sindan (*Ibid.*, p. 15). From Sindan to Malabar it was 5 days' journey. There is a reference to the crocodiles in the bay of Sindabur (Sanjan) in the Balhara kingdom by Al Masudi (10th century), who also speaks eloquently of the power of the Rashtrakutas. Al Istakhri (10th century) puts Sindan in his list of the 'cities of Hind'. Between Surabaya or Broach and Sindan it took five days to journey, and the same number of days was taken to travel from Sindan to Saimur or Chaul (*Ibid.*, p. 30). Ibn Haukal (12th century AD) repeats more or less the same information on Sindan. In the early 14th century record of Rashidu-d Din Sindabur is mentioned (*Ibid.*, p. 68) but without any detail. Al Idrisi of the 11th century writes the following about Sindan:

> Sindan is a mile-and-a half from the sea. It is populous, and the people are noted for their industry and intelligence. They are rich and of a warlike temper. The town is large, and has an extensive commerce both in exports and imports (*Ibid.*, p. 85).

The same author mentions that Sindan or Sindabur is situated on the shores of a great gulf where ships cast anchor. It was a commercial town and contained fine buildings and rich markets. Although Elliot and Dawson (*Ibid.*, p. 403) seem in favour of the idea of identifying Sindan/ Sindabur with Daman, its identification with Sanjan is conclusive.

Ranavir Chakravarti (1992) has discussed the export of Sindani indigo from India to the west in the eleventh century. He points out that Sindani indigo finds mention as a type of indigo available in Egyptian market in the late 10th and early 11th centuries AD. He points out that Gujarat has a long tradition of producing indigo, and in this connection he draws attention to the inscription of Vishnusena of AD 592, which was issued from a settlement of a community of merchants – Lohatagrama, located possibly in the gulf of Kutch area.

> Clause 19 of this charter lays down that forced labour (*vishti*) was to be extracted by merchants from workers at indigo vats (*nila-dumphaka*). A tax (*adana*) was also imposed on indigo production according to clause 48, the rate being three silver coins (*rupaka*). This is a sure evidence of regular, if not commercial, production of indigo in pre-tenth century Gujarat (Chakravarti 1992, p. 27).

It is probable that the Sindani indigo, which finds mention in the Ibn'Awkal's letters of the Geniza records, discovered in the mediaeval quarters of Cairo was so called because the Gujarati and other indigo was exported through this port. According to Chakravarti (*Ibid.*),

> "Sandani indigo, figuring in the Ibn'Awkal correspondence, was thus actually not a local product of Sanjan, but was brought from somewhere in western India to the north Konkan port. There is now a distinct possibility that Sindan actually exported Gujarati indigo and that the port of Sindan had an extensive hinterland for the purpose".

The preceding discussion has made it obvious that the importance of the modern Sanjan area has long antedated the arrival of the Parsi community in this belt. The fact that the Parsis decided to land at this place suggests that when they arrived, the place was already important. It has been claimed that "this town founded by the Parsis was named Sanjan supposedly in memory of a town in Iran bearing the same name" (Gupta *et al.* 2004, pp. 94-95). In view of the name *Samyana* in the relevant epigraphic records cited earlier, this view may be discarded.

The mediaeval and generally pre-modern history of Sanjan has been well described in the Thana district gazetteer of 1882 (*GZB, Thana District*, pp. 301-304). The Arab geographers of the 10th-12th centuries repeatedly mention it under the name of Sindan as one of the chief ports of western India.

> In the tenth century (915) it is described as famous for the export of an emerald equal to the best in brightness and colour, but harder and heavier, known as the Mecca emerald because it passed through Arabia. It is also described as a great strong city with a Jama mosque. In the twelfth century it is mentioned as populous, the people noted for industry and intelligence, rich and warlike, the town large and with a great export and import trade. Early in the sixteenth century (1534) it was taken by the Portuguese. In the first years of the seventeenth century it is noticed by the traveller Pyrard de Laval (*Ibid.*, p. 302).

The city is also known for offering, although unsuccessfully, a stiff resistance to Alph Khan, Alauddin Khiliji's general, in the 14th century.

The old city lies to the west of the modern railway station. The gazetteer describes it in the following terms:

> West of the station the site of the old city of Sanjan stretches for several miles, a bare plain with rice hollows, dry pond beds, and low rolling hillocks, some bare with old brick foundations and others shaded by clumps of trees. Towards the east and north the view is bounded by small rolling hills. To the west the plain stretches down the links of the Sanjan river about six miles to the sea. A little above the village, about a mile west of the station, the flow of the salt water is stopped, and a long reach in the river formed by a dam which is said to have been built by a Parsi during the rule of the Marathas. About half a mile below the dam, though dry at low tide, at high tide there is water enough for boats of about three tons (10 *khandis*). The country round the present Sanjan, a fair-sized village with some good houses and one broad street, is dotted with old mangoes, banyans, and huge baobab trees, one of them forty feet in girth three feet from the ground. There are the remains of several large ponds and lakes, some of them much filled with silt and now used to grow rice. The banks of the ponds are in many places topped with mounds, covered with large old bricks. Old bricks are also scattered over most of the fields and form the walls of almost all the buildings. Except these bricks, there are not many remains (*Ibid.*, p. 303).

An important old landmark for sailors in this area was Sanjan Peak or St. John Peak of the European sources, which with the name of Barat hill (1760 feet high) stands about 14 miles south of Sanjan but begins to rise about three miles from the shore. It is said to be visible to the sailors for 40 miles in clear weather.

In modern Sanjan, an area on the bank of the creek is pointed out as the port area where timber was traded as a commodity, with boats coming in from Bhavnagar in the living memory. In a village not far from the port area, there is a low but extensive mound. The surface indicates burnt brick structures below at a number of places. It has been currently estimated that the old occupational site covers an area of 2 km by 0.75 km.

The first season's excavations (Gupta *et al.* 2001-2002) identified two structural phases at the site. The first structural phase lay on the earliest layer (layer 7) and comprised mainly a burnt-brick structure of large bricks (35-40 cm x 21-25 cm x 6-7 cm) under which was a foundation of three courses of cobble interspersed with clay. The wall survived up to 15 courses of bricks. To the west of this structure was excavated a terracotta ring-well of 3.2 m depth, with straight-sided terracotta rings between 33 and 39 cm in height. The second and upper structural phase lay at a depth of 1.05 m-1.10 m from the mound surface and comprised a small burnt-brick wall, a floor made of bricks and brickbats, and two large terracotta ring-wells. A thick deposit of charcoal, potsherds and clay was noticed in a pit at the base of the ring-wells, suggesting that these ring-wells were used as soakage pits. Three coins were found associated with this upper structural phase, all indicating a context of the Indo-Sassanian period. The earliest coin is a Satavahana coin of the second century AD, but it seems to have been found along with the coins of the later period, which comprise a Sassanian issue of the 7th-8th century AD. A few coins also date from the 10th-11th century AD. Primarily on the basis of coins the excavated site has been dated between the 8th and 11th centuries AD. The excavated artefacts include iron objects, terracottas and plenty of glass. At least one glass object is said to possess analogues in the Gulf area in the 9th-10th century AD. The excavated pottery includes porcelain, a variety of glazed ware, both coarse and slipped grey ware and red ware, and glazed and plain pink ware. Parallels have been sought all over the Indian ocean region, primarily in the Gulf and Mesopotamia.

The second season's excavations, which were conducted at a different mound (Gupta *et al.* 2004), isolated a number of burials associated with the final phase of occupation at the site in the 12th-13th century AD and the traces of a number of structures along the embankment of the Varoli creek. The pottery types found in this season included celadon ware, apart from the types mentioned earlier.

A more precise estimate of the excavated chronology of Sanjan emerges from Sobhana Gokhale's comment that the measurement of the bricks of the first structural phase of Sanjan concur with the measurements of the bricks found in the Satavahana levels of such sites as Kolhapur, Nasik and Nevasa (Gokhale 2004). She also makes it clear that only the second structural phase can be placed in the 8th-9th century AD. The faunal remains comprise bones of cattle, buffalo, goat, sheep, pig, dog, horse and ass among the domesticated varieties, but a number of wild varieties are also present: gaur, wild buffalo, nilgai and other varieties of deer, wolf, mongoose, etc. Both pea-fowl and domestic fowl are reported and, interestingly, there are reports of turtle, marine crab and large to small marine fishes.

Between Sanjan and Sopara

There is a reference to presumably a small sea-port, *Dheri*, south of Umbergaon. This was in Portuguese control in AD 1583. In the same sector one notes *Gholbad* which, according to the gazetteer, had a sea-customs office. The river which flows by Dahanu has been mentioned as *Dahanuka* in a Nasik cave inscription (Senart 1905-06, p. 79), although this does not prove that Dahanu was an early historic port. The gazetteer (*GZB, Thana District*, pp. 53-55) points out that, within the outer reefs, about 4 miles to the west of the fort on the north bank of the Dahanu River, small coasting crafts find anchorage in 3 or 4 fathoms. The creek can be entered at high tide only. It came under Portuguese control in AD 1533, but by AD 1733 there was little sea-trade through Dahanu. It fell under the Maratha domination in AD 1739. South of Dahanu and Chinchani, Tarapur also was a sea-port, but by the late 19th century boats could enter it only at high tide. Six miles to the east of Dahanu and located on the Dahanu creek, *Savta* was called a *Bandar* and a large and important place of trade before the government stopped the cutting of trees in the neighbouring forests. It is apparent that towards the end of the 19th century, Savta was an important centre of trade in north Konkan for teak and general timber. *Navapur*, 4 miles south of Tarapur, was also a small sea-port.

South of Navapur, the sea-port was *Satpatti* which, during the five years ending 1878-79, accounted for average imports worth £5667 and imports worth £1386. It has been said to be a suburb of Sirgaon north of Mahim.

Mahim or Kelve-Mahim was a port and the headquarter of Mahim sub-division of the Thana district of British India. *Alibag* was another small sea-port of the area, about 3 miles south of Mahim and with a Portuguese fort. It lay on the north bank of the Kelve or Danda creek. *Agashi* stands on the southern bank of the Vaitarna River or creek and is to the west of the modern Virar railway station. Except one channel, the mouth of the bay on which the town stands was closed by a reef even towards the end of the 19th century when the bay full of shoals was navigable only for boats and small vessels. It was a centre of old timber trade and ship-building. The Portuguese records of 1530 when they burnt it refer to its rich timber trade and mention that ships as good as the Portuguese ships were built here. The Portuguese acquired the place in 1533, around the time when they acquired Bassein. In 1837 it witnessed a brisk trade with Gujarat and Bombay in grain, garden produce and salt, and used to build very good fishing boats and coasting craft. In 1881 there was a great coastal trade with Bombay in plantains and betel leaves (*Ibid.*, pp. 1-2 for Agashi).

Two forts have been mentioned by the gazetteer in the present context: Arnala and Asava forts. The Arnala fort commands the southern entrance of the Vaitarna River, the most extensive inlet of north Konkan, apart from the inlet of Bassein. It was built by the Muslim rulers of Gujarat but the Portuguese acquired it in 1530, with the British finally taking it over from the Marathas in 1817. The Asava fort was in Mahim and of special value in keeping open military communications between the great fortress of Asheri and those of Mahim, Sirgao, Chichani, Tarapur and Dahanu. The Asheri fort lay 20 miles northeast of Mahim and was the key to the Portuguese possessions in north Konkan.

Sopara

The major focus of ancient trade of north Konkan was at Sopara, which falls between Agashi in the north and Bassein in the south. The textual references to, and the finds of Asokan rock edicts at, the site make it an ancient port of outstanding importance. Archaeologically, the picture is somewhat unclear and has not got much beyond Bhagawanlal Indraji's work in the late 19th century (Indraji 1881-82).

The small-scale excavations conducted by Howell and Sinha (1994) have led to some understanding of the ceramic sequence of the site.

> Provisional study suggests that the earliest deposits contain Black and Red Ware, but not the Red Polished Ware (RPW) associated with the Indo-Roman period. There is also a tiny fragment of Northern Black Polished Ware (NBPW) from this phase, which may put the earliest occupation of the site in the third or second centuries BC (Howell and Sinha 1994, p. 192).

As far as we can judge, the co-occurrence of Black and Red Ware and NBP in the earliest phase makes it very likely that this phase is much earlier than what is thought by the excavators. One may unhesitatingly put it in the 6th century BC, if not earlier. We feel that the spread of the NBP to the Sopara area could not be much later than the date of its beginning in the Ganga plain.

Indraji's excavations at the site yielded the ruins of a *stupa* of c. AD 160. However, it is useful to mention that the cup of the gold casket, which was the last of the successively arranged relic caskets of copper, silver, stone, crystal and gold found in the *stupa*, contained "thirteen tiny pieces of earthenware" which, according to Indraji, could represent "pieces of the begging bowl of the world-honoured Gautama Buddha" (Indraji 1881-82). This may also mean that there was a much earlier *stupa* of pre-Christian era at the site and that the *stupa* of the second century AD excavated by Indraji could be a later period *stupa* incorporating the relics contained in the earlier *stupa*. Sopara was a major mart in the 10th-12th century, being mentioned by such writers as Al Masudi, Al Biruni and Al Idrisi (cf. Elliot and Dowson 1867, pp 66, 85). A clear topographic reference to the archaeological finds in the Sopara area has been made by B. Arunachalam in *Indian Cartographer* 2002 (the article was read by me on the internet).

> The early archaeological finds in the area center around Nirmal, where in a low mound called the Burud Rajache Kot, a Buddhist *stupa* was excavated by Bhagwanlal Indraji in April 1882, containing within it a coffer within a brickbuilt chamber, holding images of Maitreyi Buddha set in eight cardinal directions. The *stupa* itself is dated to the third century BC but the metal images appear to have been placed in it around 9th century AD. A silver coin of Gautamiputra Satakarni of 2nd century BC was also found in the mound. Closeby in the Brahma hill of Vakal, circular burials of unhewn boulders, dating to 2nd century BC have been noted.
>
> A second area of findings is around Sopara and Gas to its south. In the N.W. of Sopara around the shallow Chakreshwar lake and temple are noted relics of a hindu temple and memorial stones, while south of Sopara, near Ram Kund, and an old muslim grave-yard were found fragments of Asokan edicts VIII and IX. In 1956, fragments of Asokan edict XI were also found in the coastal village, Bhui (Bhuigao). Apart from the above findings, old built up areal and structural lineaments have been noted in the central depression between Nirmal and Sopara - Gas areas, beneath rice fields, and two smaller Buddha *stupas* south of the Nirmal. In a more recent excavation of 1993, a number of features have been noted – a ring well, fragments of Roman amphorae red polished ware, glass all dating to the beginning of the Christian era, a Portuguese period landing place east of Gas, and a stone paved crossing called Dagdibandh between Gas and Achole. Pali and Prakrit inscriptions in Brahmi have been found in Brahma Hill, Sopara, Gas and Bolinj. Mediaeval hindu and jain temple relics are plenty. These archaeological and historical findings fall within two N-S linear belts: Vagholi-Nirmal-Bhui (Bhuigao) on the west side and Sopara-Gas on the east. All the findings in Sopara and Gas are to the east of the line of lakes and the settlements, in or near a low terrace sloping east towards a former creek.

Regarding the location of the port of Sopara, Arunachalam on the basis of his remote-sensing image studies reaches the following conclusion:

> In the area under study though the Vagholi-Nirmal-Bhui (Bhuigao) area on the west directly faced the sea, and had small creeks parallel to the sea-face, they do not appear to have attracted a port site. The sheltered inland sea behind the Sopara and Vasi islands approached through either of the estuarine openings was far more ideal for safe sailing and anchoring. The deepest part of the sea-depression lies in the middle, to the north of Manikpur-Chulne and south and east of Gas, where the tidal flows converge from three directions. The most probable port site thus appears to have been to the south and east of Gas, with an adjoining deep water pool for safe anchorage for a few vessels. The largest archaeological findings of the Roman Era lying east of Gas in a low terrace is an indicator in this direction. The findings of the mediaeval stone pavement (Dagdibandh) leading from Gas across the terrace towards Achole, a probable landing site on the mainland face is also suggestive. The sites of ship building and a Bandar of the Portuguese times are also suggestive. A 17th century Kutchi sea manual talks of a regular cargo trade route through the Bolinj-Sopara creek from Gujarat to Mumbai and Thane. As this creek silted up, the cargo vessel traffic slowed down and receded seaward on both ends of the creek. Thus the Sopara Bandar near Nile-more, the Ranpada Bandar and the Agashi Bandar indicate three successive stages of this recession in the 19th and 20th centuries. Agashi was a ship-building center of 17th century where the Marathas as well as Portuguese built vessels upto 500 tons size. The loss of port function of Sopara by the 17th century is the outcome of the islands getting fused with the mainland.

A geomorphological examination of the Sopara area has been published by Savita Ghate (2007) who has located microliths in the Gas area and dated them around 3500 BP.

Bassein to Thana and Kalyan

South of Sopara, *Bassein* or *Vasai* is the first major trading settlement towards Mumbai. It is located on the north bank of the Thana creek. The Thana district gazetteer (*GZB, Thana,* pp. 28-43), which provides a brief history of Bassein, argues that the place could not have been important as long as Sopara, immediately north to it, retained its significance as a port. One cannot be sure if Bassein formed a district under the Yadavas of Devagiri in the 13th century. It seems to have emerged into significance under Mahmud Begra (1459-1518) during the phase of the independent Sultanate of Gujarat. In 1514 Duarte Barbosa, a Portuguese writer of the 16th century, refers to it as Baxay which was a prosperous port drawing merchandise from all parts, and especially from Malabar which sent boats loaded with arecas, coconuts and spices. The Portuguese set up a factory here in 1526, but that did not prevent them from undertaking hostilities against the Gujarat Sultans and attacking Bassein and the coast around in 1529 and 1531. To cope with this problem, the Sultans erected a well-protected fort here and put it under a large garrison. The Portuguese attacked again, defeated Gujarat's army and withdrew razing the citadel. In 1533, Bahadur Shah of Gujarat ceded Bassein to the Portuguese, mainly to obtain them as an ally against the Mughal power of Delhi. The relationship with the rulers of Gujarat deteriorated in 1539 when an attack from that quarter was repulsed by the Bassein Portuguese. By that time the Portuguese dug the foundations of a new citadel. Towards the 1580s it is reported as having a flourishing trade in rice, corn and timber for ship-building. By the beginning of the 17th century, the Portuguese settlement at Bassein was well-fortified and well-planned, having its churches and houses of the wealthy.

> The European travellers of the seventeenth century describe Bassein as a handsome well fortified town with a convenient harbour, in a country growing much rice, pulse, and other grains, oil, and coconuts. The city wall was of stone three miles round with three gates, two main gateways, one to the east the other to the west, and a smaller portal to the south, and eight bastions, some of them unfinished. On the south or sea-side, where there was little risk of an attack there was only a single wall. The garrison was (1634) 2400 strong, 400 Europeans, 200 Native Christians, and 1800 slaves. The city was set apart for the better class of Christians; neither craftsmen nor Hindus were allowed to live within the walls. It had wide straight streets and good buildings round a great square or market. The nobles lived in stately mansions, and there were six churches, four convents, and two colleges, one belonging to the Franciscans and the other to the Jesuits (*Ibid.*, p. 32).

In 1674 the Portuguese Bassein was attacked and looted by a band of 600 pirates from Muscat, and in about the same time the Marathas began to push towards the area. In 1739 Bassein fell to the Marathas. By the early 19th century, it came into the possession of the British. That some trade continued down to the late 19th century is suggested by the gazetteer's reference to its 'good landing place and a custom house'.

Along the Thana creek or the Ulhas River, there were a few trading settlements including Sassu Navghar, Ghodbandar, Thana, Kalyan and Bhiwndi. *Sassu Navghar*, 6 miles east of Bassein, was a small port and the same was true of *Ghodbandar*, about 10 miles northwest of Thana and having a sea-customs office and a Portuguese/Maratha fort. About *Thana*, it has been written that "of old Hindu or Mussulman Thana there is almost no trace" (*Ibid.*, p. 349). The *Periplus* mentions Kalyan but not Thana, which seems to have emerged strongly in focus only under the Silaharas, of whom there was a separate 'Thana' branch, in the 9th century and later. Thana has been mentioned as *Sristhanaka* in a copper-plate grant (AD 1097) of the Silahara king, Arikeshari. Tana or Thana is mentioned by Al Biruni in the early 10th century (Elliot and Dowson 1867, p. 66) and by Al Idrisi in the 11th century (Elliot and Dowson 1897, p. 89). According to Al Idrisi,

> Bana (Tanna) is a pretty town upon a great gulf where vessels anchor and from whence they set sail.

Marco Polo at the end of the 13th century refers to Thana as a centre of trade in horses, which were exported to this region from the Gulf ports. He also refers to the acts of piracy off the Thana coast (Chakravarti 1991). The gazetteer (*GZB, Thana District*, p. 347) refers to four landing places or *bandars* at Thana: Mandvi, Leberi, Bendi and Chendni. Thana possibly was also a centre of pilgrimage. The Marcella copper-plates (AD 1038) of Goa mention that the Kadamba king Sasthadeva II undertook a pilgrimage to *Sthanaka* or Thana travelling by sea (Chakravarti 1998).

Kalyan or *Kalliena* of the *Periplus* is located on the outer or east side of a deep bend of the Ulhas river upstream of Thana. No ancient remains have been reported here, but the place lies within the vast urban sprawl of greater Mumbai and offers no scope for archaeological exploration. There is a fort mound, with the fortification dating from the Mughal period and later. The gazetteer (*GZB, Thana District*, p. 113) refers to Kalyan as having considerable trade in salt and dried fish, which came from Rai Murdha, Bassein and Uran and were sent to the Deccan. Large quantities of myrobalan used to reach Kalyan by the Kusur, Bhimsankar, Nanaghat and Malsejghat passes. The history of Kalyana as a port in the early mediaeval and later contexts seems to be uncertain. Kalyan figures a number of times in the Kanheri inscriptions in the context of some donors' names. There is also a reference to *Ambaalika Mahavihara* in a Kanheri inscription, which has been identified with the Ambibvale caves near Kalyan (Gokhale 1991).

Bhiwndi to Elephanta

Bhiwndi, located on the Kamvari creek, lies roughly to the northwest of Kalyan. The Kambhari, narrow and shallow in parts, is tidal for a mile above the town. In ordinary tides no boats of more than 20 tons and in spring tides no boats of more than 42 tons could reach the town (*GZB,*

Thana District, pp. 45-49). The gazetteer says that "its position on a navigable stream on the direct line of traffic through the Thal pass must have made Bhiwndi an early centre of trade". There is no archaeological or historical evidence except that a copper-plate (AD 997) of the Silahara king Aparajita mentions a few villages near Bhiwndi. The modern Kumbharli River is mentioned as 'Kumari' in that copper-plate. In the 16th century, Bhiwndi was a centre of trade with Gujarat. In 1636 it was ceded to Bijapur by the Mughals and in 1817 it fell to the British. Near Bhiwndi there is a Portuguese fort which is a chain of forts guarding Portuguese Bassein from the Maratha territory.

Coming down from the Thana-Kalyan sector or from Bassein towards modern Mumbai, there are some ports, all of which have been subsumed under the Mumbai port, losing all their pre-modern significance. Versova, north of Mumbai, has been called a port in *GZB, Thana District*, pp. 379-381. In 1720 the harbour was described as little and narrow but deep enough for ships of the greatest burden, and in 1728 a Portuguese record speaks of it as one of the best bays on the coast. The Versova fort stands at the entrance of the creek between Versova and the island of Madh and was probably built by the Portuguese and strengthened by the Marathas. In about 1694 a fleet of Muscat Arabs raided Versova. In 1739 it was taken by the Marathas from the Portuguese, and in 1774 it fell to the British. There was a small port at Utan, 5 miles northwest of Borivli. Bandra is also called a port, although there was not much sea-trade there in the late 19th century. It was a major Portuguese centre. The Belapur fort commanded the entrance to the Panvel River, about 4 miles west of Panvel which is listed in the *GZB, Thana District*, pp. 293-296 as a port, although by that time it was poor in trade and could be used only in high water. The major ancient port of the Mumbai area was Elephanta, an island 7 miles east of Apollo Bunder or Gateway of India. The name Elephanta was given to it by the Portuguese. The island covers an area of about 4 miles (1050 hectares, according to a modern calculation) at high tide whereas at low tide it shows an area of about 6 miles (1579 hectares). It comprises three villages and landing places: Shet Bandar in the northwest, Moreh Bandar in the northeast, and Gharapuri or Raj Bandar in the south.

> Though it has long lost almost all its people and almost all its holiness, Elephanta, perhaps from about the third to about the tenth century, was the site of a city and a place of religious resort (*GZB, Thana District*, p. 60).

It has been identified with Puri, the unknown capital of the Mauryas and Silahara rulers of north Konkan from about the 6th to the 10th century. The most important epigraphic reference to it occurs in an inscription

(AD 634) of the Chalukya king Pulakesin II who invaded it. 'Golden island' and 'Sripuri' are the terms which have been used about this island in this epigraphic record.

Modern archaeological knowledge about the island has been summarized by Tripathi (2004) and Shinde, Gupta and Rajgor (2002). The latter point out that a brick wall excavated in the area of Rajbandar could be interpreted as a jetty or wharf. At Moreh or Mora Bandar there were submerged structures and finds of Roman, Kshatrapa and Gupta coins. The collected pottery includes sherds of Roman amphorae, and their chronology, as studied by Sunil Gupta (in Shinde, Gupta and Rajgor 2002), indicates a period between the 1st and 7th centuries AD. In the Morabandar area Tripathi (2004) found more amphorae sherds and classified them into four types: type I, which is said to be few and of Egyptian origin; type II, which is said to be the most common type of amphorae sherds in India with pink to whitish outer surface and gritty core; type III, which is pink to greenish yellow in colour with widely placed horizontal ridges and well distributed in the Mediterranean area; and type IV which is said to conform to the late Roman amphora type and possess pale colour with a pale slip. It is the last type which occurs profusely in Elephanta. Tripathi points out that the earliest structure in the island is a brick-built *stupa* which is located on the top of a hill in the northeast of the island. There are also rock-cut cisterns in the island. In Tripathi's explorations, Morabandar emerged as the most significant archaeological area of Elephanta (Tripathi 2004):

> The whole area between the high steep hill and the shore is strewn with remains of brick structures, stone walls and other structural remains and a large number of potsherds. Not only the land but also the sandy beaches in the north and the east of the village are virtually covered with potsherds. Many of them were there for a considerable time as they are rolled by the waves. Pottery found from Mora Bander includes Red Polished Ware, Black Slipped Ware, Red Ware and some wave-rolled black and grey sherds, looking like Rouletted Ware and a large quantity of *amphorae* pieces.

Equally importantly, he noted a large number of silver, copper and lead coins in this coastal area. Some of these coins are, according to him, of unique type and found on this island only. Moreover, from the presence of unfinished coins and lead waste he infers that Elephanta was a centre of minting coins. Although the Roman amphorae pieces have been taken here to be chronological markers, they do not necessarily represent the whole of the archaeological column in the island of Elephanta. Its beginning in the pre-Christian era seems to be very likely.

Observations

The foregoing review of the pre-modern ports in what used to be known as the Thana district of British India in the late 19th century may highlight a simple point about the location of ports in this sector of the Konkan coast. Sopara, Kalyan and Elephanta had obviously early historic beginnings. In the case of Sopara, if one considers the *Jataka* references to it, the beginning is likely to go back to c. 500 BC. If Ptolemy's Sanzantion is really ancient *Samyana*, Sanjan may be added to the list of early historic ports of this sector. This is likely to be the case because the place is mentioned in the inscription of a 4th century AD king from Nagarjunakonda. If a king of the Nagarjunakonda area of Andhra was aware of a port in the southernmost section of Gujarat, that must have been a major port of his time, and if it was a major port in the 4th century AD, it is likely to have a considerably earlier antecedence. Similarly, as the Dahanu river is said to be mentioned in a Nasik inscription as *Dahanuka*, Dahanu itself may or may not be an early historic port.

All these three or four/five places thrived throughout the early mediaeval and mediaeval periods. The epigraphic records and the relevant Arab records are clear on this issue. Centres like Thana emerged as *Sristhanaka* in the early mediaeval period and was followed by Vasai soon afterwards. However, the important point is that these important centres of maritime trade had a network of smaller places in their vicinity. The creeks or rivers which led to the interior had invariably a number of smaller trading settlements which carried on some amount of maritime trade even in the late 19th century. The whole belt no doubt constituted an important maritime zone.

The importance of this zone is also underlined by the numerous forts which dotted its landscape. Most of them dominated the creeks and some dominated possibly the entry points from the Ghats to this area. One is not sure if there has been a detailed historical study of these forts. Although it is generally assumed that they date mostly from the Portuguese and Maratha periods and are thus basically post-early 16th century, it is probable that some of them had a much earlier antecedence.

The Thana district gazetteer groups all these forts under three major headings: coastal forts, inland forts and 'Sahyadri' forts or the forts located in the Western Ghats. The coastal forts are 20 in number: 4 in Dahanu (Dahanu, Dindu, Sanjan and Umbergaon); 7 in Mahim (Alibag, Bhavangad, Dantivira, Mahim, Pankot, Sirgaon and Tarapur); 3 in Bassein (Arnala, Bassein and Kharbao); 5 in Salsette (Belapur, Dharavi, Persik, Thana and Versova); and 1 in Kalyan (Kalyan). There were 23 inland forts: 5 in Dahanu (Ballalgad, Gambhirgad, Indragad, Kanheri and Segrah); 6 in Mahim (Asava, Asheri, Kaldurg, Manor, Takmak and Tandulvadi), 1 in Vada (Koj); 2 in Bassein (Jivdhan and Kamandrug); 1 in Bhiwndi (Gumtara); 2 in Shahapur (Bhopatgad and Mahuli); 1 in Kalyan (Malangad); 3 in Panvel (Chanderi, Karnala and Peb or Vikatgad); and 3 in Karjat (Manikgad, Prabal and Vishargad). The Sahyadri forts were 9 in number: 1 in Shahapur (Balvantgad); 4 in Murbad (Bahirugad, Gorakhgad, Naldrug and Sidgad); 4 in Karjat (Bhivgad, Dhak, Kotaligad and Tungi).

> Most of these forts were built by the Musulmans or the Portuguese (1300-1600), were repaired by Shivaji about the middle of the seventeenth century, and were either taken by the British in 1774 or handed over to them in 1817 (*GZB, Thana District*, p. 98).

The point is that more than 50 forts in all were considered necessary to control what must be considered a comparatively limited stretch of the Konkan coast. This can only mean that the commercial traffic to this area must have generated enough revenue to the ruling powers of the day. The location and number of all these forts is an indirect indication of the commercial prosperity of this sector.

The configuration of its ancient monuments is also an indication of its commercial prosperity. These monuments also fall in several clusters. The most important cluster is formed by what may be called the group of caves in and around Mumbai: Kanheri Kondivti, Jogeshwar or Jogeshwari, Mandapeshwar, Magathana and Elephanta. Containing more than 100 caves and many more rock-cut water cisterns and occasional structural examples, Kanheri occupies a special place both in the history of Buddhism and the history of ancient Indian art and architecture. This is also one of the earliest Indian monuments to be described in detail by European travellers. The *GZB, Thana District*, pp. 121-190 offers one of the most detailed available descriptions of the Kanheri caves.

> The centre of trade and population, on which the Kanheri monastery originally chiefly depended, was, probably, about three miles to the west, at the mouth of the Tulsi valley, somewhere near the site of the deserted village of Magathan, which appears in one of the cave inscriptions as Mangalthan. Pilgrims, no doubt, came from the east, by Vehar and Tulsi, but the main approach was from the west, perhaps by way of Padan hill, up the Tasu valley which was probably cleared and tilled and provided with an easy road (Ibid, p. 124).

The first phase of Kanheri must have begun at least around 100 BC, and donatory inscriptions are available at least up to the 9th century AD.

According to the Thana gazetteer (*Ibid.*, p. 127), the Buddhist monks of Kanheri were building relic shrines as late as the middle of the 15th century AD. About a hundred years later, when the Portuguese took over the area, they found ascetics living in the complex and converted their leaders to Christianity. In a sense, as the gazetteer puts it, "the great Buddhist monastery of Kanheri remained in life until its leaders were made Christians by the Portuguese".

Gokhale (1991) dates the first Kanheri inscriptions in the early centuries AD, but according to her the Satavahana dynasty did not begin till 30 BC. This late date of the beginning of Satavahana chronology is, however, by no means beyond doubt. An interesting aspect of the Kanheri inscriptions is that according to the Traikutaka dynastic copper-plate of c. AD 495, Buddharuchi, a resident of the village Kanaka in the *Sindhu Vishaya* (i.e., Sindh), donated a *chaitya*. According to another inscription of c. AD 853-854, Gomin Avighnakara from *Gaudadesa* (Bengal) donated 100 *drammas* for a meditation room and clothings. That Kanheri had links with Sindh and Bengal is an important point to note.

The continued importance of the Kanheri area is also suggested by the location of later relics up to 11th/12th century in the same general area: Mandapeshwar where there are Brahmanical caves of c. 7th century, and Eksar where there are six great blocks of memorial stones recording sea and land fights of probably the 11th and 12th centuries. About half-a-mile to the east of the Borivli rail station, the gazetteer mentions "Buddhist tombs and a Buddhist monastery" of 5th/6th century AD and at Akuri, about 2 miles to the southeast, there are more relics. The Jogeshwari cave or Amboli cave, which is near Goregaon, is Brahmanical, not earlier than the 8th century AD. An early cave complex is located near Andheri: Kondivti which is famous for its pillarless circular cell with a domical but unribbed ceiling. An associated inscription puts it in the second century AD. Elephanta was important in the post-Gupta phase of Indian art, but Tripathi's report of a brick-built *stupa* structure on the top of a hill overlooking the sea suggests that it may have an earlier architectural tradition.

There are miscellaneous occurrences near Karjat: Jambrug where the spur up the incline of the Bor pass is reported to have caves; Halkhurd which is said to have a monastic cell, etc. North of Umbergaon 14 cells are said to underlie the fortifications of Indragad fort. In the area around Dahanu, on the Dahanu-Nasik road, a rock-cut cave complex has been reported by S. Nagaraju (1981).

II.2. Passes and Alignments between Umbergaon and Elephanta

The list of such miscellaneous remains may be extended, but looking at their distribution, one may make a few inferences. A few major passes lead across the Western Ghats to Thana, and, from the north to the south, they are: Shir Ghat or Shir pass which gives access to the Vaitarna valley; Tal Ghat and Pimpri Ghat or Tal and Pimpri passes which lead to a whole stretch of the Vaitarna and the Ulhas river areas; Malsej Ghat and Nana Ghat or the Malsej and Nana passes which lead straight to Kalyan; and the Bhimshankar, Kusur and Bor Ghats or passes which lead principally straight to the Karjat and Elephanta sectors.

It may be remembered that all these passes are not straight gashes across the Western Ghats; very often they are nothing more than a chain of linked alignments, and very often there are minor openings in between them. There must be openings to the north of the Shir pass, and we think that it is these openings which gave access to the area between Umbergaon-Sanjan and Dahanu. Of course, this sector could also be approached once one arrived in the Vaitarna valley near Mahim via the Shir and Tal or Thal passes. For Sopara it is these two passes which were important, just as they were for the later-day Bassein. The Thal was important for the entire Mumbai complex including Elephanta. The same is true of the passes between Malsej and Bor. They all fed the commerce of the modern Mumbai coast.

If one has to establish a relative importance among these passes, one has to give the primary importance to the Thal which was followed by the Nana and the Bor. The Thal was the most important because on the eastern flank of the Western Ghats in this sector was a major ancient settlement like Nasik. The location of the large Buddhist complex of Nasik hill in the outskirts of ancient Nasik on the approach to the Thal is another indication of the importance of this pass in ancient Indian history. The importance of the Nana pass is realised when one thinks of the importance given to it by the Satavahana kings and the location of the large Buddhist complex of Junnar at its approach. Junnar also lies on the approach to Malsej Ghat which like Nana Ghat takes one straight to the area around Kalyan and thus to the Kalyan-Thana-Mumbai chain. The most important Buddhist complexes along the Bhor alignment are those of Karle and Bhaja and possibly Kondane and Bedsa.

Once in the eastern flank of the Ghats, this northernmost part of the Konkan coast was linked to a few major alignments. The first one led, via Nasik and Chalisgaon, to Malwa across the Narmada and Aurangabad and the area to its east. The second one led to the modern Pune area from where the routes diverged towards Gulbarga in north Karnataka on the one hand and towards Satara and Kolhapur in the southwestern section of Maharashtra, on the other. In the ancient context, this section of the coast was also easily linked with the road running from Tagara or Ter to Barygaza or Broach. This road is mentioned by the *Periplus* and must have traversed through the Nasik district. Ter is near Osmanabad and from there the road probably came to Paithan, which finds a mention in the *Periplus*, and from Paithan this road would have entered Nasik to move in the direction of modern Surat from where, up the coast, Broach is within a short distance.

To the east of the Western Ghats, Pune was a focal point of communication, especially along the Poona-Solapur-Gulbarga and Poona-Satara-Kolhapur-Belgaum alignments. The importance of the Pune-Belgaum alignment also lies in the fact that there were branch roads from this alignment towards the Konkan coast. The antiquity of Pune itself has now been found to stretch back to the Satavahana period (Shinde *et al.* 2002-2003), and both in Solapur and Satara segments early historic sites have been located (cf. Joglekar *et al.* 2003-2004 for Satara; Shinde *et al.* 2003-2004, for Solapur). Kolhapur is a well-known early historic site.

II.3. From Alibag to Mahad

Around Alibag

This territory comes under the purview of the British Indian district of Kolaba. Mandva, about 12 miles north of Alibagh, is said to be 'a landing place of some importance' (*GZB, Kolaba District*, p. 350). The short broad bay here has a somewhat dangerous reef, but still a considerable quantity of rice used to be exported in the 19th century from here to the Mumbai market. There is no trace of old remains in the area. Avas is a small port, about 8 miles north of Ali Bag. Revas is located at the mouth of a creek of the same name. This creek can be used only between half and full tide and was considered a convenient spot for exporting grain. The place lies about 14 miles north of Alibag. About 10 miles north of Alibag, Dharamtar or Sabaj is the most important port of this sector. It lies on the right bank of the Amba River, and this creek is available at all times for boats of about 60 tons. Alibag lies on the coast but also at the mouth of the Sakhar creek, which is difficult to negotiate even for small boats because of the sandbanks. It was an important centre of coastal trade, exporting rice to the area from Mumbai to Ratnagiri and the southern coast. In summer mango is exported principally to Mumbai. The former importance of Alibag can be guessed from the location of Kolaba fort to its southwest, a little away from the shore. The fort is built on a rock and at high water becomes an island. Its precise history seems to be uncertain, but Shivaji selected it for defence around the middle of the 17th century. In 1662 it became one of his chief naval stations. Even after Shivaji, this fort continued to be the chief meeting point of the Maratha fleet, and became, by the early 18th century, the stronghold of that great Maratha admiral, Kanhoji Angria. Around 1840 it passed into the control of the British (for Alibag, *Ibid.*, pp. 253-265). North-east of Alibag and north of Pen, Antora is located on the Bhogavati creek, which at ordinary high tides was navigable for boats of up to 7 tons and spring tides for boats of up to 40 tons. Pen is a mile and a half south of Antora and has been described in the gazetteer as "a centre of considerable traffic between the Deccan and the sea-coast", with bullock carts coming down the Western Ghats along the Khopivli or Campoolee road bringing tobacco, molasses, pepper and onions and taking salt and rice.

> In 1668 Pen is mentioned as a port which acknowledged the Moghal as its superior, though it lay in Shivaji's territories. In 1675 it was mentioned by Fryer. In 1819 the easy communication with Bombay and with the Deccan by the Bor pass made Pen an important centre. Its chief prosperity lay in its salt beds to which many thousand bullocks came every year, some of them with a few miscellaneous articles but most of them empty. There was a considerable export of rice to Bombay. A number of carved stones about the town appear to belong to an unusually large temple of about the thirteenth or fourteenth century (Ibid, p. 356).

Six miles northwest of Alibag and 11 miles south of Bombay is the island of Khanderi, which in the Portuguese records of the 16th century was known as the Island of Chaul. Lying at the entrance to the Mumbai harbour it was of strategic importance, and although small, this island was a bone of contention between the Marathas and the British. The same is true of the smaller island of Underi, which also lies to the northwest of Alibag.

Chaul

Historically the most celebrated port of this area is Chaul on the right bank of the Kundalika River or Roha creek. It lies on the coast, about 30 miles south of Mumbai. The local Hindu traditions give its legendary names as *Champavati* or *Revatikshetra* but more dependable early references include two inscriptions of c. AD 130 from Kanheri, which mention two brothers from Chemula, who made gifts to the monastery. At about the same time Ptolemy mentions this as Symulla or Timulla from where people used to travel to Alexandria. In the middle of the 1st century AD, the *Periplus* knows it as Semulla. A Kanheri inscription of the 5th century AD refers to it as Chemula, and it is assumed that it is mentioned as Sibor by the Greek merchant and monk of the 6th century, Kosmas Indikopleustes. This was said to be a leading port between Kalyan and the Malabar ports. It has also been assumed that it was Chimolo of the Chinese pilgrim Hiuen Tsang of the 7th century AD. In the 10th to the 12th century records of Arab travellers and geographers, Chaul was known as Saimur and Jaimur. Al Masudi in the early 10th century described it as under one of the local Silahara rulers owing allegiance to the Balharas or Rashtrakuta kings. He also says that the town had an important Muslim population, some of which were locally born, but some came as merchants from Siraf, Oman, Basrah and Baghdad. The Muslims were allowed to build mosques and have their own system of adjudicating disputes. Later, in the 10th century (c. AD 970), Ibn Haukal describes Saimur as a great and strong city with abundance of mangoes, coconuts, onions and rice but no dates. A Silahara copper-plate grant of AD 1094 calls it Chemuli and describes it as a port like Surparaka and Sristhanaka. In the account of Al Idrisi in the 12th century it was a large town with coconut trees and henna in abundance, with aromatic plants in the neighbouring hills. In the 13th century Chaul probably passed into the hands of the Yadava rulers of Devagiri. Alauddin Khalji's attack on Konkan early in the 14th century did not have a permanent impact, and Chaul possibly passed into the control of the Vijayanagara kings for a short period to come under the rule of the Bahmani kings in the 14th century itself. It was the principal port of the Bahmani sultans of the Deccan. The Russian traveller Athanasius Nikitin (AD 1470) calls it Chivil, and towards the end of the 15th century Chaul passed into the hands of the kings of Ahmednagar, for whom also it was their chief port. Ludovico Varthema has left behind a description of Chaul of this period.

In the early 16th century the Portuguese had reached a rapport with the Ahmadnagar kings, under which the Portuguese would protect Chaul on condition that the Ahmadnagar kings would pay them an annual tribute as the rulers of the sea. On Chaul of 1514 we have the testimony of D. Barbosa. There was a Portuguese representative at the place which was ruled by a representative of the Ahmadnagar kings. The houses were well-built but mostly thatched. In winter large caravans of laden bullocks, about 30 to 40 of them under the care of one man, poured in with goods from the hinterland. Coconuts were exported to the Gulf and Arabia, from where dates and horses were imported. The coastal trade covered

Malabar and Goa in the south and Gujarat in the north. The Malabar trade was in coconuts, betelnuts, spices, drugs, palm-sugar and emery. Quicksilver, copper and vermilion, all of Portuguese origin, also came in Malabar boats. From Gujarat came mostly cotton. The Malabar boats took in their return journey wheat, vegetables, millet, rice, sesame and sesame oil, fine and coarse cotton. Cotton was also a staple item of the return Gujarat trade. In 1516 the Portuguese were allowed to set up a 'factory' in Chaul and have freer access to its harbour. In 1521 Chaul was attacked and burnt by the fleet of the Bijapur kings. The Portuguese were at this stage permitted to build a fort in lower Chaul. The fort was complete in 1524 but was attacked in 1528 by the Gujarati fleet aided by some Turkish ships. The attack was repulsed by the combined Ahmadnagar and Portuguese fleet but Chaul was attacked again by Gujarat. Bahadur Shah of Gujarat became an ally of Ahmadnagar at this point, but he died in 1535, after which the Ahmadnagar-Portuguese alliance became operational again. In 1570 the Ahmadnagar and the Bijapur kings combined against the Portuguese to attack the Portuguese fort of Chaul, which resulted in a treaty between them and the Portuguese.

In the last quarter of the 16th century, Chaul was described as a very prosperous port in the records of European travellers. According to Ralph Fitch, of all the places on the coast Chaul had the largest number of ships from the Red Sea and Hormuz in the Gulf. According to J.H. Linschoten (1583), it was a fortified city with a good harbour and famous for trade. Merchants came here from Cambay, Sind, Bengal, Muscat, Hormuz and the Red Sea. Many Gujarati merchants settled in Chaul. Raw silk used to be brought from China for the making of robes. There was considerable trade in rice, cotton and indigo. Around 1586, the Venetian traveller Caesar Frederick mentioned the Muslim city of Chaul located at a higher point in relation to the Portuguese city or fort located at the lower elevation of the river mouth. Both were called ports with great sea trade. Coconuts, drugs and spices came from other parts of the Indian coast, whereas from Portugal, Arabia and China came sandals, raw and manufactured silk, velvet, scarlet cloth and porcelain. The exports to other parts of India, Malacca, Macao, Hormuz, east Africa and Portugal included iron, borax, asafoetida, corn, indigo, opium, silk and great quantities of plain, painted and printed cotton goods. Among the local industries, there is mention of silk industry and the manufacture of glass beads for export to east Africa.

There were disputes between the Portuguese and the Ahmadnagar power over Chaul, but early in the 17th century, the French traveller Francois Pyrard described the Portuguese Chaul or the lower Chaul as very strong and safe from attack, whereas the upper Chaul was a great centre of manufacture, especially of lacquered chests, cabinets, beds and couches, and cotton and silk industry. In 1600 Ahmadnagar fell to the Mughals who came to control the upper Chaul by 1612. In 1623 Chaul was visited by the Italian traveller Pietro della Valle who did not offer the details of its trade, although he described the general character of the settlement.

The Portuguese Chaul of c. 1631 was described well in the Portuguese sources of the period. Unlike the Portuguese residents of Daman and Bassein, whose wealth was based mainly on land, the Portuguese of Chaul lived by trade and shipping. The chief ports with which they traded were Cambay, Muscat, Basrah, Mozambique, Manila and China. There was great demand for fine gold-bordered Deccan cloth in Persia and other trade goods included glass beads, iron, silk, rice, wheat and vegetables. In fair weather even small boats could easily sail to Cambay with spices and other products, but the coast was then so infested with pirates that the Chaul boats never sailed except in large groups protected by escorts of war ships. Only two voyages were possible each season. The ships bound for the Gulf left Chaul at any time between October and the end of April and returned generally in September-October or in March to May. To Mozambique a ship went every January carrying mostly cloth and Deccanese glass beads, bringing back ivory, gold and slaves. The export of glass beads was highly profitable and a monopoly of the Portuguese Captain of Chaul. Boats left for Manila and China between the end of March and the end of May. Iron came to Chaul in great quantities from the Deccan and were used for the manufacture of anchors, small guns called falcons, and nails. To China went Cambay cloth, linen, almonds, raisins, frankincense and a type of wood. The goods bound for Manila included, in addition to those sent to China, much wheat flour and iron.

For a short while around 1636 Chaul passed into the hands of the Bijapur power, but that was the period of the rise of the Marathas, and after protracted struggle between the Marathas, the Portuguese and the British, the Marathas took possession of Chaul from the Portuguese in 1740. Chaul did not regain its earlier prosperity, but as late as 1781, Upper Chaul was called a considerable sea-port.

The remains of the Portuguese buildings of Lower Chaul have been described in detail by the Kolaba district gazetteer (*Ibid.*, pp. 287-301).

The archaeological excavations in the Chaul area have been conducted by V.D. Gogte (Gogte *et al.* 2006). The report is only briefly published. However, it has been noted that the Satavahana period pottery, and ring-wells, coins, saddle querns, glass beads and bangles of the Satavahana period (put by him between 230 BC and AD 230) have been located at several places in the old mud flats of the Kundalika River. A body sherd of Roman amphora has also been found in this context. An ancient embankment wall and a dilapidated stone structure looking like a jetty occur at the edge of the old mud flats. It has further been argued that the Hinglaj hill, which has Buddhist caves, served as an anchorage point of Chaul.

Gogte's estimate is that pre-modern Chaul is spread over 2 km along the Kundalika River, with a breadth varying between 400 and 900 m. One excavation trench yielded rich evidence of glass production including beads of the 'Indo-Pacific' type, bangles and vessels.

> The total number of beads recovered from this small trench is 517. Within 1 m depth, all salient features of glass bead production were observed. The Indo-Pacific beads are of various colours: blue, green, yellow and brick red. The lengths vary from 1.5 mm to 5 mm. Hundreds of beads could be collected from the surface in this area, particularly after the rains. This area is clearly a production centre of Indo-Pacific beads. ... A large number of antiquities containing glass beads, fragments of glass bangles and very thin glass bangles having golden and bluish patina, glass debitage, iron ring, knife, spatula, nails and small rods of iron, copper wires and hooks, small stones of garnet, furnace linings, etc. were also recovered. Lumps of fine siliceous rocks, possibly used as raw material in glass production, and a half terracotta mould of an Indo-Sassanian coin were also discovered. The pottery consists of early mediaeval glazed pottery from west Asia, monochrome ware, and the Chinese blue-on-white ware, besides a large number of coarse wares (Gogte *et al.* 2006).

At a lower level, this trench also yielded two large ring wells, each individual ring being 75 cm in diameter, 35 cm in height and 3 cm in thickness. These and other reported terracotta ring wells in the Chaul area were possibly dug to procure fresh water.

Another excavated trench yielded a complete stratigraphic column of the site from the third century BC onward. A major feature of this trench was the discovery of a Satavahana period burnt-brick plinth wall, which was 85 cm high and rested on a solid foundation of about 1 m thick bedding made of boulders and rammed soil. Below this bedding, black-and-red ware was found in a calcified pit dug into beach sand. In the first phase the identified pottery included black-and-red ware and black-slipped ware. The next phase contains red polished ware, red-slipped ware and possibly sherds of Roman amphorae, all of which can be dated between the 1st-2nd century BC and c. 5th-7th century AD. This phase is followed by the appearance of glazed wares from West Asia and what has been called 'crude, large Stoneware sherds of the Chinese origin'. In the uppermost phase is found a large quantity of West Asian glazed pottery and different varieties of Chinese pottery. The seven sherds of Roman amphorae have been supposed to be identical with those from Nevasa in the interior and bear 'striking resemblance' with those from Qana at the mouth of the Red Sea.

Two caves of the 2nd-3rd century AD have been located in the vicinity of Chaul at Agrav and Chinchoti. It has also been asserted by Gogte *et al.* (2006) that the trade routes which led from Chaul to the interior of the Deccan passed by the cave at Agashi on the right bank of the Kundalika River, which could be reached via the caves at Agrav, Chinchjoti and Ashtami. They also outline the courses of the following major routes starting from Chaul.

The first alignment followed the ancient caves of Agrav, Ashtami, Gomashi, Gothe and Mann to reach Pune. This went through the Pimpri pass which has another pass called the Paratewadi pass close to it.

The second alignment branched off at Gothe to follow the alignment of ancient caves of Pomgaon, Tikona, Bedsa, Shelarwadi and Bhandara to reach Junnar and then to Nasik or Nevasa.

The third alignment followed the approach to the ancient cave of Thanale, crossed the Vaghlaj pass to the areas of Karle, Bhaja and Bhandara on the way to Junnar and beyond.

The fourth alignment also went to the Junnar segment but did so by crossing the Kivni pass. The fifth alignment went to Mahad and then crossed the Varandah pass to reach Khandala from where the Khambataki pass was crossed to reach the Satara-Karad side of the Western Ghats to reach Kolhapur. The sixth alignment took one through Karad to Chiplun, from where the Kumbharli pass was crossed to be in the area of Kolhapur. Gogte *et al.* (2006) point out the existence of three further alignments to reach the Junnar area in the first instance. These alignments could use any of the three passes – the Vaghjai pass, the Tamhini pass and the Bor pass. From Junnar one could travel almost due north to Nasik or proceed somewhat northeast to Nevasa from where Paithan was within easy distance down the Godavari.

One of the important results of Gogte's Chaul excavations is that it has shown the earliest settlement at the site to be 1.98 m below the present high tide sea level. Assuming that the original settlement was located, for the sake of safety, about 2 m higher than the sea-level of the day, one has to infer that "since the first Mauryan habitation around 300 BCE, the sea level has risen to anything between 4 to 5 metres". Further, attention has

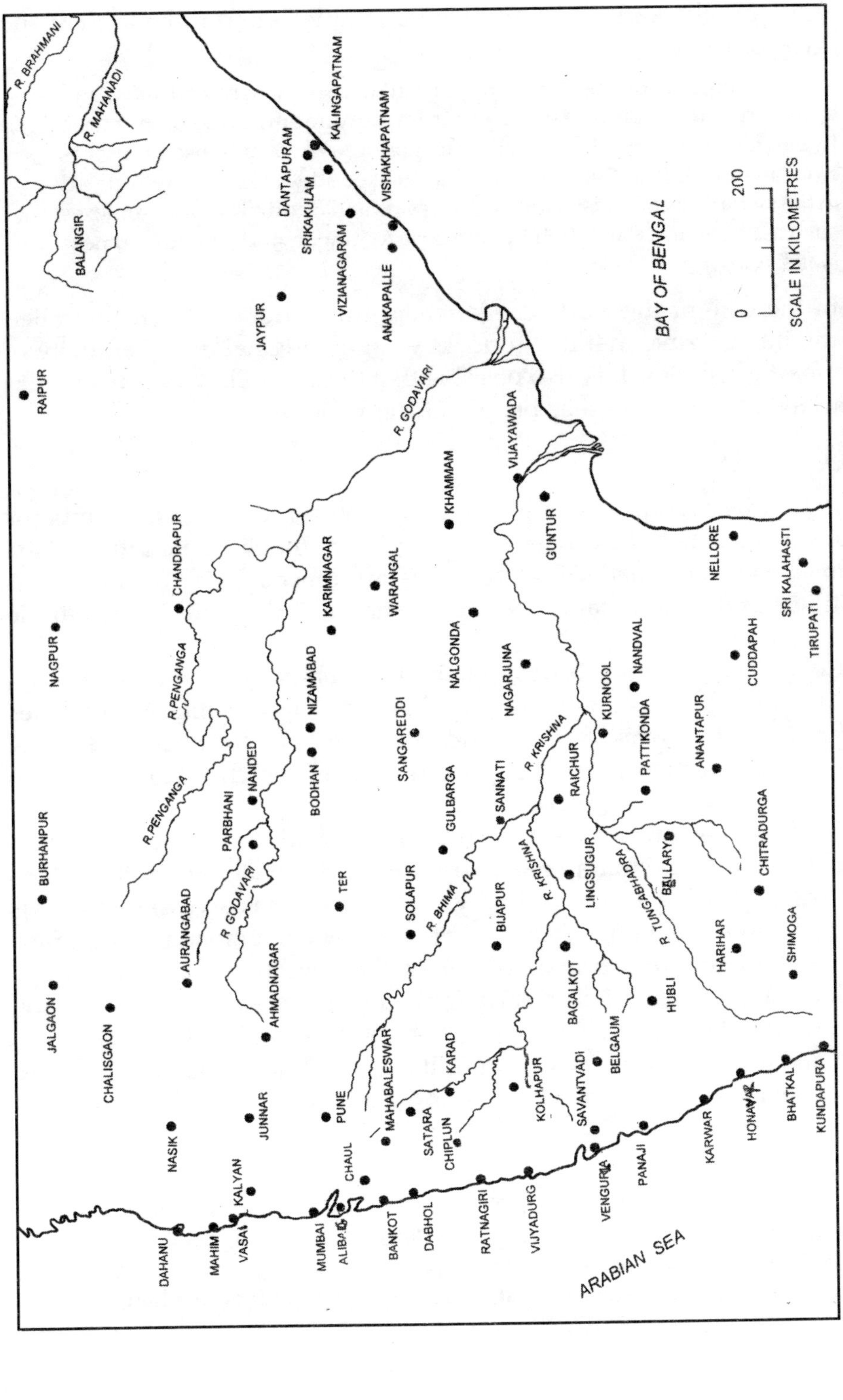

Map 1. The Konkan Coast and its hinterland in Maharashtra and Parts of Karnataka and Andhra.

been drawn to the location of an Ekavira temple between the ancient site and caves of Chaul.

> The worshippers of this deity are particularly the fishermen (*Kolis*) and sailors from the Mumbai island and from surrounding areas of the coast. In the coastal area of Maharashtra, the goddess Ekavira is also known as Konkan devi. Interestingly, other temples of goddess Ekavira are situated in the vicinity of early historic cities, sea ports and Buddhist cave complexes such as at Sopara, Karle, Behergaon close to Junnar, and Chandwad near Nasik (Gogte *et al.* 2006).

In the case of the Karle caves where the goddess Ekavira is called Veherai, it is possible that the goddess was the original guardian deity of the monastic complex. It is also possible that the deity Ekavira was popular among the traders and other people of the region.

Nagothna to Mahad

About 15 miles south of Pen is Nagothna, on the bank of the Amba or Nagothna creek, about 24 miles from its mouth. In 1883 when the Kolaba gazetteer was published, Nagothna was approachable by boats only at high tide, but it is said that in the fair season there was considerable trade in rice, salt and fish.

Roha lies on the north bank of the Kundalika River, about 24 miles from its mouth. It has a stone-built wharf which at ordinary high tides could be used for boats of 5 tons and at spring tides for boats of 15 tons. Roha has been called a great rice market from which exports went to Mumbai and the Ratnagiri coast.

Mandad lies on the bank of the Mandad River 8 miles above its confluence with the Janjira creek. At spring tides boats of up to 70 tons could reach Mandad and at ordinary high tides it was accessible to boats of up to 12-and-a-half tons. As it is supposed to be mentioned as Mandava in the second century AD inscriptions of the neighbouring Kuda caves, Mandad may be considered an early trade centre. However, the correlation between 'Mandava' of a Kuda inscription (cf. *GZB, Kolaba District*, p. 333) and Mandad is by no means certain. It has been assumed that Mandad was the Mandagora of the *Periplus* and Ptolemy. In 1883 the situation was the following:

> *Machvas* and other vessels of fifty to 125 tons from Bombay, Habsan, Goa and Balsar visit Mandad anchoring from fifty to seventy feet from the landing place. The exports are myrobalans, coarse cloth, rice, mustard seed, tobacco, and live stock; the imports are cloth, drugs, coconuts, iron, coffee, fish, betelnut, spices, sugar, and tobacco. The traders are Bhandaris

> and Musulmans, most of them men of capital, who stay in Mandad from November to May (*GZB, Kolaba District*, p. 349).

There is an unconfirmed report of the habitation of the Satavahana period in the vicinity of Mandad. The area can be approached only during low tide and has yielded typical Satavahana period pottery including drinking cups and dishes. A sherd of a Roman amphora has also been reported.

North of the Savitri River, there are a few small trading settlements in and around the Rajapuri creek of Janjira. Murud is surrounded on three sides by the sea and a shallow creek is about a mile north of Janjira. There was brisk trade in 1883, the leading articles of trade being rice, coconuts, dried fish and firewood. Mhasla at the head of the Rajapur creek has been assumed to be Ptolemy's Musopalli, but there is no evidence except that it lies at the head of a great gulf. The trade of the town was poor in 1883. Janjira is a fortified island just at the entrance of the Rajapuri creek and known principally as the stronghold of the Sidis, the descendants of the Abyssinian slaves imported to the Konkan coast. The Sidi naval force along with that of the Marathas was an important factor in the history of this coast in the 17th-18th century. Danda-Rajpuri, on the south bank of the Rajapuri creek at its mouth, was an important port in the 14th/15th to the 18th centuries. It figures as a rich trading town with a good harbour in the European records.

Dasgaon is on the bank of the Savitri River, 5 miles west of Mahad, and 24 miles above Bankot at the mouth of the river. The river is navigable up to Dasgaon where there is a stone-built jetty. Further up along the Savitri is Mahad which, because of its proximity to two groups of Buddhist rock-cut caves, has been called an early trade centre by the Kolaba gazetteer (*Ibid.*, 344). In 1538 a Portuguese record describes it as a large town with a great trade in wheat. Even in 1883 Mahad had considerable import and export trade. Fresh and salted fish came from Goa and elsewhere on the coast and there was considerable commercial traffic with Mumbai. Considerable quantities of rice went across the Varandah pass to the Deccan and also south to Ratnagiri.

> In 1820 Mahad is described as standing at the foot of a principal pass through the mountain leading to Poona, and as the emporium of the Bankot river where all merchandise whether leaving or entering the river was embarked. There was a large Vanjari traffic, caravans of pack-bullocks coming from the Deccan to be laden with rice and salt (*Ibid.*, p. 345).

The following inland forts are important in understanding the exercise of power in this sector: Sagargad fort which dominates both the Alibag and Dharamtar landing places, in addition to looking over Chaul; Songiri and Sankshi forts, both around Pen; Avchitgad, Birvadhgad, Ghosalgad and Surgad, all positioned near Roha on the Kundalika River and thus suitable for controlling access to Chaul which is located at the mouth of this river; Mangad and Visramgad near Mangaon; and finally Raygad, 'Gibraltar of the East', according to the early Europeans, looking over the entire Mangaon - Mahad sector and the approaches from this side to the Ratnagiri coast. These are not ancient forts but demonstrate, like the Thana forts, the importance of the commercial traffic of the area between Alibag and Mahad. Besides, as it appears, there is a chain of forts on the rocky islands off the coast between Alibag and Janjira.

It has been argued that, when the political condition was favourable, "the whole traffic across the Sahyadris from the Par pass in the south to the Tal pass in the north centred at Chaul."(*Ibid.*, p. 110). It has further been claimed that the largest share of the traffic to Chaul came through the Bor pass, first by the Bor pass to Panvel, from Panvel by boat to Nagothna, from Nagothna by road to Roha, and from Roha down the Kundalika River to Chaul. One cannot cite any special evidence in this regard but this impression comes from people who knew the concerned terrain well and deserves every consideration.

II.4. Passes and Alignments between Alibag and Mahad

If one begins in the south and moves toward the north in the direction of Alibag, first one gets Parghat or Par pass which is 15 miles southeast of Mahad and leads toward Mahabaleshwar. Till 1826 it was much frequented by the Vanjaras bringing grain and salt from Satara to Konkan, although in 1883 it is called a mere footpath. Half a mile north of the Par pass is the FitzGerald pass which runs to Satara and enjoyed much traffic in 1883 between Vai and Neher in Satara and Mahad in Konkan. The Dhavla and Kamtha passes lie 5½ miles north of the FitzGerald pass and lead to Vai in Satara but were not much used in 1883. Five miles north of the Kamtha pass is the Varandah pass, which forms part of the road to Poona and is the scene of much traffic. A quarter of a mile north of the Varandah pass is the Umbarda pass which was fit for men and unladen cattle but was infrequented in the late 19th century. Four miles north of Umbarda is the Gopya pass which leads through Gonde to Poona. It was fit for men and with difficulty, for laden cattle. One mile north of the Gopya pass is the Ambenal pass which leads to Poona. It is fit for men. One mile north of the Ambenal pass is the Madhya pass which also leads to Poona. In 1826 it was fit for cattle. Half a mile north of Madhya is the

Shevtya pass aligned in the direction of Poona. It is fit for men and unladen cattle. Six miles north of Shevtya is the Kavaliya pass which led to Poona and was used by the Vanjaras. Eight miles north of Kavaliya is the Kumbha pass which was considered suitable for men and cattle but not for carts. Four miles north of the Kumbha pass is the *Linga* pass which was fit for men and laden cattle. Two miles north of the *Linga* pass is the Nisni pass which is merely a footpath but fit for men with light burdens. Six miles north of Nisni are the Tamhana, Devasthali and Thiba passes, which are merely footpaths. Four miles north of the Tamhana pass is the Pimpri pass. It was fit for men and laden cattle and was much used.

Apart from these main passes through the Western Ghats, this sector from Alibag to Mahad has also eleven gorges or *Khinds* through the smaller ranges of hills. Of these eleven gorges, two are in Alibag, five in Pen, two in Roha, and two in Mahad. In Alibag they are the Karli and Pir passes. In Pen there are Khachar, Gagode, Dahivali, Govirle and Sukeli passes. In Roha there are Chavee and Bhise passes, and in Mahad we have Dasgaon pass and Chambhar pass. All these passes are generally fit for cart traffic. Regarding Pir pass it has been written that when Chaul was a great port, this must have been one of the highways of traffic.

The distribution of ancient remains in the form of Buddhist caves is limited to the Hinglaj spur near Chaul, Kuda, also close to Chaul, and the Pali and Kol cave complexes, both around Mahad. The Mahad caves date from the 1st to the 3rd centuries AD and as the term Pali or Pale is echoed in 'Palalipatmai' of the *Periplus* and 'Balipatna 'of Ptolemy, it has been argued that Mahad might be identified with Balipatna/Palaipatmai of the Classical sources. Kuda is a major cave complex and has been described in detail in the Kolaba district gazetteer:

> It is remarkable for a group of twenty-six Buddhist caves and eleven cisterns, from 150 to 200 feet above sea-level, cut in the side of a hill which is about 250 feet high. ...The walls of almost all the caves were plastered with earth and rice-chaff, and several of them have remains of painting. Many have inscriptions, the sixth cave having as many as six. Five, all in the sixth cave, belong to the fifth or sixth century after Christ. The rest are in letters of about the first century before Christ, and record the names of the giver and the nature of the gift, whether a cave, a cistern, or both. Several of the givers are women and one of them is a Brahman's wife (*GZB, Kolaba District*, pp. 332-333).

A number of Kuda inscriptions refer to traders.

Pale/Pali is a group of twenty-nine Buddhist caves of the first-second century AD and lies about 2 miles to the northwest of Mahad. As the name appears as Valipavana or Palipattana in a Silahara copper-plate of AD 1094, it is generally identified with Balipatana of Ptolemy or Palaipatmai of the *Periplus*. One of the inscriptions in the verandah outside Cave 28 seems to mention a rich merchant or *Sresthi* whose name was Sangharakshita. His name also figures in an inscription of the Kol caves, which lie about a mile to the southwest of Mahad. There is also a third group of caves to the southeast of Mahad but that consists of only a few cells and cisterns. There is also a cell by the side of the road leading from Mahad to Nagothna.

It is the Chaul and Mahad sectors which were prominent on the coast as the centres of maritime trade, and one wonders which passes were more important in leading to them. For the northern Alibag-Pen – Nagothna belt the Bor pass was likely to have played a role, because, once inside the Ghats, there could be feeder routes in the direction of Alibag, Pen and Nagothna. One learns that in the late 19th century there was a straight route from Poona to Nagothna.

II.5. The Ratnagiri Sector

Bankot to Burondi

Regarding the movement of goods in pre-British Ratnagiri, it may be useful to cite what the Ratnagiri and Savantbadi gazetteer of 1880 (*GZB, Ratnagiri District*) states:

> At the beginning of British rule (1818-1820) carriage was almost entirely by water. The government grain stores, the chief centres of local traffic, were all near the banks of creeks, and from no part of the district, except where water carriage was at hand, was the forest produce gathered and exported (*Ibid.*, p. 167).

The chain of ports in Ratnagiri begins with Bankot on the Savitri River in the north. Next to Mumbai, it was the earliest English possession in western India. It lies on the south shore of the entrance to the Bankot or Savitri River. The port remains closed during the southwest monsoon, but opens earlier and remains longer than most Ratnagiri ports. For vessels of 16 feet draught, the river is navigable up to Mahapral, and for vessels of 7 feet draught, it is navigable for further ten miles up to Mahad. There was some trade in 1880, but in 1548 it was destroyed by the Portuguese along with the other coastal towns controlled by the Bijapur rulers. In 1775 it passed into the hands of the British. *Mahapral* is closely linked to Bankot as a trading centre, and although the area of Mandangarh fort in the same area has been identified by some with Mandagora mentioned by the *Periplus* and Ptolemy, there is an opinion which puts Mandagora "on the coast at the mouth of the Bankot creek, on the site of the present villages of Bagmandla and Kolmandla" (*Ibid.*, p. 352). Kelshi, whose principal export was betelnut, lies at the mouth of the Kelshi river 3 miles southeast of Bankot. It is mentioned by the Portuguese Dom Joao de Castro (1538) and P. della Valle (1624), but the latter did not go on shore here because of the fear of pirates. It was a small trading place with few Vanjaras and little export of grain in 1819. Ade is a port 3 miles south of Kelshi. It has been described as a port with a small trade in corn and fish. Anjarla, a small port at the mouth of the Jog river and about 3 miles south of Ade, had a little trade in salt, fish and corn in 1819. Harnai, about 2 miles south of Anjarla, has a small rocky bay offering shelter to coasting craft in southwest monsoon and is noted for its proximity to a number of forts: the island fortress of Suvarnadurg, a little to the north; Kanakdurg and Fatehgad on the mainland across a narrow channel; and Gova, also an island fort but much smaller than Suvarnadurg. The area seems to be noted for its market in fish and manufacture of coarse cotton, but was linked to Satara by Khed and Ambavli passes. Suvarnadurg and other forts seem to go back to the rulers of Bijapur but were taken over later by the Marathas. In the late 17th and early 18th centuries, Suvarnadurg was an important base of the Maratha admiral Kanhoji Angria. It fell to the British in 1818.

Dapoli on the bank of the Jagbudi river does not appear to be a trading settlement, but Khed, located at the head of this river, carries on trade both with Harnai via Dapoli and with Satara via the Ambola pass. Six miles south of Harnai, Burondi is called a small port.

Dabhol

Dabhol lies on the north bank of the Anjanvel or Vashisht river and is a narrow strip of land between the high steep hills and the river. Its early occupation possibly stretched along the river for 3/4 miles. Although Dabhol has still a landing place, there is little of trade now. The gazetteer (*Ibid.*, p. 327) notes that large remains are found at Dabhol several feet underground and that there is supposedly epigraphic record to state that in the 11th century Dabhol was the seat of a Jaina ruler. In the mediaeval period, and possibly early mediaeval period as well, Dabhol was an important place. It was destroyed by Malik Kafur, Alauddin Khalji's general in AD 1312. By 1357 it became the western limit of the Bahmani power of Bidar. In the 15th century it was a great centre of trade. According to Athanasius Nikitin in 1570 it was a great town, an extensive sea-port and a centre of horse trade with Mysore, Arabia, Khorasan and Nighostan. It was also a place connected by trade with Ethiopia. At the beginning of the 16th century Dabhol fell to the power of Bijapur, and around 1508, in Ludovice Varhema's account,

> Dabhol was one of the most noted coast towns with a considerable trade and stately and magnificent buildings, girt with a wall, surrounded by country houses, and fortified by a strong castle garrisoned by 6000 men of whom 500 were Turks (*Ibid.*, p. 328).

The Portuguese kept on either attacking, or creating harassment for Dabhol throughout the 16th century, and in the 17th century it was much reduced in prosperity. It fell to the British in 1818.

On Dabhol and Chaul and the Deccanese trade through them, the testimony of *The Suma Oriental of Tome Pires* (Cortesao 1944, vol. 1, pp. 52-54) is important. Tome Pires wrote his account between 1512 and 1515.

> The Deccan used to do a great deal of trade, chiefly in Dabhol. It was a rich and honoured port of call, a good port, with many ships; ... This kingdom of the Deccan produces the following merchandise: calicos – cloths in white and countless colours – and *beatilhas*, which the Moors and Klings generally use for their turbans. They make enough of these things to furnish the world. They also make black beads in this kingdom which are good for *Diua* (Diu? the Maldives ? the latter more probable) and Abyssinia. Most of the betel, which is called *folio Indo*, goes from here to Cambay, Ormuz and Aden. As the ports of this kingdom were conveniently situated, the merchandise from all over Asia and Europe was to be found there; and the port of Chaul was very famous, but it is already on the decline.

Anjanvel, on the south shore of the entrance to the Vashishti or Dabhol River gave good anchorage during the fair weather to vessels passing and to and fro from Chiplun up the river.

The gazetteer's description of Chiplun as a trading centre is vivid and gives a thorough idea of how the trade across the Western Ghats used to be conducted in the pre-modern period:

> At the head of a navigable river and near the entrance to the Kumbharli pass, one of the easiest routes from the Deccan to the sea, Chiplun must always have been a centre of trade. Of late, by the opening of a cart road through the pass, traffic has much increased. Its leading merchants are local Brahmans and Bhatias, with, in the fair season, a few agents of Bombay firms. All goods passing through Chiplun are, in the first instance, consigned to local merchants in accordance with the orders given by them to their correspondents in Bombay or the Deccan. Bulk is broken on arrival, and the goods are sold in large or small lots to the petty dealers and agents

> of Bombay firms. After changing hands, most of the imports are, in the course of two or three months, again exported. The chief articles received from the Deccan are cotton, molasses, clarified butter, oil, grain, turmeric, and chillies; and from Bombay, most of them to be sent on to the Deccan, are piece goods, metals, and other miscellaneous articles.... During the busy season, February to May, from 300 to 400 carts pass daily into Chiplun by this route. The merchants deal in every kind of goods, but never largely in any particular commodity. The trade is carried on in the fair season only. During these months (November-June) every empty space near the market or the landing place, and even in the river bed is covered by sheds or booths. This large trading camp is broken up on the first sign of the south-west monsoon, and during the rains almost the whole site is flooded (*GZB, Ratnagiri District*, pp. 324-325).

Guhagar on the coast, about 6 miles south of Anjanvel, which has been called an open roadstead without any shelter, has never been a place of trade. However, Gogte (2004) has tried to locate Palaipatmai mentioned by the *Periplus* at Palshet, which seems to lie in this sector. This modern village, apparently full of old but undated structural ruins, lies on the bank of the Sundari River, and although large walls of undressed stones have been located at the site and odd pieces of pottery claiming 'Satavahana affinity', there is absolutely nothing to suggest that the place can be identified with *Palaipatmai*.

Boria or *Adur* lies midway between the mouths of the Vashishti and Shastri rivers and is a small port offering safe anchorage during the northerly gales.

Jaygad lies on the south shore of the entrance to the Shastri or Sangameshwar River and is overlooked by a fort. Known for trade in salt and fish, Jaygad has a good bay and offered safe harbour. The fort at Jaygad was built in the 16th century by Bijapur, falling to the British in 1818 along with other Ratnagiri forts.

Sangameshwar is up the Shastri River, which was navigable even for the largest vessels up to this trading centre which lies about 20 miles from the coast. It lies at the mouth of the Mala pass and was thus a major centre of trade with the Deccan hinterland.

Ratnagiri in the late 19th century was a port of some local importance. It has a good bay overlooked by a fort with Bahmani/Bijapur ancestry.

Rajapur lies at the head of a tidal creek about 15 miles from the coast, and although the creek was largely silted up in the late 19th century, earlier it was a major port. It also derived its importance from the fact that it was directly linked with Kolhapur by the Phonda and Anaskura passes. The importance of Rajapur can be deduced from the fact that even in the late 19th century, a few Arab vessels from Zanzibar and the African coast used to bring to it every year fresh and dry dates to exchange for molasses and other produce (*GZB, Ratnagiri District*, p. 357). In the 14th century Jajapur is recorded as an important town of the area. In the 17th century, the European traveller Mandelslo considered it one of the best Deccan maritime towns. There was a British 'factory' here between 1649 and 1708. A French 'factory' was set up in 1673.

> In 1819 Rajapur was, in the extent of its trade and in the number and wealth of its people, much ahead of any other south Konkan port. The river was not very good, large boats having at one-third of the way up to move their cargoes into small boats. But trade was encouraged by specially easy rates. The inland trade was through the Anaskura pass to all the chief towns of the Maratha states (*Ibid.*, p. 360).

The system of trade which has been described by the gazetteer in the case of Rajapur was possibly true of other Konkan ports as well.

> The system of trade is similar to that of Chiplun and other old-fashioned isolated Konkan towns. Business is in the hands of local merchants, chiefly Bhatias, Brahmans and Musulmans. A few paid agents of Bombay firms come down for fair season to buy cotton and other goods, and arrange for freight to Bombay. Goods from the Deccan and Bombay are consigned to the local merchants. On arrival they are sold and re-sold to petty dealers, continually changing hands until they are distributed amongst the consumers or re-exported. The through trade is limited to the fair season (October-May), and as at Chiplun, during this busty time a large trading camp is formed, every available space near the market and the landing place being filled by temporary booths and warehouses. The chief streets are well kept and paved, and the permanent shops are substantially built. During the hot months, March, April, and May, the streets are shaded from the sun by a continuous canopy of plaited coconut leaves, stretching from house to house and making a temporary arcade (*Ibid.*, p. 358)

Jaytapur lies at the head of the Rajapur River and was thus in a way the sea outlet of the trading centre of Rajapur. The early European records give it importance, although in the late 19th century only smaller boats discharged and loaded. The 17th and 18th century sources speak of it as one of the best coast harbours, if not one of the best harbours in the world.

Vijaydurg is on the south shore of the entrance to the Vaghotan River and considered "one of the best harbours on the western coast" which can be entered in all weathers, offering shelter even to large ships during the south-west monsoon. Through the Fonda pass the commerce of this port was linked with the Deccan hinterland. Vijaydurg is also famous for its sea-fort, which lies on the neck of rocky land forming the south side of the bay. The gazetteer records that there is an old dock (355 ft by 227 ft) hollowed out of the rock by the Marathi admiral Kanhoji Angria, about 2 miles from the fort, on the same side of the river. According to the gazetteer (*Ibid.*, p. 379, note 2), "its great natural advantages make it probable that the mouth of Vaghotan River is one of the oldest coast settlements. There seems reason to suppose that it is Ptolemy's Byzantium, a Greek corruption of Vijayanta". It is connected with the Phonda pass across the Western Ghats.

Kharepatan, 25 miles up the Vaghotan or Vijaydurg River, was the inland port linked with Vijaydurg, and had in the late 19th century trade in salt and fish. According to Duarte Barbosa (1514), the Malabar vessels used to take on board here cheap rice and vegetables. In the 17th century it was described as the best port on the Konkan coast. The largest boat could sail up to it and it was only 15 miles from the Bavda pass. However, it has direct communication with the interior by the Phonda pass and is on the main line of road from Ratnagiri to Vengurla.

Achra is listed as a small port located on a creek of the same name. It is about 10 miles north of Malvan. It was once under the control of Bijapur.

Malvan, said to be a busy port in the late 19th century, is also known primarily for Sindhudurg fort which is located on an island about a mile offshore. It was also well linked with the hinterland around Belgaum through the Western Ghats passes. Sindhudurg was built by Shivaji in the middle of the 17th century along with the smaller fort of Padamgarh nearby. Sindhudurg covers an area of 48 acres and its ramparts measure less than two miles in periphery. The walls are 29-30 feet high and their width about 12 feet. Malvan has been said to be formerly a port of call for the Arab vessels who brought dates and umbrellas and took in return, at least up to Mumbai, cotton, coconuts and foodgrains. In the 16th century Malvan was an important centre of trade with access to the Deccan hinterlands. It has been fought over between the Marathas and the Portuguese, and the British tried to have a 'factory' here. A Classical association has also been assumed, as the following extract from the gazetteer demonstrates.

> The similarity of the name Melizigeris, the island of Meli, and the fact that the chief export was pepper would seem to make it probable that Ptolemy's island of Melizigeris and the *Periplus*' mart of Melizeigara, and perhaps Pliny's Zigerus, and Strabo's Sigerdis, were the island-town of Milandi or Malvan (*Ibid.*, p. 348, note 4).

South of Malvan and north of Vengurla is the fort of *Nivti*, which stands at the mouth of a small creek with a good bay. In 1819 its trade was insignificant but the fact that a fort guards its entrance suggests its importance as a port in the pre-modern period.

Vengurla, at the mouth of a swampy creek leading to a bay, is well connected with the hinterland from Belgaum downward. Vengurla figures prominently in the early European records as the place where both the Dutch (1635) and the British (1766?) set up 'factories'. The French traveller Tavernier mentions (1660) it as Mingrela which had ships from Batavia, Japan, Bengal, Sri Lanka, Surat, Hormuz and the Red Sea. Both the water and rice were excellent and the area famous for its cardamom and cloth. Vengurla was annexed by the British in 1812. It is connected with Belgaum by two routes, one over the Parpoli pass and the other by the Ram pass. Although except in the south the bay is sheltered, the port even in the fair season can be dangerous and remains closed between mid-June to the end of August. This, however, has not prevented it from monopolising the traffic with Belgaum and the neighbouring districts from Nipani to Gokak, both near Belgaum.

Observations

As in the sector between Umbergaon-Sanjan and Elephanta, there is a large number of forts in this sector, with the gazetteer listing 43 of them. The main island forts are Suvarnadurg and Sindhudurg whereas the main headland forts located on the banks of some rivers are, from north to south, Bankot, Anjanvel or Gopalgad, Govlkot, Jaygad, Ratnagiri, Purangad, Satavli, Rajapur, Jaytapur, Vijaydurg, Kharepatan, Devgad, Bhagvantgad, Ramgad, Sidhgad, Nivti, Vengurla and Redi. Their locations give an idea both of the importance of both maritime and inland trade passing through this sector and of the routes which linked this sector with its hinterland on the other side of the Ghats.

The Ratnagiri district gazetteer offers a general picture of trade of the region. In the 16th century the Ratnagiri ports were frequented by the Muslim traders of India herself and those from the Arab countries and Iran, the Hindu traders from Malabar, Konkan and the Deccan, and the Gujarati Hindus from Gujarat. There were large ships from Mecca, Aden and Hormuz and smaller coasting vessels from Cambay and Diu in the north and Malabar in the south. The chief trade routes followed the Bankot River up to Mahad and from Dabhol, Chiplun and Khed by the Ambavli pass to Bidar. Later in this century, the rise of Bijapur brought about the significance of another route up the Muchkundi River by Satavli through the Amba or Visalgad pass, by Kolhapur or Panhala to Bijapur and Golconda. A third route from Konkan to Bijapur lay from Jaytapur and Rajapur through Bavda and Kolhapur.

Of imports, there were, from the Red Sea and Persian Gulf, copper, quicksilver, vermilion, and horses; from the Malabar coast, coconuts, betelnuts, spices, copper, and quicksilver; from places along the Konkan coast, salt; and from the Deccan and Karnatak, wheat and fine cotton cloth. The exports were, to Gujarat, the copper and quicksilver brought from Arabia and the Malabar coast; to Malabar wheat and cotton cloth brought from the Deccan, and vegetables grown in Ratnagiri; and to the Red Sea and Persian Gulf, great quantities of cloth and coconuts, pepper, and other spices and drugs brought from the Malabar coast. Besides these, honey is mentioned as exported from the Bankot river; pepper as produced in small quantities (1540) near Dabhol, and as an export from Sangameshvar; and cheap rice and vegetables as an export from Kharepatan. Betel was grown in great quantities. The Muchkundi river was so famous for its betel gardens that it was known as the Betel river. The only local manufacture that seems to have been exported was iron from Sangameshvar. This trade, which centring in Dabhol had risen to great importance in the early part of the sixteenth century, was, from the refusal of the Bijapur kings to acknowledge their supremacy at sea, greatly harassed by the Portuguese.

In the beginning of the seventeenth century, with the decline of Portuguese power and increase of trade by the competition of the English, Dutch, and French, Dabhol, Rajapur and Vengurla again became important centres of traffic. In 1611, when the English first visited Dabhol, they found the merchants almost all Musulmans, carrying on trade with the Red Sea in ships some as much as 1200 tons burden. The Dabhol people 'made a noise of' fine cloth, indigo, and pepper, but showed none. They bought some broadcloth, kersies, lead bars, iron, ivory, and indigo. In 1639, salt and pepper are mentioned as the chief articles of trade at Dabhol. In 1649, its pepper and cardamom trade was the chief attraction that brought the English Company's factory to Rajapur. In 1660, Vengurla is spoken of as a great place of call for ships from Batavia, Japan, and Ceylon on the one side, and the Persian Gulf and Red Sea on the other. It is said to have been famous for its pepper and cardamoms, and it and Ratnagiri ports had much trade in calicoes, silks, grain, and coarse lacquer (*Ibid.*, pp. 174-175).

The gazetteer's summary of the Ratnagiri ports is no less interesting:

The Ratnagiri seaboard, stretching north and south for 160 miles, contains twenty-nine ports and harbours. Of the whole number, nine, Bankot, Harnai, Chiplun, Sangameshvar, Ratnagiri, Rajapur, Kharepatan, Malvan, and Vengurla, are places of some trade and consequence; the rest are small, offering during the fair season more or less complete shelter to coasting craft, but with little or no trade.

> Ratnagiri ports are of two classes, coast ports on sheltered bays and river mouths, and inland ports up the tidal creeks generally at the point where navigation ceases. Dabhol in former times, and now Ratnagiri, Malvan, and Vengurla are exceptions. But from the ruggedness of the inland country, and in former times from their freedom from pirate attacks, trade has always centred at the inland harbours. The coast settlements have been little more than fishing villages with, in the fair season, some stranger merchants and a small traffic chiefly in salt and grain (*Ibid.*, p. 356)

II.6. Passes and Alignments in the Ratnagiri Sector

The major Western Ghats passes, from north to south, are Hatlot, Ambavli, north Tivra, Kumbharli, Mala, south Tivra, Kundi, Amba, Vishalgad, Shevgad, Anaskura, Narduvaghat, Ghotgaghat, Ambolighat, Ramghat and Phonda. We quote from a source dated 1826 (*Ibid.*, p. 167):

> HATLOT, seven miles south of Par and leading from Makrangad fort to Khed, was little used; neither the pass nor its approach was practicable for carriages. AMBAVLI, nine miles south of Hatlot, the line of route from Satara to Khed and Dapoli, was passable but hard for cattle which in places had to be unladen; from the west mouth of the pass, the whole way to Khed was extremely bad and still worse to Dapoli. NORTH TIVRA, about half way (23 miles) between Satara and Chiplun, though used by Vanjara and others, was hardly practicable for loaded cattle; the fourteen miles from Tivra to Chiplun were very bad. KUMBHARLI, about 13-½ miles south of Tivra, winding, long, and of easy ascent, though generally rocky and bad, was the best in that part of the range; it had lately been repaired and was the high road from the coast to Karhad, Satara, Sholapur and other places. MALA, about nine miles south of Kumbharli, was about three miles long, leading from Karhad in Satara to Makhjan. SOUTH TIVRA, six miles south of Mala, was exceedingly steep for two miles, the road running up a river bed; this was a route between Sangameshvar and Miraj. KUNDI, five and a half miles south of Tivra, was a bad pass. AMBA, eleven miles south of Kundi, led from Devrukh to Kolhapur and Miraj; Vishalgad fort at the mouth of this pass divided it into two, Devara on the north, unpracticable for cattle, and Prabhavali on the south, little used except by people going to Vishalgad. ANASKURA or ANSKURA, nine miles south of Amba, was the direct route from Karhad to Malvan, and the usual route from Miraj to Rajapur and Kharepatan; though in no part possible to wheeled carriages, the road was good and in steep places paved with large rough stones; it was much used by Vanjaris; the approach from the Konkan side was very bad, but a little labour might make it practicable for guns. KAJIRDA, the straight road between Kolhapur

and Rajapur, formerly passable to laden cattle, was stopped. BAVDA, about seven miles north of Shevgad, also a route from Kolhapur to Rajapur, a road for foot passengers, was frequented by laden cattle. SHEVGAD, about six miles north of Phonda, from Kolhapur to Malvan, frequented by cattle, was out of repair; formerly guns had been brought up it. PHONDA, the direct line from Kolhapur to Malvan, one of the easiest passes to the Deccan, had a few years before been made practicable for ordnance; with little labour it might be put in good repair; it was not much used. GHOTGA, the route from Kolhapur and Miraj to Malvan, though bad near the top, was much used by cattle. RANGNA, or PRACHITGAD, was frequented by laden cattle from Kolhapur to Malvan. HANUMANT, or TALKAT, was a very bad cattle road; the Konkan mouth was four miles from Banda. AMBOLI, or PARPOLI, stony and in no part very steep, was from zigzag difficult for heavy ordnance; it had been used by Colonel Dowse when going to invest Redi (1818); in three days the pioneers made it passable for small guns; merchants from Goa to the Deccan went along this route. RAM was the great pass to the upper country from Vadi, Malvan, Vengurla, and Goa. The approach to the pass, both above and below, was a made road, the ascent easy and passable for every sort of carriage. The general breadth of the new road, finished in March 1821, was thirty feet. Before this time, in 1790, two detachments of troops on their way to Sangameshvar to Dharwar passed through the steep Amba pass, on which some trouble had been taken. Light baggage and good weather enabled them without much difficulty to go up the pass in a day.

The main Buddhist rock-cut complexes are centred around Chiplun, Dabhol, Khed, Kol and Sangameshwar. There are presumably only Brahmanical caves around Vaghotan. At Chiplun the series of rock temples is located about a quarter of a mile south of the town. One of them showed a 22 ft x 15 ft hall with a *stupa* at its far end. On the road from Chiplun to Karhad is another group of Buddhist caves. On the side of a low hill to the east of the town are three small rock-cut caves at Khed. There are three short inscriptions in one of the two groups of rock-cut caves at Kol.

An idea of the major ancient points on the eastern side of the Western Ghats in this section can be had by concentrating on the distribution of Buddist caves on this side. Of these the northernmost complex seems to be located at Shirval in the northwest corner of the Satara district. It has a group of 15 early Buddhist caves. Both these complexes are oriented towards Mahad by the Par pass. Wai in the uppermost reaches of the Krishna has been called 'one of the most sacred places' associated with this river and has a large number of temples as well. The most important

Buddhist complex of the Satara area lies in Karad, about 31 miles south of Satara and located at the junction of the Krishna and the Koyna rivers. It was also linked by a road to Bijapur, which lies considerably away to the southeast. In addition to the 63 Buddhist caves here, there are many small excavations and innumerable rock-cut water cisterns, often two to a single cave. Kundal, about 22 miles southeast of Karad and thus broadly in the direction of Bijapur, has a set of Brahmanical rock-cut caves. Around Patan to the northwest of Karad, there is Tamkane which has two early Buddhist caves.

The gazetteer points out that under the British rule three Satara passes were made fit for cart traffic:

> In 1857 the opening of the Varandha pass put Wai within sixty miles of Mahad by cart road; in 1864 the opening of the Kumbharli pass put Karad within sixty miles of Chiplun; and in 1876 the opening of the FitzGerald pass placed Wai and Satara within fifty miles of Mahad. At present these three passes form the chief outlets to the coast (*Ibid.*, p. 196).

The gazetteer further states that among the Satara passes, the Mala, north and south Tivra, and Varandah passes were used for pack bullocks between Satara and the coast from the earliest times. One also gets descriptions of Mala and north Tivra passes in the gazetteer. Though a mere pack-bullock track, the north Tivra pass carried a considerable traffic in chiefly grain, molasses, tobacco, chillies and oil from Satara to Ratnagiri and rice, coconuts, spices, dates and salt from Ratnagiri to Satara. The Mala pass takes one to Sangameshwar in Ratnagiri from the direction of Patan in Satara. The track is said to be fit for pack bullocks and carried a large traffic in chillies, groundnut, myrobalans, oil and tobacco from Patan to Sangameshwar and in betelnuts, coconut-kernels and dates from Ratnagiri to Satara.

In addition, there are many gorges. For instance, there are nine gorges in the Wai area alone. During the rains, the tracks along such gorges may be impassable, but in fair weather these are suitable as footpaths and for pack bullocks.

In the Kolhapur stretch, Kolhapur itself is an ancient site. The main routes which go the coast across the Ghats are the Kolhapur-Amba pass road to Ratnagiri, the Kolhapur-Phonda pass route to Vijaydurg, Devgad and Malvan, and the Kolhapur-Sankeshvar-Parpoli pass road to Malvan and Vengurla. The Kolhapur-Amba pass road crosses at Brahmapuri in the outskirts of Kolhapur the Panchganga and reaches Amba through the Panhala gorge. From Amba the road descends by the Amba pass to Ratnagiri. It is said to be the shortest coast road for the whole of Kolhapur-

Sangli-Miraj-Athni sector. The Kolhapur-Phonda pass road first goes to Dajipur in the Ghats, and once beyond the Phonda pass, branches in three directions, one going northwest to Vijaydurg, another going west to Devgad, and a third southwest to Malvan. A branch of this road on the eastern side of the Ghats goes to Nipani near Belgaum. The Kolhapur-Sankeshvar-Parploi pass road goes to Dhangormola in the Ghats and after crossing the Parpoli pass, goes northwest to Malvan and southwest to Vengurla. Within the limits of the Belgaum sector there are eight main passes across the Ghats. The northernmost one is the Amboli or Parpoli pass on the Belgaum-Vengurla road, which is called "an excellent pass nine and a half miles long with an easy gradient". The next is the Ram pass, about 30 miles west of Belgaum on the Belgaum-Vengurla road. The ascent was easy and passable for wheeled carriage but was little frequented in 1883 except by traders from Goa and the Vanjaras carrying salt from the coast and grain from inland on bullocks. About 25 miles southwest of Belgaum is the Chorle pass, a foot-track which was used with difficulty by pack bullocks carrying salt. To the southeast of the Chorle pass and only a little away from it, is the Parva pass, and about 8 miles to its southeast is the Kel pass which begins at Khanapur near Belgaum and goes in a southern direction. Both the Parva and Kel passes are only foot-tracks with difficulty for cattle. About 12 miles to the southeast of the Kel pass is the Tameri pass and about 12 miles to the southeast of the Tameri pass is the Tinai pass. The Tameri pass is a foot-track but the Tinai pass is well-suited for the descent of carts.

The stretch between the Savitri and the Terekhol rivers, which denotes the Ratnagiri section of the coast, is thus linked to the Satara and Belgaum areas in the hinterland by a network of routes. Belgaum itself was a major centre of trade in the early mediaeval period, and its importance in the earlier period is reflected by the location of the site of now-destroyed site of Bhatgaon-Madhopur in its outskirts.

It may be interesting to reflect here that after Kalyana or Kalliena, the *Periplus* puts the following under the category of "other local marts": Semulla (Chaul), Mandagora (Bankot at the mouth of the Savgitri; alternatively, Mandangad, a little south of Bankot), Palaipatmai (Dabhol, cf. Huntingford 1980: 114), Melizeigara (Jaigad, south of Dabhol, cf. Huntingford 1980: 114), Buzantion (Vijaydurg cf. Huntingford 1980: 114), Toparan and Erannaboas (the last two basically unidentified but may be Jaygad and Malvan, respectively, cf. Huntingford 1980: 114-115). A chain of islands is mentioned next: Sesekreienai (the Vengurla rocks south of Malvan, cf. Huntingford 1980: 115), Aigidion (Anjediva island, a little south of Karwar, cf. Huntingford 1980: 115), Kaneiton (Oyster rock, west of Karwar, cf. Huntingford 1980: 115), and White islands (Hog/Pigeon island south of Karwar).

II.7. The Goa Section of the Coast and the Routes across the Western Ghats

The Goa section of the coast is about 100 km long and is dominated by the mouth of the combined Mandovi and Zuari rivers, which creates the most important harbour of Goa. The Portuguese took over Goa from the Adil Shahi kings of Bijapur, and soon after this conquest around 1510, Goa was described by Duarte Barbosa as an important port to which came ships from Arabia, the Gulf, Cambay and Malabar. Among its imports were horses and slaves from the African coast. Throughout the 16th century this trade was profitable as was the trade with Southeast Asia, China and Japan. There are also references to the coming of caravans from Balaghat in Madhya Pradesh with cotton. Apart from Goa or Old Goa, the major mercantile centres were Mapusa on a branch of the Mandovi river and Margao on the Sal River. Both these were important trading centres when the Portuguese came. It has been claimed that there were four old trade routes in the area. One came through the Kele pass and went to Mapusa via Sanquelim and Bicholim. The second one came by the Tinai pass and proceeded via Usgao, Ponda and Mardol, while the third one was linked to Sanquem and Margao. Another route went to Pernem at the mouth of the Terkol River. It is interesting that the only major complex of rock-cut caves – Arvalem in Goa – is near Bicholim, the area through which the route coming through the Kele Ghat passes.

Abbe Carre who travelled in India between 1672 and 1674 has briefly described the route between Goa and Bijapur. One started from Bicholim and went through the Ramghat pass, which crossed the Western Ghats about 2 miles south of Pargad fort and 30 miles west of Belgaum. The French Tavernier also took this route. This was a narrow, precipitious path ascended with much difficulty. On the top of the pass there were some houses and a temple. He also referred to a group of people who lived on the coast of Goa but gained their livelihood by carrying loads of dried fish, coconuts, arrack, and other commodities to sell in Bijapur. They were paid by loads, and each return trip lasted 25-30 days (Fawcett 1947, vol. 1, pp. 223-224).

Chandrapur or modern Chandor is located in the Salcete sector which also has modern Margao. As reported by V.T. Gune (1979), the ancient town of Chandrapur, mentioned in the Siroda copper-plate grant of the

Bhoja dynasty king Devaraya of the 3rd-4th century AD, extended over a large area and was protected by a mud fortification wall on the northwest, and a canal and the river Paroda on the other sides. The fortification section was also protected by a moat. The red ware of the Satavahana period was located along the river-side, and the trial excavations indicated that the city was occupied from the 2nd-3rd century BC to the 11th-12th century AD. There are also early ruins at the Brahmavatara site of Mapusa (Satavahana period pottery ?) and at Nunden in the Sanquem area (an inscription of the 5th-6th century AD). On the whole, it seems possible to argue that the coastal belt of Goa had settlements dating from the early historic period. However, it is interesting to note that the *Periplus* does not seem to refer to any place on the Goan coast.

Tome Pires' early 16th century account of trade through Goa is illuminating. By that time Goa had fallen to the Portuguese, and Pires was rapturous about this triumph of the Cross over the Moors or Muslims. However, his account of Goa as a trade centre deserves notice:

> The kingdom of Goa always had the advantage over Chaul. It traded lavishly. It had many merchants of all nationalities, people of large means. It has a good port, and not only that, but it was especially suited to the business of raising armadas which was carried on there, on account of the wood and of the craftsmen, and also because it had plentiful supplies and was very strong.... They used to bring horses to Goa from all the kingdoms in Arabia Petrae, from Ormuz, from Persia and from the kingdom of Cambay; and from Goa they were sent to the kingdoms of the Deccan and Narsinga. After Goa was taken from the Moors, Narsinga got its horses through Bhatkal. And Goa also collected all the merchandise of those parts and they took back calico, fine muslin, rice, areca, betel and many *pardaos* and *oraos*, because horses here are worth a great deal... the seamen who sailed the ships were natives of the country, because the kingdom of Goa produces good seamen who can stand hard work (Cortesao 1944, vol. 1, pp. 57-58).

Another important point of Pires' account of Goa is his enumeration of all the ports of his time along the Goan coast: Devgarh, Banda, Old Goa, New Goa, Liga, *Ancoll*, Pale, Sal River, Cape Ramas, Cintacorra, and Anjediva. "Between these ports there are rivers, which ships used to – and still do – navigate". When he writes about the export of rice and betel from Goa, he possibly speaks of the commodities passing through all these ports. Both areca-nut and betel from Goa are said to be superior to the specimens from the other areas, and from Goa betel used to be exported to Aden, Ormuz and Cambay. "Cargoes of rice are taken from here, and great trains of oxen loaded with merchandise used to come in to Goa from very distant kingdoms in the interior" (Cortesao 1944, vol. 1, p. 57).

Belgaum is across the Western Ghats from Goa, and was, along with Dharwar, a major hub of communication in various directions. Its importance as an early mediaeval trade centre is well-known from inscriptions (Burnett undated), and its prosperity in the earlier periods is attested by the 40 hectare-site of Vadgaon-Madhavpur which in its 4.25 m thick deposit has yielded three phases of occupation from the 3rd century BC to the 2nd century AD (Ghosh 1989, p. 456). The site has been completely destroyed by a modern housing colony.

II.8. North Kanara: From Karwar to Bhatkal, and the Major Alignments

South of Margao in Goa, the coastal strip seems to gain width with vast paddy-fields and villages dotting a placid countryside. There is no prominent inlet or river-mouth till one comes to Karwar, which is located on the coast but close to the mouth of the Kalinadi. Karwar also marks the northern extremity of the present North Kanara district of Karnataka. The major historical ports of North Kanara are Karwar, Kumta, Honavar and Bhatkal.

Karwar (the *Imperial Gazetteer of India*, vol. 15, pp. 65-67) is located on the Kali Nadi, and the old port is 3 miles east of the present town. Around 1510 it was known as Caribal and in the first half of the 17th century it was a revenue unit of the Bijapur kingdom. The importance of pepper of the Sonda area (a village in the Sirsi taluk) led in 1638 to the establishment of a British factory here. The factory was known as prosperous in 1660, exporting the finest muslin in western India, the weaving country being located at Hubli and other centres where as many as 50000 weavers were employed. Known primarily for its export of muslin, Karwar also exported pepper, cardamoms, cassia and coarse blue cotton cloth (*dungari*). In 1697, after an attack by the Marathas, the Karwar began to decline, and by 1801 old Karwar was in ruins.

The Imperial Gazetteer describes Karwar as the only safe harbour between Bombay and Cochin during all seasons of the year. There is a cluster of islets, called the Oyster Rocks, in the bay where there are also two smaller islands affording protection to the smaller vessels during the northwest winds between February and April.

Bhatkal is near the mouth of a small stream which falls into the Arabian Sea. This was the centre of a group of Muslims known locally as *Navyats* or the 'newly arrived ones', thus named because they were Sunni muslims driven out of the Gulf by the Shiahs in the 8th century. Many of them were wealthy traders. Under the names of Batticala in the European travellers' records, Bhatkal was a flourishing centre of trade in the 14th-16th centuries. Ships from Ormuz and Goa used to come here to load rice and sugar. To the Portuguese who established a factory here in 1505, its importance was overshadowed by their annexation of Goa. The British set up factory here in 1638 and 1668, but on both occasions it failed. The chief articles of trade in Bhatkal were rice, betelnuts, coconuts and cotton cloth (for the details, the *IGI*, vol. 8, p. 90).

The testimony of Tome Pires on Bhatkal is detailed.

> The port of Bhatkal comes next in importance to Goa and Chaul, and has a great deal of trade. It is the port which serves the kingdom of Narsinga, and through which the horses come.... Bhatkal used to be the most important of all the ports in the kingdoms of Canara, on account of its many merchants, and many horses from all parts were landed here, and much other merchandise. These horses were brought for the kingdom of Narsinga, and heavy duties were paid on them. The merchants returned from this land of Kanara with quantities of the best rice there is in this part of the world, that is *giracal* which is the finest and whitest and most expensive and considered the best; after this comes *chambacal* and after *chambacal* comes the *pacharil* from Goa and the kingdom of the Deccan. They also took back iron and a great deal of sugar which there is in this country, and many sugar preserves which are made in Bhatkal; these (were products) of the land. And many of the merchants from Malabar used to go there so that its trade was of great account. This is the most important possession the king of Narsinga has in Kanara (Cortesao 1944, vol. 1, pp. 61-62).

Robert Sewell in his account of the kingdom of Vijayanagara and the city of Hampi points out that Bhatkal was connected with Vijayanagara via Bankapur.

> Bankapur was one of the most important fortresses in the Karnataka country, situated 40 miles south of Dharwar on the direct road from Honawar to Vijayanagar. The road from Bhatkal, a favourite landing place, first went northwards to Honawar, thence inland to Bankapur, and thence to Banavasi, Ranibennur, and over to the plains to Hospett and Vijayanagar. It was known as early as AD 848, and remained in possession of Hindu rulers down to 1573, when it was captured by Ali Adil Shah and its beautiful temple was destroyed (Sewell 1924 reprint, p. 122, note 1).

Apart from Karwar and Bhatkal, there are two important ports in the North Kanara sector. They are Kumta and Honawar/Honavar. *Kumta* lies to the south of Karwar, on the north side of the Kumta creek. *The*

Imperial Gazetteer of India (vol. 16, 1908, pp. 23-24) writes that although it is an open roadstead, it was formerly a large trade centre because it was connected with the cotton marts of Dharwar by roads. Cotton came chiefly from the Dharwar area and spices and grain came from the uplands of North Kanara. *Honavar (The Imperial Gazetteer of India*, vol. 13, pp. 160-161) lies to the north of an extensive inlet of the sea. At its southeastern extremity this inlet receives the Sharavati River. Among the travellers who reported on it, the most famous name is that of Ibn Batuta who in the 14th century found it a rich and well-governed place. In the 16th century, it is known to have exported rice. The Portuguese built a fort here in 1505 but burnt down the town in a dispute with the Vijayanagara kings. The Portuguese, however, continued to be powerful here, and from them the place was acquired by the local power of the chiefs of Bednur. From them again, the place went to Haider Ali of Mysore.

When the British came, the hill passes in use in North Kanara were the following (Kamath 1985): Tinai, Anshi, Kaiga, Arebail, Devimane and Gersoppa. The British (1802) dragged guns and military supplies from Goa to Huliyal via the Tinai pass. During the second half of the 19th century, there were 17 main passes in use – two in Karwar – Gopshitta and Kaiga; two in Honavar – Hogevadi and Gundilkatta; six in Supa –Tinai, Kuveshi, Digi, Kundal, Dhokarpa and Anshi; two in Yellapur – Ganeshgudi and Arebail; four in Sirsi – Vaddi, Devimane, Nilkund, and Dodmane; and one in Siddapur – Gersoppa. Of these the important ones are Arebail, Devimane and Gersoppa. Peter Mundy travelled from Bhatkal to Ikkeri through the Hogewadi pass, which is 30 km from Bhatkal. The Kadra-Belgaum road through the Anshi pass was connected with Supa through roads en route the passes of Tinai, Kuveshi, Digi and Hundal. From Tinai to Supa there is a 40 km road. The Kuveshi pass on the Goa frontier. The Dig-Sanjhode road is linked to the Anshi pass road leading to Supa. the Karwar-Dharwad road is linked to another road leading to Supa by the Anshi pass. The Kadra-Belgaum road is connected to Yellapur through the Ganeshgudi hill pass road. The Arebail pass lies 20 km south of Yellapur with the Karwar-Dharwar road passing through it (one of the chief passes of the district – passable by foot and bullock carts). Among the Sirsi passes, the Vaddi pass had a road of 60 km from Sirsi to Hillur (not negotiable for carts). The Nilkund hill pass is about 30 km west of Sirsi and the Dodmane hill pass is about 50 km west of Sirsi. The Gersoppa hill pass, about 25 km southwest of Siddapur, had a road from Gersoppa to Talguppa passing through it. This was the position in the 19th century.

The most important ancient historical site of this sector is Banavasi in the Sirsi taluk of North Kanara, which is approachable from the coast between Karwar and Honavar. A large section of Karnataka hinterland – Harihar, Shimoga and Chitradurg, and all the other places they are linked to – can be accessed through the Sirsi-Banavasi area. The general archaeological knowledge of the site is marginal (Ghosh 1989). The epigraphical and textual references to the site, however, are many. It figure in the *Mahabharata* as *Vanavasaka*. According to the *Mahavamsa*, Asoka sent monks here to propagate Buddhism. A merchant from this place donated the expense of constructing the Karle rock-cut complex. Among the inscriptions found at the site, the following one (Inscription 1186 of Luders' list) was of the time of the king 'Haritiputa Vinhukada-Chutukulananda-Satakamni' and records the

> gift of a naga, a tank (*tadaga*) and a vihara by the mahabhuvi (*mahabhoji* ?), the daughter of a maharaja, whose son and progeny (?) was alive, together with (?) the prince Sada or Sivakhandanagasiri. The minister Khadasati (Skandasvati) was the superintendent of the work. The naga was made by Nataka (Nartaka ?), pupil of the teacher Idamoraka (Indramayuraka), the Sajayataka (inhabitant of Sanjayanti) (Luders 1912, p. 136).

It is important to note that Sanjayanti is ancient Sanjan, and Banavasi was linked both to Karle and Sanjan.

The place is also mentioned in the Aihole inscription of Pulakesin II and a host of later inscriptions including those of the Vijayanagara kings. In the 4th century AD it became the capital of the Kadamba kings, one of whom – 'Sivakhandavamman Haritiputta' – calls himself 'the lord of Vaijayanti' (Mallavalli pillar inscription – Inscription 1196 of Luders' list).

II.9. South Kanara: Barkur, Udupi and Mangalore, and the Major Alignments

The passes seem to be far less frequent in this sector. Three alignments stand out: the Agumba Ghat alignment which links both Udupi and Mangalore sectors and leads one through Shimoga and Bhadravati to Chitradurg and thus the wide network of routes in the Deccan part of Karnataka; the Kodkal Ghat alignment which goes via Buntwal, Charmadi and Chikmagalur to Kadur where it meets the Shimoga-Arsikere-Tumkur alignment from which the whole of Karnataka is wide open; and finally, the modern Mangalore-Hassan alignment, with Hassan occupying a nodal point in the communication network of southern Karnataka. One is not sure if the Mangalore-Hassan road via Shiradi and Saklespur, which has been converted into a National Highway, is an ancient route. The Hulikal pass road, which lies to the north of Agumbe Ghat alignment, also links Udupi with Shimoga. There is also an alignment from Mangalore in the direction of Kodagu or Coorg and thus towards Mysore. This route goes by the Samajpe Ghat (Parthasarathy 2003).

Mangalore is the most important port of this sector. The two rivers – the Netravati and Sharavati – join near Mangalore and form a lagoon, which is about 3.5 miles long and a little less than half a mile wide. A sandbank separates this backwater from the sea and enables it to provide a safe all-weather shelter to the ships.

J. Sturrock's *South Kanara Manual, Volume 1, 1894* (Sturrock 1894, p. 29) describes in some detail the trade conducted through Mangalore.

> Three-fourths of the whole sea-borne trade …is carried on at the port of Mangalore…. The ports of Coondapur (Gongoli), Barkur (Hangarkatta) and Udupi (Malpe) have each about one-fourth of the trade of Mangalore; Mulky has from a third to a half of the trade carried on at these latter, and Kasadgad, Kumbla, and Manjesvar have from one to two lakhs. At Baindur, the most northern part of the district, the trade is under a lakh.

This *Manual* (p. 29) refers to the presence of both steamers and large sailing vessels in the Mangalore harbour. However,

> The trade at the other ports and the remainder of the trade at Mangalore is carried on by means of buggalows from Arabia and the Persian Gulf with a capacity of from 30 to 50 tons, and country craft commonly called Pattimars and Machwas with an average capacity of about 20 tons, the Machwas as a rule being smaller than the Pattimars. About 2000 of these vessels enter annually at the port of Mangalore, and from 500 to 1000 at each of the large ports mentioned above.

Malpe is about 5 km west of Udupi and 64 km north of Mangalore. It lies at the mouth of the Udayavara River and has the additional advantage of being sheltered from the sea by a chain of granitic islands running parallel to the coast. The Udupi-Karkal-Agumbe sector forms the hinterland of Malpe port. *The Imperial Gazetteer of India* (vol. 17, p. 94) calls it "the best natural port in South Kanara, the roadstead being sheltered by the island of Darya Bahadurgarh". *Hangarkatta* lies to the north of Malpe and is located at the estuary of the confluence of the Sitanadi and Swarnanadi rivers. It is mainly a riverine port with a limited stretch of hinterland. Of basically the same type of riverine port is the *Kundapur* port at the confluence of the rivers Haladi and Chakranadi. *The Imperial Gazetteer of India* (vol. 11, pp. 1-2) points out that in the late 19th century trade was carried on from Gongoli, which lies on the north bank of the estuary and is located more suitably for shipping. The *Baindur* port lies in the northernmost part of South Kanara and is on the bank of the Baindur River.

Barkur or old Barakanur was related to the ports both at Kundapur and Hangarkatta. It was the capital of the Alupa dynasty of the area, which comes in the limelight in the 6th/7th century AD. It was under the Chola domination in the 11th century and later on it came under the rule of the Hoyasalas and the kings of Vijayanagara. The place witnessed extensive temple construction activities at least from the 8th century AD onwards. The Panchalingeshwara temple is the earliest surviving temple of Barkur and has three stages of development – Chalukyan, Hoyasala and Vijayanagara. It appears that the temples were built in different stages up to the 14th century, if not still later.

Basrur, which lies to the east of the port of Kundapur, has been mentioned as an important trading place by the Arab geographers. According to Duarte Barbosa, it received ships from Malabar to Aden. In the late 16th century the town was under the control of the kings of Bijapur from whom it was taken by the Portuguese. The Dutch set up a 'factory' here in the early 18th century. The area was also within the area of influence of Vijayanagara. Two temples of the place go back to the 10th/11th century.

Udyavara or *Udayavara* near Udupi was a capital of the Alupa kings in the 8th century AD. There are not many archaeological relics around but a few inscriptions date back to the 7th century AD. *Udupi* is a major religious town associated with the *Mathas* associated with Madhavacharya of the 14th century AD. The temples of the place bear the influence of Vijayanagara.

C.B. Patil (2006) has offered a synoptic survey of the early historic finds in both North and South Kanara. The citadel at Balerugudda in the vicinity of Udayavara is supposed to possess three gateways and a lower town facing the sea. The site has yielded megalithic black-and-red ware, black polished ware, plain red ware, and cream ware. A chert blade in apparent association with cream ware has also been mentioned (for Udayavara, also *IAR* 1968-69). At Haigunda in the Honavar sector, he reports the remains of a brick temple with a *Shivalinga*, besides drawing attention to a 'palace mound'/citadel of an unspecified period. A 'commercial town', again of an unspecified period, has been reported at Hattiangadi near Udupi. Banavasi near Sirsi has shown the succession of Chutu, Satavahana, Kadamba and post-Kadamba periods. The first phase does not show any structure, but the next phase of the Satavahanas has revealed an enclosure wall (sections of a fortification wall around the site) and an apsidal burnt brick structure which can be a temple or a Buddhist *chaitya*. Further, a square brick platform was noticed. The Banavasi mound encloses an area of over 1 square km in extent within a fortification made of burnt bricks and set on a rubble foundation. The Sonda-Sirsi area where Banavasi is situated is known as a pepper-producing area and the site lies on a route from the Honavar-Kumta sector of the coast to the Karnataka hinterland. Another early historic site of this general area is Vadgaon-Madhavpur/Madhopur (Ghosh 1989, p. 456), which goes back to the 3rd century BC but when we visited it, we found it completely destroyed by a Housing Society.

If one takes a broad overview of the historical geography of the coast from Umbergaon-Sanjan to Mangalore and its hinterland areas of Maharashtra and Karnataka, one realizes that the goals of the passes across the Western Ghats were to maintain links with certain key areas both in Karnataka and Maharashtra. These key areas derived their importance not merely from their being the sources of different economic products but also from their being centres of political powers which exercised control in different segments of the coast at various points of history. The southernmost relevant section in Karnataka was Hassan where the Hoyasala power had its capital at Halebid. The Hoyasalas maintained in their time control over the north and south Kanara coasts. Hasan is also directly connected with the most important historical port of the area, Mangalore. North of Hasan, there is a chain of three areas along the central section of the eastern edge of Kartnataka – Chitradurg, Bellary, Kopbal and Raichur – all interconnected and all bearing Asokan edicts and thus in the limelight of early historic India. The evidence of early historic occupation in the Karnataka coastal stretch is limited and available positively only at Banavasi. There is no evidence of Mauryan occupation here, but scholars have been satisfied with the Satavahana presence at the site. Banavasi is to the southeast of the inland town of Sirsi in North Kanara, and its location suggests that its main inland alignments were with the Dharwar sector in the north and the Shimoga sector in the south. Through Shimoga the Chitradurg area was easily accessible, and through Dharwar one could easily reach the Kopbal-Bellary-Raichur belt. This belt was also the epicentre of the Vijayanagara power, and the Vijayanagara kingdom had close links with the Karnataka coast. Although Goa does not have any indisputable evidence of occupation of the pre-Christian period, it is possibly due to the lack of work in the region. In the outskirts of modern Belgaum the site of Vadgaon-Madhopur is an early historic site, although currently destroyed. Goa is well connected with Belgaum. Similarly, Kolhapur in Maharashtra, which has historic roots of the pre-Christian era is well connected with Belgaum, and through

Belgaum, with Bijapur, Gulbarga and Bidar. The Bidar-Gulbarga-Bijapur sector was politically a crucial sector in the history of the Deccan. Bidar was the centre of the Bahmani power in the 14th century and later. Gulbarga had a major Mauryan period city at Sannati on the bank of the Bhima River. Manyakhet or Malkhed in Gulbarga was the centre of the Rashtrakuta power in the 8th century. Bijapur was the centre of the Adil Shahi kings of the 15th-17th centuries but, more importantly, the Bagalkot sector to its south had the centre of Chalukyan power at Badami. The Kolhapur-Satara sector of Maharashtra, which lies on the eastern side of the Western Ghats, maintained a major role in maintaining the links between the Konkan coast and the whole of the northern segment of Karnataka, from where one could easily come south to Raichur-Kopbal-Bellary-Chitradurga.

2

Tamil Nadu and Kerala

I. THE ROUTES TO TAMIL NADU FROM MYSORE AND ANDHRA

In the case of the Tamil Nadu hinterland, the initial problem is two-fold: how to enter it from the Mysore-Bangalore tract of Karnataka, on the one hand, and from the Chittoor-Nellore segment of Andhra, on the other. In both cases there are hill-ranges to be crossed – the outliers of the Eastern Ghats including the Javadi hills near Chittoor and Nellore, and the chain of hills which link the Eastern Ghats near Chittoor with the Nilgiri outliers near Coimbatore. Mysore and Bangalore lie on the other side of the latter chain of hills whereas its eastern and southern extensions are composed of the Shevaroy, Kalrayan, Pachaimalai and Kolimalai groups of hills. One is not sure if the route from Nellore to Chennai followed the alignment of the modern Kolkata-Chennai railway line down the coast, but that one of the major routes to Tamil Nadu from Andhra came by Renigunta, keeping the Tirupati hills a little to the west, and Vellore and Tiruvallur, is beyond question because the famous second century BC Siva of Gudimallam lies on this way. Once inside the boundary of modern Tamil Nadu, this route can, if necessary, follow the Palar River to the coast for the area around Chennai.

I.1. From the Mysore Plateau to Tamil Nadu

F.J. Richards' *Gazetteer of the Salem District* (Richards 1918, pp. 108 ff) lists four major routes between the Mysore plateau and the Dharampuri-Salem sections of Tamil Nadu:

1. Budikota Pass leads from Krishnagiri on the Tamil Nadu side to Budikota in the Bowringpet *Taluk* of the Kolar district in Mysore. The pass follows the Markanda River.
2. Sulagiri Pass leads through Sulagiri to the Hosur area in the Mysore plateau.
3. Anchetti Ghat or Pass between Denkanikota and Pennagaram goes from Denkanikota to Pennagaram via Anchetti and Geratti, and from there goes to the Toppur River via Morawsara-halli and Donnakutta-halli.
4. Palakodu-Rayakota Pass, which lies wholly in the Krishnagiri *Taluk* of Tamil Nadu.

Regarding the Budikota pass, Richards points out the following:

> The Budikota Pass, now almost forgotten, was one of the principal routes between the Baramahal and the Balaghat in the days of Haidar and Tipu. Its approach was guarded by the Fort of Krishnagiri, and its entrance was flanked by the Durgams of Balakonda-Rayan and Ankusagiri. No doubt the selection of Kundani as a capital of the Hoyasala kingdom of Ramanatha, in the latter half of the thirteenth century, was due to its proximity to this Pass, which must even then have served as a main channel of communication between the upland and lowland territories of the Hoyasala king. Its former military importance is testified to by the rough track which still bears the name, *Dandu Oni* or Army Road, which branches from the Krishnagiri-Sulagiri Road at the 7th mile from Krishnagiri, near the village of Puliyanjeri, and passes by way of Nidusal to Manavarana-palli. There it splits. The eastern branch passes east of the Palmal Ridge via Singiri-palli to Kama-samudram in Kolar District. The western branch runs from Mavarana-palli via Sigarala-palli, and west of the Palmal Ridge to Budikota (Richards 1918, p. 108).

The Sulagiri pass is said to be rather steep, with the road for about 8 miles east of Sulagiri 'undulating tediously'. The pass begins at the 167th mile from Chennai and dips down past the foot of Balakonda-Rayan fort. At the point the road comes down to the Baramahal or the Tamil Nadu side of the area, the roadside is strewn with enormous blocks of gneiss in wild confusion. As it offers a more direct route between Bangalore and Chennai, the pass had sprung into significance since the British occupation.

The Anchetti pass area seems to mark a complex of routes which also seems to include the Palakodu-Rayakota section. Richards argues that the area was better populated before the villages were looted by the Lambadis accompanying the army of Lord Cornwallis, which was mobilised against Mysore.

> There is little doubt that the regular trade-routes existed in the eighteenth century between the Balaghat and the lowlands, by way of the Kaveri valley, and that the commissariat requirements of both Tipu and the British were a heavy drain on the resources of the villagers, who tenanted the adjoining tracts. The British occupation, in the course of a century, has had the effect of advancing the Tamil at the expense of the Kanarese, and the Lingayat population has gravitated towards their natural home in the Mysore State. The Great Famine of 1877-78 led to the complete desertion of many villages and Forest Reservation followed before the ryots could reclaim their lands. Hence it is that many square miles of cultivated land have in the course of a century lapsed into jungle (Richards 1918, p. 110)

The main Anchetti pass route from Denkanikota to the Baramahal or the lowland basin of Dharampuri and Salem led, via Kundukota, Anchetti and Natara-palaiyam, to Biligundlu in the Kaveri system. The pass could be negotiated by pack bullocks and ponies. It thus provided an almost direct route from the Mysore plateau to the Kaveri valley of Tamil Nadu.

The higher region of Balaghat, which falls mostly in the Mysore plateau, is protected from incursions from the plains by a chain of hill forts, such as Ankusagiri and Kundanimalai forts which flank the Markanda-nadi valley, and the forts of Rayakota and Virabhadra which guard the ascents from Krishnagiri and Palakodu respectively. Each of these forts is protected in turn by other forts. More interestingly,

> At the foot of most of these mountain strongholds are the remains of fortified *petas*. Many of these are now deserted, and overgrown with prickly-pear and scrub jungle, but their sides are still marked by traces of earthen ramparts topped by a crumbling mud wall, by fragments of brick and pottery, one or two revetted walls, a few grindstones or oilmills, sometimes a ruined temple or a tamarind grove. Many of these *peta* sites lie on the saddle which joins two or more hills, each hill being fortified, and the *peta* site itself, in many cases, appears to have been artificially levelled before the town was built. The foot of the *durgam* is often entirely girt by a line of ramparts, and tier after tier of ramparts, pierced by cleverly fortified gateways, protected all accessible approaches. The last two few hundred feet of the ascent usually lead across a glacis of smooth rock, perfectly commanded by the ramparts of the main stronghold, and down these rocky inclines the garrison, it is said, poured oil in time of war, to impede the approach of an assailing force (Richards 1918, p. 111).

The foregoing description clearly demonstrates the significance of this region in the chain of routes between the Mysore plateau and Tamil Nadu. Richards mentions that in the Hosur *Taluk* of the Mysore plateau almost every village was fortified or had a fort attached to it. The fort did not have any dwelling inside it but "when raiders came, the villagers would take refuge in the fort with their wives, children, chattels and grain, and they would be fairly safe", especially with the services of a few musketeers who would be positioned behind the fort's loopholes. Regarding Hosur town he adds that the place was once of military importance for it commands all lines of communication between the Baramahal and Mysore. In fact, any force advancing from the low country (i.e., the Tamil Nadu side) by the Rayakota or Sulagiri Ghat roads, or even by the Anchetti tract, or through the rough country between Veppana-palli and Berikari, must pass within easy striking distance of Hosur (Richards 1918, p. 131)

Apart from this complex of routes between the Mysore plateau and what is basically Dharampuri-Salem tract of Tamil Nadu, another major Tamil Nadu area with which the Mysore plateau is well connected is the section of Coimbatore and Erode. The Satyamangalam *Taluk* of this region is flanked by the Nilagiris on the west and by the hills to the south of the Mysore plateau on the north-west and north. Three passes penetrate this area: the Talamalai, Gazzalhatti and Hasanur passes. The Gazzalhatti pass lies in the northeastern corner of the Moyar River valley. Formerly the principal pass between Coimbatore and Mysore, one track leads from Satyamangalam while another track goes from Coimbatore via Danyakkankottai. This route was used extensively in the Mysore wars of the East India Company against Hyder Ali and Tipu Sultan. Danyakkankottai is currently submerged under the waters of the Bhavanisagar dam which was constructed in 1949-1955, but there are reports of a mud fort and temples near the place. It was an important strategic point not merely in the Mysore wars but also in the history of the Hoyasala and later Nayaka kingdoms.

I.2. From Andhra to Tamil Nadu

The North Arcot area of Tamil Nadu is bordered on the north by the Eastern Ghats, which are spread in this section as far east as the Tirupati hills. A long valley leads through the Ghats northward to the Cuddapah district through the villages of Karkambadi and Manundur and offers passage for the Mumbai-Chennai railway. However, there are many passes which link North Arcot with Andhra.

> Numerous passes lead from the lowland taluks to those above the ghats, but only three of these admit of wheeled traffic, viz., the Kallur, Mogiliu and Sainagunta passes. The Kallur pass, in the Chendragiri taluk, runs along the Damalcheruvu valley and through the Kallur palaiyam to the

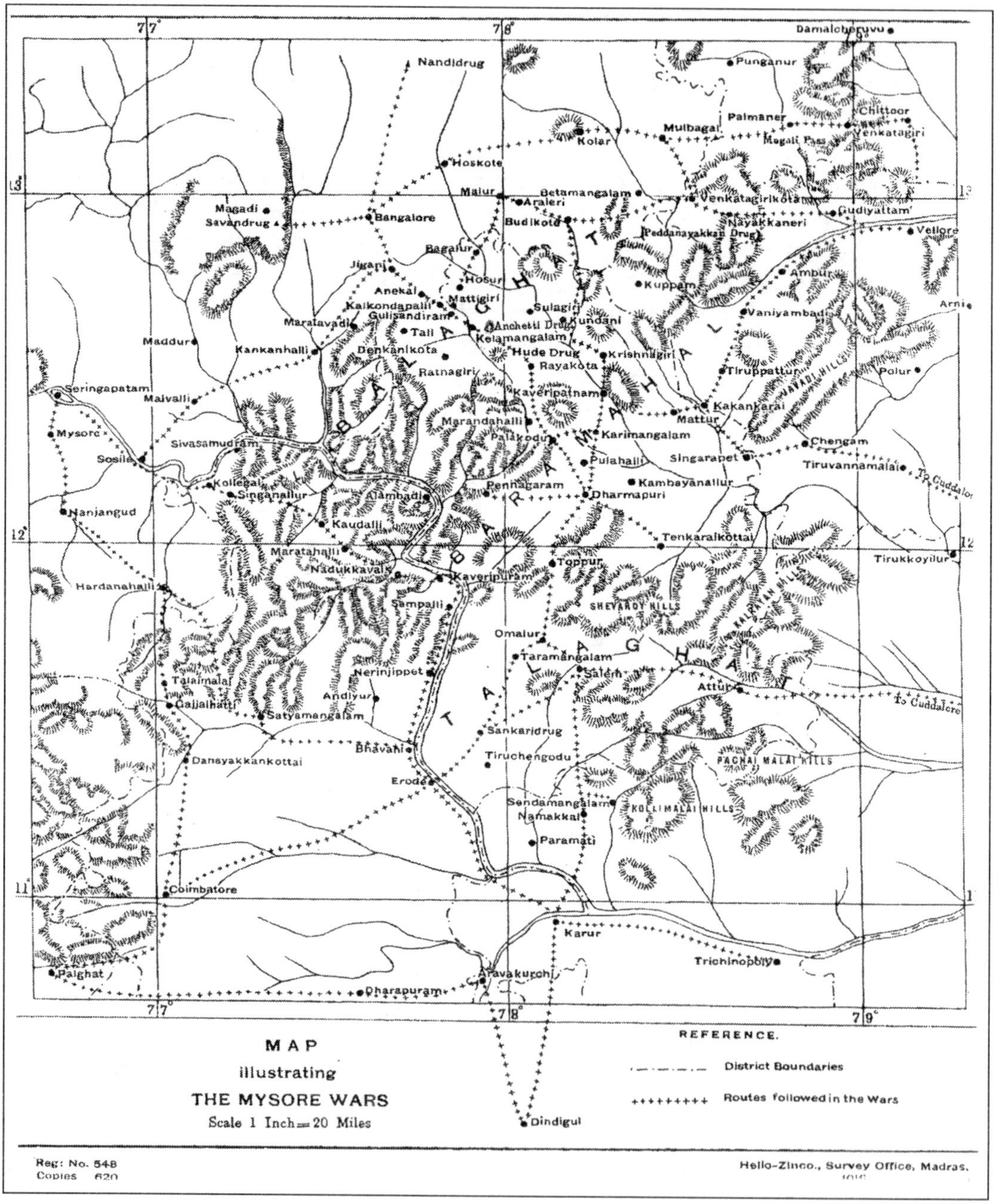

Map 2. The general entry-points to Tamil Nadu from Karnataka and Andhra, and also some major alighments in Tamil Nadu (after the Madras Presidency Gazetters).

> Piler taluk of Cuddapah. Along it passes the trunk road from Madras to Cuddapah.... The Mogili pass, in the Chittoor taluk, commences at a point almost directly west of, and at a distance of some twenty miles from, Chittoor, the head-quarters of the district. Through it runs the main road from Palamner to Bangalore, and also to the sub-division of Cuddapah. The rise of the ghat is gradual.... The Sainagunta pass leads from the taluk of Gudiyattam to Palamner, where it unites with the road from Mogili. The ascent is steep, but the scenery very picturesque. The principal ascent from the plains to the plateau used to be formerly by way of the Nayakkaneri pass, on the western borders of Gudiyattam, not far from Satghur. Through this ascended the great trunk road to Bangalore.... Besides the above, many other passes without regularly made roads lead to the plateau. They are little more than mountain pathways, along which laden cattle are driven with some difficulty (Cox 1881: 4-5)

II. SOME MAJOR INTERNAL ROUTES IN TAMIL NADU

If the foregoing passes link Tamil Nadu with the Mysore plateau and Andhra, there are some other passes which offer links between the different areas of the State. For instance, Dharampuri is linked with Salem by the Toppur pass in the south and the Manjabadi pass in the east. More importantly, through the Chengam pass which lies to the northwest of Tiruvannamalai, one can easily approach Tirukkoyilur in the Ponnaiyar valley on the way to Cuddalore on the coast. In fact, through the Chengam pass, which lies between the Javadi hills in the north and the Kalrayan hills in the south, virtually the whole of the northern Tamil Nadu coast between Pulicat and Cuddalore is open. This comprises the two Arcots (North and South) and Chingleput.

South of Dharampuri, Salem too is linked with the coast around Cuddalore, but this time the route goes through Attur between the Kalrayan and Pachaimalai hills. Moving southwest from Salem to Erode, one can move either straight to Coimbatore to enter the Palghat pass to the Kerala coast or travel southeastward along the Kaveri to Karur and from there to Trichinopoly and eventually the Kaveri delta. In this section, it is a fairly open country. From Trichinopoly there is a somewhat indirect but easily accessible route to the Palghat gap via Dindigul and Pollachi. A more direct route lies through Dharapuram. The Trichinopoly – Dindigul-Palghat link is joined at Dindigul by a route coming northward from Madurai. Dindigul commands a strategic gap between the Palni hills, Annamalai hills and the Sirumalai hills. These ranges continue through the Cardamom hills in the south almost to the tip of the Peninsula, dividing the Malabar coast south of the Palghat gap almost completely from this part of Tamil Nadu.

III. FROM TAMIL NADU TO KERALA

Apart from the tip of the Peninsula where there is a gap linking Kerala with Tamil Nadu, the only other opening is through the Cumbum valley (Uthamapalayam *Taluk* of the Theni area), which follows the Periyar river system. The Bodinayikanur and Aryankavu gaps are also in the same region. Bodinaikannur pass connects Bodinaikannur in the Madura district and the High Range of the Palni-Cardamom highlands and leads to Devicolam and Munnar. The Tevaram pass, Kambam pass, Kumili pass and the Arienkavu pass are other examples of the major openings between Tamil Nadu and Kerala in this section. Among the less important passes in the same area are the Kottachimala pass, the Thirukkuramgudy Birla pass and Yedamala pass.

If Thanjavur lies at the mouth of the Kaveri delta, Madurai commands the Vaigai system to its south, and is linked with the Rameshwaram tip of the Ramanathapuram district on the Gulf of Mannar. Further south, Tinnevelly is connected with Tiruvananthapuram of Kerala through Nagercoil which overlooks the Aramboli gap in the hills. The most important gap linking Tamil Nadu with Kerala is, of course, the famous Palghat gap, a 32-42 km wide natural depression linking the Ponani-Trichur sector of Kerala with Coimbatore of Tamil Nadu. The gap, although well-marked, is also clearly defined between the two ranges of hills which are about 1100 m high on the northern side and about 2000 m high on the southern side. The gap also acts as a channel of the monsoonal wind from the Kerala coast to Tamil Nadu.

IV. THE ROUTES FROM MYSORE TO KERALA: THE IMPORTANCE OF THE WYNAD PLATEAU

Regarding the Kottayam and the adjacent regions of Kerala, it has been said that "up to the time of the Mysorean invasion, the rivers and backwaters of the district were the main channel of trade". However, there had to be some major routes across the Western Ghats, apart from those via the Cumbum valley and of course, the gap of Palghat. The record is obtained from the movements of Tipu's army in the direction of Kerala. However, the general line of movements can be applicable to the much earlier periods as well.

Tipu invaded the coastal area of Kerala both from Mysore by way of the passes through the Western Ghats and from the area lower down through the Palghat Gap. While Seringapatam was "the grand termination of these intercommunications", many of the roads converged upon the Tamaresseri and other passes into the Wynad plateau. Palghat was also an important road centre. Not much is known of his routes in North Malabar except that the majority started from Mount Deli, and had for "their general direction" the Tamarasseri and Periya ghats.

> The Tamarasseri ghat, up which a steep gun road ran, was the meeting place of no less than four roads. Two led by different routes from Malappuram and two from Calicut, one following more or less the line of the present Mysore road, and the other passing through Ferok and Chattamangalam. Ferok, Tipu's capital in Malabar, was connected with the Karakkur ghat by a road which runs through Kondotti, Edavanna and Nilambur, and with Coimbatore by two alternative routes. A road led via Tirurangadi to Venkatakotta (the modern Kotakkal) in the Ernad taluk, and then bifurcated, one branch gointg to Coimbatore by Angadippuram, Mannarghat and the Attapadi valley, and the other by Kavalappara, Mankara and Valayar. The coast road from Beypore to Cranganore via Tanur, Ponnani, Veliyangod and Chettuvayi was another gun road, as was also the existing road from Tanur to Palghat by way of Pudiyangadi, Trittala and Lakkidi. Palghat was also connected with Dindigul and Kollangod by lines of communication (Logan 1887, pp. 268-269).

By the mid-19th century, there were important bullock tracks up the Perambadi, Kuttiyadi, Tamarasseri and Sispara ghats, all in north Malabar, orienting the traffic towards Mysore through the Wynad plateau. It may be noted that Mount Deli, to which a reference has been made in the foregoing extract is locally known as Eli-Mala. This is the northernmost boundary of Malabar. There is also little doubt that there was a direct link between the Nilgiri-Wynad region with Calicut on the coast via the Karakkur and Sispara ghats. Ferok, the capital of Tipu in Malabar, was six miles south of Calicut. From Cannanore further up the coast there was a road to Coorg. In the same area, the ghat near Kutttiyadi, also oriented towards Coorg, was impossible for carts but extensively used for pedestrian traffic and pack animals. The main Calicut-Mysore road is by the Tamarasseri ghat, Vyaittiri and Sultan's Battery. An important branch road leads in the direction of the Nilgiris from Chundale. In the north of the Wynad taluk the main road passes through Manantoddy from the Periya ghat to Gundalpet in Mysore. The Tamarasseri and Periya ghats are the only two passes into the Wynad which are fit for cart traffic. The Kuttiyadi ghat is much used by coolies and pack bullocks; but the other passes, the Ellacheram and Tariyot passes descending on Kuttiyadi, the Smugglers' pass from Dindima to Manattana and the Choladi pass into the Nilambur valley, are mere foot-paths (Logan 1887, p. 500).

V. THE EARLY HISTORICAL CONTEXT OF THE SATIYAPUTRA, CHERA, CHOLA, PANDYA TERRITORIES

The traditional division of Tamil Nadu into Tondaimandalam, Cholamandalam, Pandyamandalam, Cheramandalam and Kongumandalam seems to have firm roots in geography, although politically, their boundaries could be more fluid and diverse. Tondaimandalam possibly denotes the territory from the Tirupati hills of Andhra to the Ponnaiyar river valley of Tamil Nadu – basically the districts of Chittoor, North and South Arcot, and Chingleput. The hills in the north which provide gaps to maintain north-south interconnections, and the river valleys of the Pennar, Palar and Ponnaiyar tie up these districts as a historical entity, and they are mentioned as such in the Sangam literature. Cholamandalam is primarily the Kaveri delta, and one is not sure if the Pudukottai area falls in Cholamandalam or in the Pandyamandalam, the latter meaning the Vaigai valley and delta to its south. Cheramandalam contains the coastal north-south transect of Malabar, Cochin and Travancore (i.e., the whole of Kerala) and possibly a large chunk of the Palghat gap as well. Kongumandalam is *prima facie* Coimbatore including the relevant section of the Kaveri valley. One is not sure how to put Dharampuri in this context. There is no justification to bracket it with Coimbatore and thus with Kongumandalam, but on the other hand it does not figure as a separate and traditional geographical unit of Tamil Nadu.

It is indeed fortunate that there is no confusion about the location of the four ancient territorial formations of Tamil Nadu – Satiyaputra, Chola, Pandya and Chera of the Asokan edicts (Rock Edicts II and XIII, the latter in Kalsi version) of the third century BC. In view of the fact that these were full-fledged states worth mentioning in the Asokan edicts and also in view of the fact that in each of these areas there is a sizeable cultural deposit of the pre-3rd century BC, there is a good deal of justification to assume that the basic antiquity of these territorial formations may go back to the *Mahajanapada* phase of the north Indian and Deccanese history. We believe that there is convincing evidence to date the beginning of the early historic period in the Kaveri delta as early as c. 500 BC. We also believe that in view of the mid-5th century BC antiquity of the potsherds inscribed in Tamil-Brahmi, which were excavated at Anuradhapura in Sri Lanka, some Tamil-Brahmi inscriptions discovered both on pottery and in the rock-cut caverns in Tamil Nadu are likely to date from the same period (for a detailed discussion of this problem, Chakrabarti 2006, pp. 312-314, 346-347).

The discovery and the recognition of the authenticity of the Jambai inscription found in a rock-cut cave near Tirukkoyilur in the Ponnaiyar valley in South Arcot clearly throw light on the territory of Satiyaputra. The inscription reads *Satiyaputo Atiyan Natuman Anci* or "the abode (Pali) given by (itta) Atiyan Neduman Anci (name), the Satiyaputo (title)". As the title Satiyaputo is given to the Atiyaman chief Neduman Anci, this inscription sets at rest the controversy regarding the identity and location of the territorial unit of Satiyaputra. The point is that this inscription also provides a clear example of correlation between the Sangam literature and archaeology. Neduman Anci is an important character in the Sangam literature, being described well in the poems of the poet Paranar and the poetess Avvaiyar. He had his capital at Tagadur which has been identified with the area of the modern town of Dharampuri. He was also reputedly a great performer of the Vedic sacrifices and one of his ancestors is credited with the introduction of sugarcane cultivation. The poetess Avvaiyar went on his behalf as an emissary to Tondaiman. The Satiyaputra king of the Jambai inscription, Atiyaman, donated the rock-cut cavern where the inscription occurs to the Jaina monks. He was known to be a Saivite and he also reputedly defeated a confederacy of seven unknown rulers and captured Tirukkoiyulur. The Jambai inscription was engraved apparently after his capture of Tirukkoiyulur. However, Atiyaman was eventually defeated by the combined forces of the Tondaiman ruler Malaiyaman Thirumudi Kari and the Chera ruler Perum Cheral Irumporai, the latter mentioned in the Pugalur inscription found in the Kaveri valley near Karur. The Pugalur inscription records the gift of a rock-cut cave to the Jaina monk Cenkayapan. Atiyaman joined a confederacy of Valvil Ori of the Kolli or Kalrayan hills (east of Salem and overlooking the Chengam pass on its south) and the Chola and Pandya kings. The Chera king won the battle between these two confederacies. This Chera king is also credited with the conquest of the Kolli hills. The 'Kollipurai coin' (a circular inscribed silver coin found in the river bed at Karur, bearing the legend Kollipurai) has been argued by R. Nagaswamy (1995) to have been issued by Ko-Perum Cheral Irumporai, the conqueror of Tagadur and the Kolli hills. Nagaswamy puts the coin in the first century AD.

That there is a cogent body of evidence testifying to a clear correlation between the basic evidence of the Sangam literature and the various archaeological finds cannot be doubted. The names of rulers known from the Sangam literature occur routinely in the various Tamil-Brahmi inscriptions (for the details of these inscriptions, Mahadevan 2003) including the one at Mangulam near Madurai, which records the gift of a monastery by the Pandyan king Nedunj Cheliyan to a Jaina monk. The problem lies with the general chronological range postulated for these inscriptions and the date of the beginning of the early historic period in Tamil Nadu and Kerala. The third century BC when Asoka mentions four kingdoms of Tamil Nadu and Kerala is the defining line, but, as has been pointed out elsewhere (Chakrabarti 2006, pp. 312-314), there is impeccable evidence to argue that the date of the inscribed potsherds found in the lowest levels of such sites as Kodumanal should go back to the 5th century BC and bring the Tamil Nadu and Kerala picture in line with the date obtained for the occurrence of the Tamil-Brahmi script at Anuradhapura in Sri Lanka in the mid-5th century BC. The neat chronological classification of the early Tamil-Brahmi inscriptions, that I. Mahadevan (2003) undertakes in his *Early Tamil Epigraphy – From the Earliest Times to the Sixth Century AD* seems to be nothing more than a subjective exercise based on the assumption that even the earliest of these inscriptions can date only from the second century BC, i.e., a hundred years later than the Asokan edicts. We have noted that Nagaswamy (1995) puts the Kollipurai coin of Perum Cheral Irimporai, the Chera king, who defeated and killed Atiyaman of the Jambai inscription, in the first century AD. On the other hand, there can be nothing against the assumption that the reference to 'Satiyaputra' in the Jambai inscription may well date from the third century BC itself, when Asoka referred to this kingdom on his border. Mahadevan also puts the Jambai record in the first century AD. The Kollipurai coin itself, as illustrated by Mahadevan (2003), is completely free of any Roman influence, despite the opinion of Nagaswamy (1995) to the contrary. In the writings of some historians and archaeologists the Roman contact seems to be the only defining point of the early history of Tamil Nadu and Kerala. It is perhaps time that some attempt is made to look at the history of this region without its traditional umbilical cords of megaliths and Roman contact. In his estimate of the date of the archaeological sequence at Alagunkalam (located on the way to Rameswaram from Madurai), Mahadevan mentions that the site dates between c. 300 BC and 5th century AD. There is an uncalibrated radiocarbon date of 380 BC for the NBP deposit at the depth of 2.8 m from the surface, whereas the total occupational depth of the site is 4 m and its earliest level is marked by black-and-red ware and not by the NBP, as Mahadevan writes. The site of Korkai in Tirunelveli has a single date for its NBP-bearing level, whose calibrated date-range is 906-795 BC, a date which fits in with the early dates now emerging in the Ganga valley for this pottery. The chronology of the early historic Tamil Nadu needs serious revision and also calls for a change in attitude.

The Jambai inscription is particularly important because it specifically proves the existence of the Satiyaputra kingdom on the border of the Mauryan state. The rest of the political picture related to the Satiyaputra king mentioned in the Jambai edict is obtained primarily from what is known about him from the Sangam literature.

The next political unit – that of the Cholas – is securely rooted in the Kaveri delta, although one would suggest that in the beginning of the early historic period the Kaveri was likely to be a free-flowing river which was not brought under the network of irrigation canals, as it happened under the later Chola kings. It is also not clear if in the early historic period the Kaveri was flowing into the sea in many mouths, as it does now. The early Chola rulers are not mentioned in any contemporary inscription, nor do they figure in any inscribed coin, although the Chola symbol of tiger occurs in a number of coins. However, Mahadevan (2003) has pointed out that there is a possibility of the occurrence of one or more early Chola princes on some miscellaneous bits of inscribed evidence.

The reference to the Chera kings in the Pugalur inscription has already been noted. On the southern slope of a hill overlooking the Kaveri at Pugalur, about 15 km northwest of Karur, two caves contain inscriptions on their brow and on the stone beds. A cave on the northern side of the hill has another inscription on a stone bed. Out of the twelve Pugalur inscriptions, the Jaina monk Cenkayapan of Yarrur is mentioned in three, and the Chera ruling family is mentioned in two:

> Pugalur-1: The abode of the senior Jaina monk, Cenkayapan of Yarrur. The rock (shelter) was carved when (I)lankatunko, the son of Perunkatunkon, the son of king Atan Cel Irumporai, became the heir apparent.
>
> Pugalur-2: The abode of the senior Jaina monk, Yarru Cenkayapan. The rock (shelter) was caused to be carved when Katunkon (I)lankastunko, the son of Perunkatunkon, the son of King A (tan Ce) I Irumpurai, became the heir apparent.

Mahadevan's date for these two Pugalur inscriptions is the 2nd century AD. The fact that these names indicate the Chera ruling family is obtained from the Sangam literature. The postulated second century AD date for the two Pugalur inscriptions mentioning Irumporai is based on his contemporaneity (according to the *Silappadikaram* of the Sangam literature) with the Sri Lankan king Gajabahu, whose date in the second century AD is known independently from the Sri Lankan sources. The authenticity of another Chera king, Katumiputta Cera has been established from the inscription reproduced by Mahadevan as his Tamil-Brahmi inscription number 80 (Edakal-A-2) and put by him in the third century AD. The Edakal hill is located 6 km southwest of Sultan's Battery in the Wynad district of Kerala.

The ruling family of the Pandya territory based in the Vaigai delta near Madura is mentioned in the form of a celebrated Sangam literature Pandya king Netuncaliyan in the two cave inscriptions at Mangulam near Madura.

> Mangulam-1: Charity to Nanta-siri Kuvan, the kani. Behold ! The hermitage was caused to be carved by Katalan Valuti, the servant of Netuncaliyan.
> Mangulam-2: Charity (to)Nanta-siri Ku(v)an, the kani. Behold ! The hermitage was made by Catikan, the father of Ilancatikan, the husband of the sister-in-law of Netuncaliyan.

The total number of inscriptions at Mangulam is six, but only two of them mention the Pandya ruler Netuncaliyan. Mahadevan's date for these two Mangulam inscriptions is the 2nd century BC. Copper coins inscribed with the legend *Peruvaluti* and dated in the second century BC also establish the authenticity of another early Pandya king.

In addition to these four politically defined territories of the Satiyaputras, Chera, Cholas and Pandyas, there were various chieftainships in the early historic Tamil Nadu. The primary evidence is obtained from the Sangam literature. For instance, the Pudukottai area between Thanjavur in the Chola domain and Madura in the Pandya domain is suposed to have been associated with the Vellalars. It is difficult to define such groups of people historically unless they figure in inscriptions, which in some cases they do.

Whatever may be the date of these inscriptions, there is no doubt that they throw light on different aspects of political, economic, social and cultural life of the first phase of the historic period in Tamil Nadu. Mahadevan has systematically compiled the relevant references, and here we may cite some of them to denote the historical context in which the early historic Tamil Nadu and its states – Satiyaputra, Chera, Chola, Pandya – took shape. Among the institutions, the village assembly ("the assembly (Ur) of Vempil (Vempirrur) constructed the large tank") and the assembly of learned persons (the term *katikai* in the Mannarkoil inscription of the second century AD – cf. Mahadevan 2003: 125) deserve notice, and so do the references to agriculture (paddy, ploughshare, irrigation), trade (the merchant guild, merchants and traders, commodities of trade – cloth, salt, oil, ploughshare, molasses, gold) and professions (mason and master mason, producer or seller of salt, carpenter, *mahut*, and goldsmith). Sri Lanka is possibly mentioned, and the only territory mentioned outside modern Tamil Nadu is Erumi-Nadu identified with the *Mahisha-mandala* or the Mysore region. The places mentioned include cities and ports like Madura, Tondi, the sea-port of the Pandyas, Karur and Muziris. There are also references to various lesser towns and villages in Tamil Nadu. The names of a few trees and animals also occur. There is possibly a reference to the musical notations in an inscription.

If one compares this general picture with the basic settlement evidence and the evidence of craft specialization in the form of the use of different raw materials and products in the excavated materials of the early historic levels of Tamil Nadu's early historic sites, one finds a close generic similarity. The evidence is also hardly dissimilar with what we know of the material sphere of life in early historic northern India. One may go to the extent of claiming that the function which the north Indian *Jatakas* fulfil in providing a literary backdrop to the archaeological picture is fulfilled here by the Sangam literature. This literature could have been set down in later periods, but basically they depict the historical reality of Tamil Nadu in the second half of the first millennium BC. The mention of *Damilarattha* in the *Akitti Jataka* suggests that Tamil Nadu figured as a geographical territory in the *Jatakas*. We have argued elsewhere (Chakrabarti 2005) that the *Jatakas* are more likely to reflect the socio-political and economic conditions of the central Ganga plain of c. 500 BC than anything later. In all likelihood, the beginning of the early historic Tamil Nadu dates from around this chronological point.

At this point, it should be noted that a historian of the stature of K.A. Nilakanta Sastri thought that the Sangam literature was not earlier than the early centuries AD. The basis of his opinion was an apparent similarity between the evidence furnished by this literature and that furnished by the classical writers like the *Periplus* of the mid-1st century AD and Ptolemy of the 2nd century AD.

> There is a perfect concord between the Sangam anthologies, the notices of South India by classical works of the early centuries of the Christian era, like the *Periplus* and Ptolemy's geography, and the numerous finds of Roman coins of the early Roman Empire in several places in Southern India. This would lead any unbiased student to the conclusion that the Tamil anthologies were contemporary with the classical works and the Roman coins (Sastri 1935, p. 69).

Elsewhere he writes,

> If we compare this evidence with that of the classical writers of the early centuries of the Christian era, we shall see that the data drawn from these

> two disparate sources work into one another so closely that it becomes quite obvious that they relate to the same period of history (Sastri 1935, p. 100).

Sastri wrote at a time when the evidence of Roman contact with Tamil Nadu was based only on unstratified numismatic evidence. Trade contacts between Arikamedu and the Mediterranean region are now considered to have begun in the late 3rd century BC (Suresh 2007), with the possibility of the trade between South India and the Mediterranean region going back earlier (cf. Sewell). That the Mediterranean contact of the Coromandel coast antedates the testimony of Megasthenes in the later part of the 4th century BC is clear from a detailed consideration of what Megasthenes wrote:

> Next come the Pandae, the only race in India, ruled by women. They say that Hercules, having but one daughter, who was on that account all the more beloved, endowed her with a noble kingdom. Her descendants rule over 300 cities, and command an army of 150000 foot and 500 elephants (McCrindle 1926, pp. 150-151)

> The Pandaean nation is governed by females, and their first queen is said to have been the daughter of Hercules (McCrindle 1926, p. 161).

> Heracles begat a daughter in India whom he called Pandaia. To her he assigned that portion of India which lies to the southward and extends to the sea (McCrindle 1926, pp. 163-164).

Megasthenes' notion of the geography and trade of the region is clear from the following:

> The island, then, in the great sea, which they call Taprobane, has palm-groves.... It has also herds of elephants.... The islanders export them to the mainland opposite in boats ..., and they dispose off their cargoes to the king of the Kalingai (McCrindle 1926, pp. 174-175).

Megasthenes clearly refers to an organized kingdom – the kingdom of the Pandyas – which had a large army of foot-soldiers and elephants. He also had a clear idea of its geographical location, including the fact that the Sri Lankans were selling their cargoes to 'the king of the Kalingai'. He was, thus, aware of the trade conducted in that region, and he was unlikely to have been aware of this unless the Greeks were participating in that. Megasthenes offers measurements of distances from point to point on the Indian coastline:

> From the mouth of the Ganges to Cape Calingon and the town of Dandagula 625 miles; to Tropina 1225; to the cape of Perimula, where

> there is the greatest emporium of trade in India, 750 miles (McCrindle 1926, pp. 144-145)

J.W. McCrindle (1926, pp. 144-145) who translated and edited Megasthenes' 'fragments' adds Alexander Cunningham's notes on the identification of Cape Calingon, Tropina and Cape Perimula. Cape Calingon was identified with the port town of Coringa at the Godavari mouth and Tropina with Tripontai or Tirupantara, opposite Cochin. The island of Salsette was considered to be Perimula. While there can be little doubt about the identification of 'Cape Calingon', the two other identifications are somewhat arbitrary. However, what is striking is that Megasthenes, a Greek resident in the court of Chandragupta Maurya at Pataliputra, was aware of a great emporium of trade located somewhere on the west coast of India but probably in the area of Mumbai-Sopara. It is highly unlikely that without a knowledge of this emporium in the Mediterranean world, Megasthenes would have been so clearly aware of it.

That the Greeks were participating in the Coromandel coast trade is clear from what Arrian, a Roman Senator of the 2nd century AD wrote later on India, basing himself on Megasthenes and Nearchus.

> (Heracles) found in the sea an ornament for women, which even to this day the Indian traders who bring us their wares eagerly buy up and carry away to foreign markets, while it is even more eagerly brought up by the wealthy Romans of today, *as it was wont to be by the wealthy Greeks long ago* (italics ours). This article is sea-pearl, called in the Indian tongue *margarita* (McCrindle 1926, pp. 206-207).

Arrian also mentions the tradition of the queen of Pandaia being a daughter of Heracles and given by her father an army of 500 elephants, 'a force of cavalry 4000 strong' and 130,000 foot-soldiers or infantry. Megasthenes does not mention cavalry, but Arrian does, and as cavalry is based on horses, we may infer from this that the import of horses which was an ubiquitous feature at Indian ports right up to the end of the pre-modern period was already known in the 2nd century AD.

The classical references we have cited above mention not merely the kingdom of the Pandyas and pearl-fishery in the south but also clearly allude to the classical familiarity with the existence of trade all along the Indian coastline including Sri Lanka by the 4th century BC.

This evidence has also to be considered along with the evidence of Kautilya's *Arthasastra* of the 3rd century BC. In his chapter 11, entitled "examination of gems that are to be entered into the treasury", Kautilya refers to a variety of pearl necklaces and the following types of gems:

> Tamraparnika, that which is produced in the Tamraparni, Pandyakavataka, that which is produced in Pandyakavata (Shamasastry 1923, p. 83).

'Pandyakavata,' according to R. Shamasastry, the first translator of the *Arthasastra*, means a mountain known as Malayakoti in the Pandya country.

Thus, as far as Nilakanta Sastri's opinion regarding the date of the maritime trade of South India is concerned, we cannot accept the main basis of his argument that this trade dates in its earliest from the 1st century AD. We do so not merely in the light of the revised chronology of trade through Arikamedu (i.e., the 3rd century BC) but also in view of the rather categorical evidence provided by Megasthenes, Arrian and Kautilya, which establishes that the historical knowledge of the Pandya country, its pearls and trade through Indian coast came into focus by the 4th century BC at the latest. Our general dating of the beginning of the early historical period in South India – at least in the Pandyan area – at c. 500 BC is not, on the basis of the literary evidence alone, an eminently justifiable exercise.

VI. THE DISTRIBUTION OF CAVE INSCRIPTIONS, INSCRIBED SHERDS AND PUNCH-MARKED COINS IN TAMIL NADU AND KERALA, AND ITS IMPLICATIONS IN THE STUDY OF THE EARLY HISTORIC ROUTES OF THE REGION

Mahadevan (2003) puts the Tamil-Brahmi inscriptions between the second century BC and fourth century AD in two chronological groups: between the second century BC and the first century AD, and between the second century AD and the fourth century AD. We have argued before that the basic antiquity of writing in Tamil Nadu should date from at least c. 500 BC. However, chronology is not the major issue in this section. For our purpose, we can take the whole series of inscriptions, which Mahadevan dates up to the 4th century AD, as a historical block representing in essence the pattern of life embedded in the Sangam literature. The problem is to determine if this block of inscriptions throws any light on the routes in circulation during that period.

Mahadevan shows that out of a total of 89 cave inscriptions limited to 30 sites, 28 sites and 84 inscriptions are associated with the Jaina religion. The two other sites and their five inscriptions do not ostensibly represent any religious faith. They are secular. Mahadevan's maps convincingly demonstrate that the densest concentration of what he calls the early group of inscriptions between the second century BC and the first century AD is

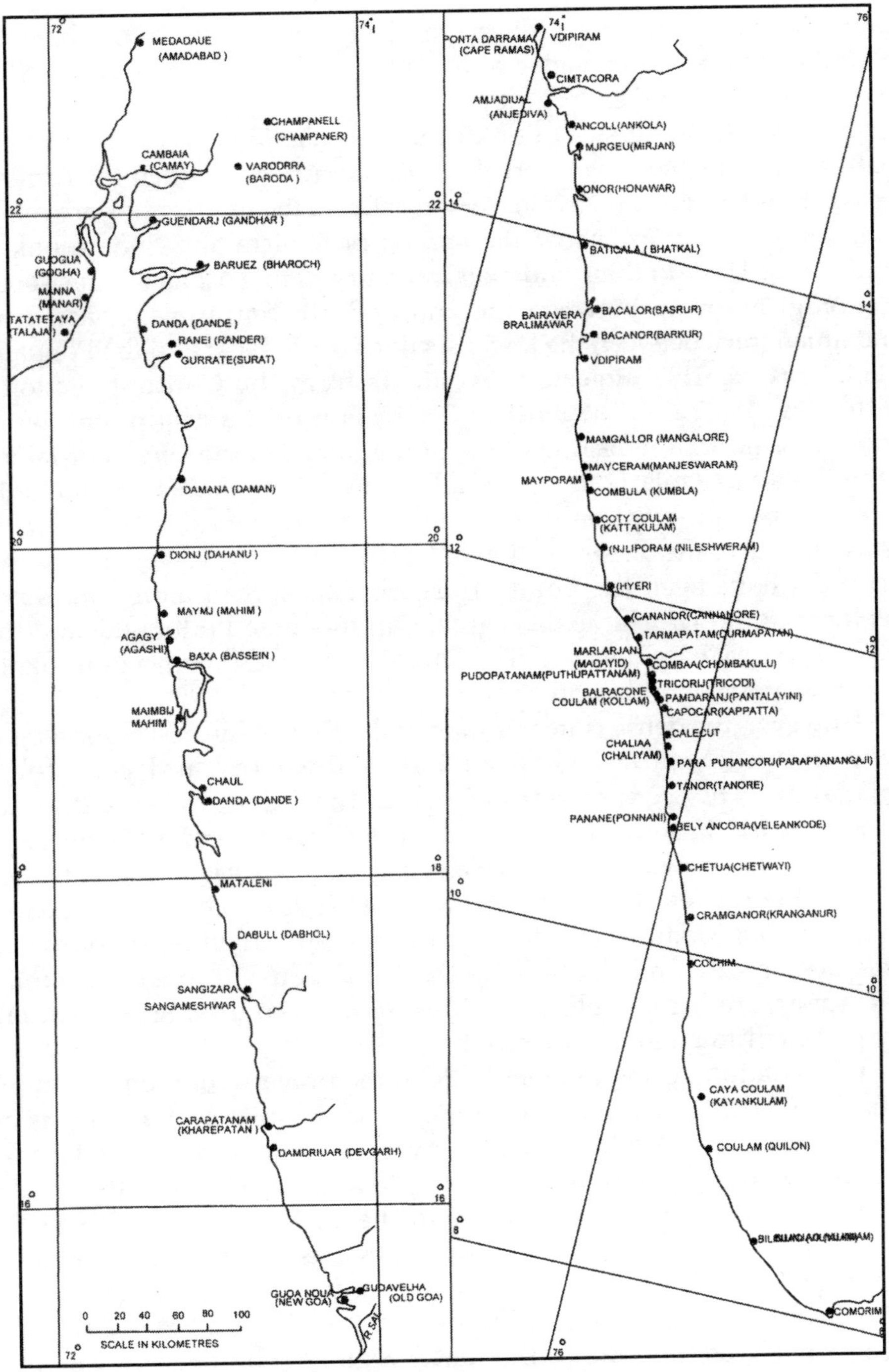

Map 3. The major places along the west coast (after Tome Pires).

around Madurai, including Sittanavasal in Pudukottai. Two other sites, Aiyarmalai in the Kaveri valley and Jambai in the Ponnaiyar valley, show the occurrence of this early group.

In any case, the distribution of these inscriptions gives us an idea of what emerged as the major corridors of interaction between the different areas of Tamil Nadu and Kerala. As virtually all the inscriptions are related to the Jaina faith, these show the spread of Jainism and Jaina monks in Tamil Nadu. Three of their findspots, all representing Mahadevan's second chronological group between the 2nd and 4th centuries AD, are in the Tondaiman tract, between the lower sections of the Palar and the Ponnaiyar rivers. This clearly suggests movements from the Chittoor section of Andhra. As Jambai is the earliest inscription of the group, one would argue that Andhra Pradesh was one of the points of the spread of Jainism in Tamil Nadu. Similarly, there are a few sites along the Kaveri, including the Aiyarmalai inscription of the earliest chronological group. For this particular case of the dissemination of Jainism along the Kaveri, the Mysore tract must have been the point of origin. This spread along the Kaveri took them to the Tiruchirapalli segment, from where Pudukottai and then Madurai were at easy distance. The Sittanavasal inscriptions in Pudukottai are a clear pointer in this direction.

However, the dense concentration of the sites of the first chronological group around Madurai is singularly noteworthy and calls for an explanation. This concentration implies that Madurai was the most important early historic city-site of the pre-Christian era in Tamil Nadu. Madurai is not known to have an especially holy association with Jainism, and thus the concentration of the abode of Jaina monks in this area can only mean that Madurai was the most important urban centre of the day in the deep south, and that is why the Jaina monks thronged around it. They apparently came both from Mysore and Andhra, and eventually they preferred to be in the vicinity of Madurai.

Why Madurai came to loom large in the universe of the Jaina monks of the pre-Christian era cannot be understood completely, but there is one element which gave Madurai an edge over the contemporary south Indian cities. As the pearl fishery of the Gulf of Mannar was known to Kautilya, one may argue, as we have argued in the earlier section with further evidence from Megasthenes and Kautilya, that its basic antiquity is earlier. As Madurai was the chief city of the Vaigai valley, one can also assume that it became a major centre of trade in pearls by the time of Kautilya, and this was possibly one of the major regions why the city was more important than the rest of its southern contemporaries.

The three inscriptions at Edakal have major geographical significance of their own. The place, a large cave near the summit of a 4000 feet high hill near Sultan's Battery in the Wynad district of Kerala, has four inscriptions. The first one refers to a 'writer/scribe' called Oppanappa Vira(n). The second one mentions "Katumiputta, the Chera". The third one mentions a chieftain called Puti Vira, and the fourth one mentions a king – "Atan, the king". As we have earlier noted, the main Calicut-Mysore road is by the Tamarasseri ghat, Vyaittiri and Sultan's Battery. Even if we assume that Mahadevan's dating of the Edakal inscriptions in the 3rd century AD does not need revision, we have to say that one of the important links between Mysore and the coastal Kerala through the Wynad plateau was operational by the third century AD.

If one compares the distribution of the Tamil Nadu and Kerala rock-cut inscriptions with the distribution of those explored and excavated sites which contain Tamil-Brahmi inscriptions incised in potsherds, one finds a remarkable similarity between them. It may be noted that no site in Kerala has yet yielded potsherds inscribed in Tamil-Brahmi and, thus, for this category we have to think only of the Tamil Nadu sites. There are four relevant sites in the Tondaiman area between the Palar and the Ponnaiyar: Kanchipuram, Arikamedu, Maligaimedu and Jambai. The Kaveri valley has five of them: Attur, Karur, Alagarai, Uraiyur and Vallam, and there are three of them in the Coimbatore-Erode mouth of the Palghat gap: Poluvampatti, Daikalpalaiyam, and Kodumanal. The Vaigai valley possesses seven such sites: Kovalanpottal, S. Pappinayakkanpatti, Kallupatti (these three around Madurai), Sivakasi, Teriruveli, Alagankulam, and Korkai. Sivakasi suggests a link with the region south of Madura. On the whole, it is clear from the distribution of Tamil-Brahmi inscriptions (both rock-cut cave inscriptions and inscriptions incised on potsherds) that by the early centuries AD, the different areas of Tamil Nadu were fully opened up for intercommunications, and this took in also the Wynad plateau and the adjacent coastal regions of Kerala.

This picture becomes sharper when we take into consideration the evidence of the distribution of punch-marked coins in Tamil Nadu and Kerala. Even without going into the details of these finds, one notes that in Tamil Nadu punch-marked coin hoards have been found, among other places, at Mambalam (Chennai city area), Kayadi (in or at the edge of the Palni hills), Navalai (Dharampuri), Tirunelveli, and Bodinayakkanur (at the edge of the Cardamom hills, north of Cumbum). In addition, this coin-type has been found at Alagankulam (along with the NBP, in excavations) and in the Amaravati River-bed at Karur. It has been pointed

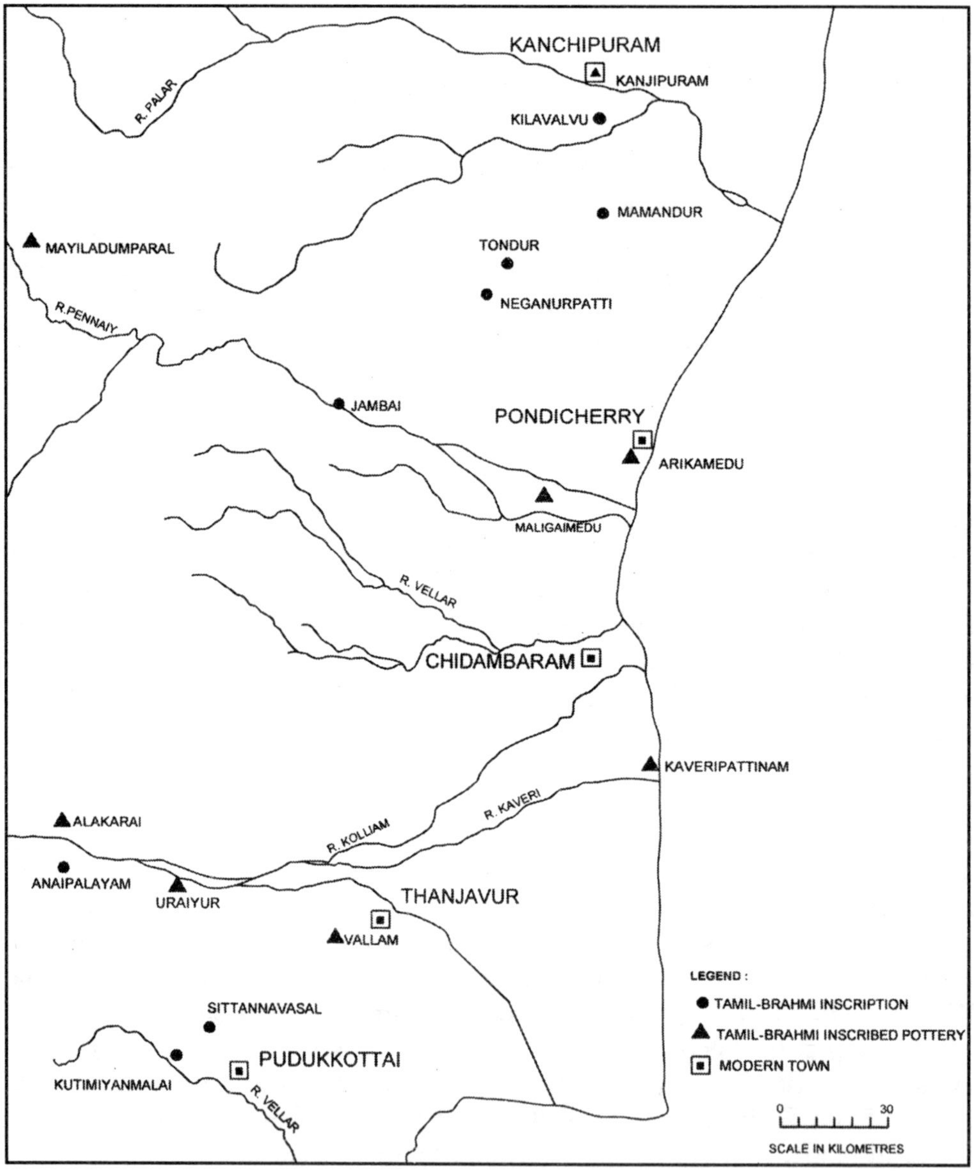

Map 4. Tamil-Brahmi inscriptions in northeastern Tamil Nadu (after K. Rajan, V.P. Yathees Kumar and S. Selvakumar, *Catalogue of Archaeological Sites in Tamil Nadu*, Vol. 1. Thanjavur, Heritage India Trust, 2009; cited hereafter as *Catalogue*).

out that the Mambalam hoard of punch-marked coins included a coin of the Roman emperor Augustus. In the punch-marked coin hoards from Kottayam and Iyyal in Kerala there were coins of the Roman emperors Augustus, Tiberius, Claudius, Nero and Trajan. On the basis of these hoards it is possible to argue that the punch-marked coins continued to be in use in Tamil Nadu as late as the first or even the beginning of the second century AD. *However, it is possible to argue with equal justification that the punch-marked coins marked the relic of a long by-gone era and were hoarded as such, and not as something which was valid currency at the time of the deposition of the hoard in question.* This argument gains in strength if one considers that the Roman coins which came as bullion in exchange for goods were unlikely to have been used in India as a valid currency. Their importance lay in their metallic value. *So, the find of a hoard of Roman and silver punch-marked coins simply means that the hoard was deposited mainly for its worth in metals. If a Victorian gold coin is found in the collection of coins of modern Indian families, that does no mean that the gold coin in question is now valid currency.*

Whether the Pandya kings issued classic punch-marked coins is a question which cannot be settled, but the hoards of such coins at Bodikkayanur and Tirunelveli can be explained more simply as marking the line of the routes from Madurai to the Thekkadi-Periyar section of Kerala through the Cumbam valley. On the Kerala side, the find of a punch-marked coin hoard in the Kottayam area similarly suggests the use of the Thekkadi-Periyar route from Tamil Nadu to Kerala. The Iyyal hoard of punch-marked coins near Cochin and the find of a similar hoard at Angamalai in the same area further sharpen the focus of this route. The Mala hoard of punch-marked coins in the Thrissur area points out the importance of the Palghat gap. Thrissur lies near its mouth on the Kerala side. The occurrence of punch-marked coins at Mambalam in Chennai and Navalai in Dharampuri underscores the importance of the movements from Andhra and Mysore tract in this regard.

If one takes up M. Mitchiner's *Coin Circulation in Southernmost India* (Mitchiner 1995), one realizes that the finds of punch-marked coins are comparatively limited both in Tamil Nadu and Kerala. In Kerala he mentions Kottayam and Iyyal, Cochin/Ernakulam (6 coins of Magadhan and Mauryan affiliation, including 2 found at Kottayam), Palghat (2 copper, originally silver-plated), Coimbatore, Perur and Vellalore (several, mainly of Magadhan types, plus copper but originally silver-plated specimens), Karur (silver punch-marked types, including "dies for counterfeit silver punch-marked coins"), Madurai (both Magadhan and

Mauryan silver punch-marked coins, Pandyan silver punch-marked coins which add the Pandyan symbol fish to the repertoire of punch-marks), Tirunelveli (Magadhan-Mauryan and Pandyan silver punch-marked coins), and Tirukoiyulur (silver punch-marked). The Magadhan types of punch-marked coins are pre-Mauryan and thus pre-4th century BC. The finds of these types, although occasionally with the admixture of Roman coins, at Cochin, Kottayam, Palghat and Karur argues, at least indirectly, for the opening up of the Palghat gap route before the fourth century BC. More importantly, the occurrence of this type at Madurai and Tirunelveli argues for the emergence of the Pandyan kingdom before the fourth century BC. From this point of view also, our idea that Tamil Nadu and Kerala were incorporated in the early historic development of states, urbanism and literacy by at least 500 BC makes sound sense. The geographically feasible routes of the region too were in circulation by that time.

By making the Roman contact and Roman coins the hub of the Tamil Nadu and Kerala archaeological universe, one suspects that grave injustice has been done to a proper historical understanding of this region. The fact that dies of counterfeit silver punch-marked coins have been found in the Amaravati River-bed of Karur, the river-bed from which most of the antiquities reported from Karur have been obtained, suggests that some of the punch-marked coins which have been cited as evidence of their continuation as currency till the beginning of the second century AD may be nothing more than such counterfeit coins. Further, the fact that pre-4th century BC Magadhan coins have been found in the Madurai area and the fact that the Pandyan kings were the only southern kings to adopt the use of punch-marked coins as their own coins by adding their own symbol fish to it, may suggest that the Pandyan kingdom was the first to emerge as a state in ancient Tamil Nadu and that its date may securely be put in a period earlier than the fourth century BC.

VII. THE PRE-EARLY HISTORIC CONTEXT

Whatever the date, what evidence is there of movements from the north to Tamil Nadu and Kerala before their early historic phase? The issue which is generally ignored is the occurrence of Gangetic valley copper hoard specimens along a well-defined route (for discussion, Chakrabarti and Lahiri 1996), first at Vellore (information from Professor K. Rajan) and then at Shavinipatti in the Ramanathapuram district. On the other hand, it has been reported from the Annamalai hills area of Idukki in Kerala. The shape of the reported antennae-hilted swords is as distinctive as the Gangetic specimens, and one may remember that an example of this type of implement was also found at Kallur in the Raichur area of the Deccan. There was in all probability a southern dispersal of this type of copper implement, and its occurrence both at Vellore and in the Ramanathapuram district would indicate a general movement in the direction of Madurai and from there to Ramanathapuram. Vellore lies at the entrance from the Chittoor section of Andhra. Idukki lies in the Periyar area, and the find could be the result of a movement from Madurai to the Periyar section via the Kambam valley or the adjacent areas.

If one goes back to the earlier period, one finds that the only Tamil Nadu area from where there is definitive evidence of neolithic habitation sites is the Tiripattur taluk of North Arcot at the foot of the Javadi hills. The adjacent Krishnagiri and Harur taluks of Dharampuri also belong to this neolithic belt. The point is that the neolithic culture of the type which has been identified stratigraphically at Paiyampalli and Mayilaidumparai (for Paiyampalli, Ghosh 1989; for Mayilaidumparai, Rajan, Athiyaman and Jayakumar 2004) in Tamil Nadu belongs to the general range of the South Indian neolithic culture, which has been extensively identified in Karnataka and Andhra. Both Krishnagiri and Tirupattur lie in the hilly belt which offers openings for movements to Tamil Nadu from Karnataka and Andhra. The same trend has been observed by K. Rajan (1997) in his survey of megalithic burials in the Coimbatore, Dharampuri, North and South Arcot districts. In the Coimbatore region he puts emphasis on the significance of the Moyyar valley as the route of interaction with Mysore. He adds that the Dimpam and Kadambur passes near the Moyyar valley could also have played a minor role in this regard. In the case of the distribution of megaliths in Dharampuri, he argues that the area shows the evidence of inflow of three megalithic traits from three geographical regions. The trait of 'cairn circle' came from the Mandya area of Mysore along the Kaveri valley. The second trait of dolmens and dolmenoid cists came by the Kuppam and other passes from the Kolar area of Mysore and the Chittoor area of Andhra. The third trait of cairn circles with portholed cists occur in the Hosur, Dencanikotta and Krishnagiri area of the Balaghat region which is an extension of the Mysore plateau. In North Arcot he argues that the cairn circle trait travelled along the Ponnaiyar River from Dharampuri. The stone circle variety entered the eastern part of the area from the eastern part of the Chittoor district. The dolmens could have come from the Palamaner taluk in the western part of Chittoor. The dolmenoid cists with orthostats could have developed in North Arcot itself or come from Chingleput where they seem to be common. According to

Rajan, the sarcophagus burial trait is the earlier burial trait of North Arcot, and the other megalithic traits were superimposed on it. Also, the megalithic feature of large and standing anthropomorphic figures noticed at places such as Mottur in the Chengam pass area came in all probability from the Chittoor section of Andhra. Regarding the distribution of sarcophagi, Rajan writes the following:

> The available evidence suggests that the sarcophagus had its origin in the eastern coastal plain between Godavari and Pennaiyar and moves slowly westward and merged with the local tradition of the respective areas. In district Chingleput and northern part of South Arcot district, particularly in the coastal area, it was found in the pits and pit circles. While moving westward it is found as an interment in the cists, dolmenoid cists and dolmens (Rajan 1997, p. 208).

The point which emerges is that the Iron Age phase of Tamil Nadu had in its northern section a close tie-up with the adjacent regions of the Mysore plateau and Andhra, and displayed the same type of interaction through the gaps in the Eastern Ghats and other hills that we see in other contexts.

This survey by Rajan has also highlighted the distribution of major habitation sites in the region along with its megalithic remains. In the Coimbatore sector the explored habitation sites with habitational area of 25 acres or more are the following: Kaniyampundi (50 acres, Avinashi taluk), Kanjapalli (30 acres, Avinashi taluk), Irugur (25 acres, Avinashi taluk), Kovilpalayam (30 acres, Avinashi taluk), Vellalur (the enire habitation site covered by the modern village, Avinashi taluk), Idayapalayam (30 acres, Palladam taluk), Muthukaundanpudur/Sulur (50 acres, Palladam taluk), Agilandapuram (more than 25 acres, Kangayam taluk), Kodumanal (the size of the habitational area not mentioned but this a major excavated site, Perundurai taluk), and Sircar Periyapalayam (more than 100 acres of habitation-cum-burial area – the habitational area more than 20 acres – Perundurai taluk).

In Dharampuri such sites comprise the following: Adiyamankottai (2 km south of Dharampuri – 100 acres), Kolahattur (more than 75 acres – 3 km from Dharampuri), Kottaimedu (75 acres – 15 km northwest of Dharampuri), Nattapatti (50 acres, 12 km from Dharampuri), Nerkunti (75 acres, 16 km southwest of Dharampuri), the Kottaimedu mound at Palaya Indur, 13 km west of Dharampuri – 50 acres), Chennachandram (75 acres, Krishnagiri taluk), Pachchihanapalli (more than 200 acres – the most extensive site noticed so far in the Dharampuri district – left bank of the Ponnaiyar – Krishnagiri taluk), Adanur (75 acres, Pennagaram taluk),

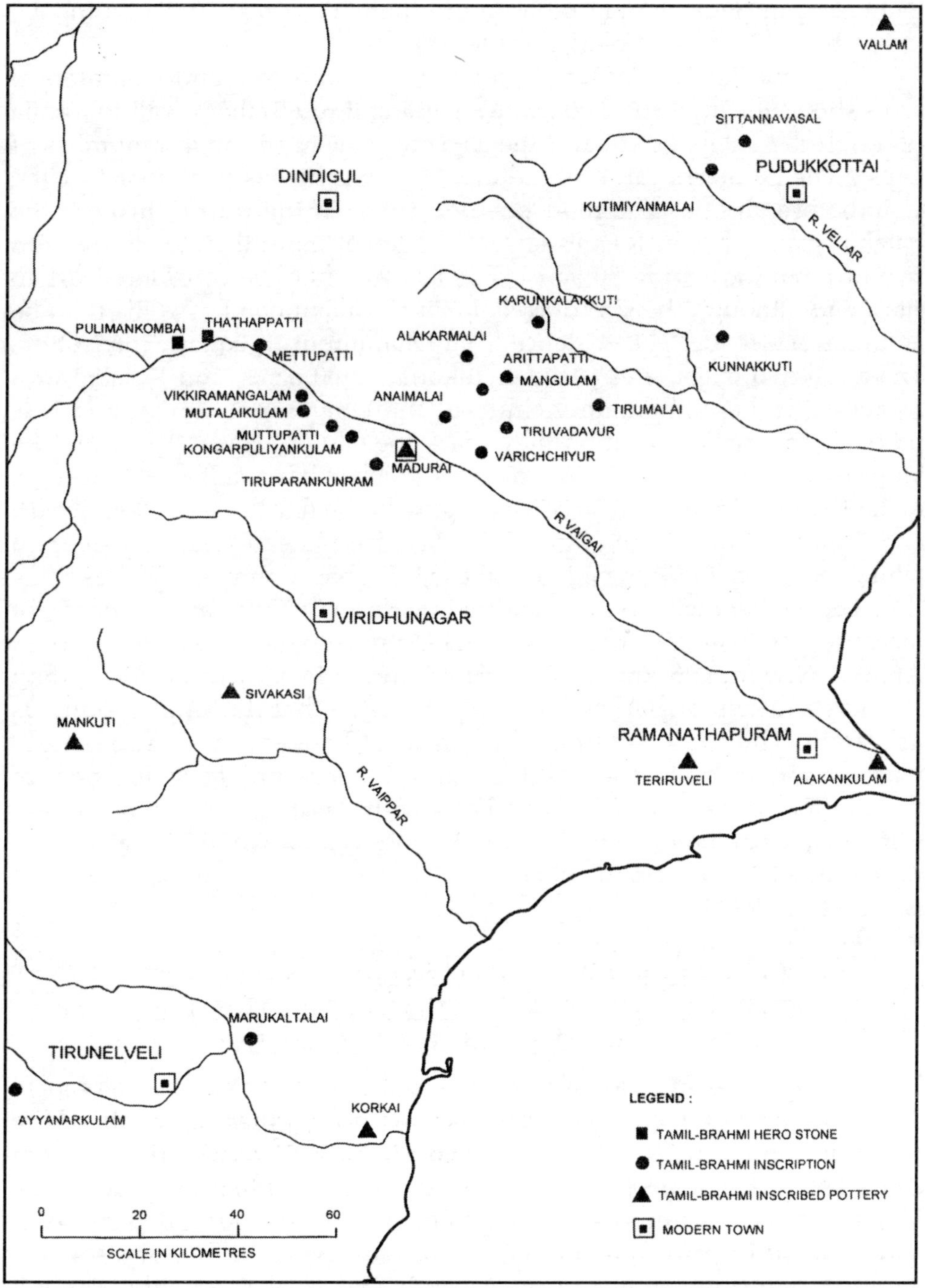

Map 5. Tamil-Brahmi inscriptions in southern Tamil Nadu (after *Catalogue*).

Pannaikulam (Pennagaram taluk, more than 100 acres), and Perumbalai (more than 75 acres, Pennagaram taluk).

The concentration of large sites in the Coimbatore and Dharampuri areas shows the importance of routes passing through them both to Kerala (through the Palghat gap) and the Mysore plateau (through a number of gaps). The Avinashi taluk of Coimbatore, which lies to the east of the Coimbatore city, is in a good position to catch the traffic through the Palghat gap. It has in Rajan's survey 5 sites of more than 25 acres, with two of them measuring 50 acres. The last two may be considered urban sites, and although the size of Vellalur is not mentioned, it is likely to be an urban centre too. The evidence from Dharampuri is equally interesting. There are two major sites (Adiyamankottai – 100 acres, and Kolahattur – 75 acres) in the immediate vicinity of the Dharampuri town, and it is probable that in combination they mark the site of ancient Tagadur. The largest habitational site in Dharampuri (Pachchihanapalli – 200 acres) is in the Krishnagiri taluk, which lies roughly to the northeast of Dharampuri and is in the hills at the edge of the Mysore plateau. The Pennagaram taluk, another taluk at the edge of these hills, has a number of large sites.

The habitational mounds reported by Rajan in North and South Arcot measure less than 25 acres but one habitational-cum-burial site in South Arcot – Nayanur, 5 km from Tirukkoyilur – is said to be more than 100 acres in extent. However, the size of its habitational mound is uncertain. The route coming through the Chengam opening possibly played a role in the location of these sites. Considering the significance of the Chittoor gaps in maintaining links with Andhra, one would expect some major habitational sites in the Vellore region where these Andhra routes enter Tamil Nadu. It appears that this zone has not yet been surveyed in detail.

VIII. SOME EXCAVATED COASTAL AND INLAND SITES OF TAMIL NADU AND KERALA IN THEIR DYNASTIC AND MARITIME CONTEXTS

It is logical to assume that by the time the four early states emerged in Tamil Nadu, they were connected well with the other segments of the region including the Kerala coast. From Madurai there would have been a link towards Alagankulam. This is more or less a straight link down the Vaigai, via Manamadurai and Ramanathapuram. Another link is by Avur and Tiruchuli up to Ramanathapuram. However, the literary sources mention two other major ports – Tondi and Korkai – of the Pandya territory. The coastline of this section is also dotted by other ports, of whose antiquity one is seldom certain. From Madurai there are two routes to connect Trichinopoly / Tiruchirapally or ancient Uraiyur, the Chola capital, one, the longer one, via Dindigul, and the second one via Tirupattur. From Madurai, Tirunelveli / Tinnevelly is directly linked via Sattur and Kovilpattu. There is also a route from Madurai to Tenkasi, which eventually takes one to Quilon in Kerala through the Shencottah gap. Two other Madurai-Kerala routes run through Bodinayakannnur to Kottayam, on the one hand, and to Alwaye via Periyakulam, on the other.

VIII.1. The Pandya Territory

Although never subjected to excavations, Madurai as the capital of the Pandya territory has a rich textual history, beginning with the first Pandya kings mentioned in the Sangam literature. One of them, Nedun-Cheliyan II, defeated a confederacy of the Cholas, Cheras and five minor chieftains. Apart from the Sangam literature, the reference by Megasthenes, already considered in detail by us, to the Pandaia country which lies to the southward and extends to the sea is important. Pliny in the first century AD refers both to 'Pandae, king Pandion' and its emporium 'Modoura'. Reputedly, the king Pandion sent an embassy to Augustus Caesar in c. 20 BC. In a sense, the Mediterranean association of Madurai has been proved by the number of Roman coin finds in the region. It has been suggested on this basis that a Roman colony must once have existed there. The next major identifiable stage in the history of the Pandyas and Madurai is the end of the sixth century AD when the Pallava kings Simhavishnu and Narasimhavarman I, ruling from Kanchipuram towards the end of the sixth century AD, claim to have conquered the Cholas and invaded the country of the Pandyas and Cheras. The Pallava pressure on the Pandya kingdom was lifted by the growth of the power of the Western Chalukyas of Badami who early in the 7th century overshadowed the Pallava power in the south. However, in the middle of the 8th century AD a Pallava king, Nandivarman Pallavamalla, claims to have defeated the Pandyas in a battle at an unidentified place called Mannaikuddi. In the 9th century the Ganga-Pallavas ruled from Kanchipuram, but it was also in this century that the Pandyas became powerful. Their inscriptions of this period have been found in the Chola territory and also to its north, in North Arcot. The Pandyas also reputedly invaded Sri Lanka around the middle of the 9th century. In the first half of the 10th century, the Pandya territory was conquered by the Cholas under Parantaka I but after his defeat by the Rashtrakutas of Malkhed / Manyakhet who supplanted the Western Chalukyas of Badami in the Deccan, the Pandyas had a brief phase of independence under Vira-Pandya. However, under the Chola Rajaraja I (AD 985-1013), Madurai and Tirunelveli became part of the Chola dominions. According to the Madurai district gazetteer, this is evidenced by the immense number of Chola inscriptions which occur in Madura and Tinnevelly districts, by the very large number of copper coins of Rajaraja which are even now found in the former of these, and by the fact that the name of the old Pandya capital of Korkai was changed to the Chola term *Cholendrasimha-chaturvedimangalam* and that of the Pandya country itself to *Rajaraja-Pandi-nadu* (p. 31).

The Pandyas, the Cheras and the Sri Lankans rebelled against Rajadhiraja I (1018-53) of the Cholas, but were defeated. The Pandyas rebelled, unsuccessfully again, during the time of the Chola Vira-Rajendra I (1062-70) who gave the Pandya territory to his son Gangai-Konda Chola. This Chola king took the title of Chola-Pandya. The Chola supremacy over the Pandyas continued through the reign of the Chola Kulottinga I to c. AD 1119, but by the end of the 12th century there were two Pandya contenders for the Pandya power, with one of them being supported by the contemporary Sri Lankan king. The Sri Lankan army returned to Sri Lanka, and the Chola-Pandya strife continued intermittently till the end of the Chola power at the hands of the Hoyasala dynasty of Halebid of Mysore in the first half of the 13th century AD. From the beginning of the 13th century AD there is a dated sequence of 15 Pandya kings who continued to rule from Madura from c. AD 1190 to c. AD 1567. The political history of the Pandyas of this period is marked by their struggles with the Hoyasalas and occasionally the Cholas and the Kakatiyas (of Warangal). Jatavarman Sundara-Pandya I (AD 1251-61) invaded Sri Lanka, looted the tooth relic of Kandy, covered the Srirangam temple of Trichy with gold and established his power in the north as far as Nellore, entering into a struggle with the Kakatiyas of Warangal and the Hoyasalas of Halebid. The wealth and magnificence of the Pandya kingdom of Madura at the end of the 13th and the beginning of the 14th centuries are documented in various sources including the account of Marco Polo. Early in the 14th century a Pandya claimant for the throne sought the help of Ala-ud-din of Delhi who sent Malik Kafur on an expedition against the Deccan and the south up to Madurai and Rameshwaram. Kafur returned to Delhi but the Pandya power was weakened to the point of being taken over by a king of the Cheras in AD 1313. This Chera power was short-lived and succeeded by a brief rule by a Muslim dynasty to be overthrown in 1365 by the Vijayanagara kings who remained as the overlords of the Pandya territory up to c. AD 1565. There were problems from the Cheras or Travancore of that time, but there was not much interruption of the Vijayanagara supremacy. In 1559 the Nayaka dynasty became powerful around Madurai and ruled till the Sultan of Arcot came to dominate this area in 1736. The Nayakas had their occasional troubles with the powers based in Bijapur and Golconda in the Deccan. There was a brief Maratha interlude in 1740-43 but the Muslim power was re-established. In 1780 the territory was invaded by Haidar Ali of Mysore and came into the possession of the East India Company in 1801.

As far as the political interaction of the Madurai region is concerned, it was initially limited to the Cheras, Cholas and the Tondaiman territory, but soon through the Pallava extension of power to the area, had entered into interaction with the powers like the Western Chalukyas and Rashtrakutas of the Deccan, and the Hoyasalas of the Mysore plateau. Basically, it is this Deccanese orbit of power which could reach as far south as the ancient Pandya territory. Sri Lanka's appearance in its political horizon was more or less sporadic but it was certainly a fact to consider.

Madurai has not been excavated. Excavations have been limited to only two port sites – Alagankulam and Korkai – in the Pandyan territory. Both these excavations have thrown a flood of light on the early historic period of the region.

While assessing the results of excavations at Alagankulam, it is important to draw attention to the evidence of its contact with Sri Lanka. As Sridhar writes in the preface to the report on Alagankulam excavations:

> The letter and symbols found in the inscribed potsherds at Alagankulam digs resemble that of the letters and symbols of inscriptions present in the caves of Sri Lanka. This in fact reveals not only the commercial activity between Alagankulam and Sri Lanka but also the cultural and social contacts between the two countries (Sridhar 2005).

The river Vaigai, which passes through the Alagankulam area, is now dry, only the traces of its bed joining the sea at Attankarai being currently visible. During the period of the Sangam literature it was a perennial river but by the 12th century AD or even earlier it had ceased to be so. Periapattinam is a port of c. 10th century AD across the Vaigai near Alagangulam. Sridhar identifies Alagankulam with the ancient Unur and Marungurppattinam mentioned in the Sangam literature. The excavated sequence of the Alagunkalam site reveals the following:

> Period I – black-and-red, grey and red wares, pottery with mat design and NBP ware – black-and-red and red wares dominant in the lower level – grey ware and pottery with mat design in the mid-level – the NBP only in the upper level – shell bangles, terracotta beads, iron objects, potsherds

with graffiti marks, sherds inscribed with Tamil-Brahmi, bone arrowheads and terracotta discs.
Period II – continuation of black-and-red ware, red ware, grey ware, and pottery with mat design – a few NBP sherds in the lower levels – amphorae pieces, stamped pottery and Rouletted Ware (in bulk quantity) – grooved roofing tiles, stone beads and beads of glass, shell, coral and terracotta, conch bangles, and terracotta gamesmen, spindle-whorls and spouted knobs – a rouletted ware sherd bearing graffiti and a mule- rider, Pandya square copper coins and punch-marked coins – a few Arretine sherds in the upper level.
Period III – the appearance of red rouletted ware 'in profuse quantity' the only feature of difference between the pottery types of Period II and Period III – L-shaped roofing tiles in the upper level – also semi-precious stone beads, shell bangles – a sherd of rouletted ware showing a three-masted ship in incised form – sherds of rouletted ware with elephant and bull symbols – Roman coins – terracotta dice.
Period IV – coarse red ware without any slip – shell bangles, black glass bangles – Chinese Celadon ware and porcelain ware.

It appears that Alagankulam has rouletted ware in two forms, one black inside with rouletted designs on the inner side of the base and red or brown on the outside, and another reddish on both sides with various rouletted designs on the inner base of the ware. The profusion of both these types implies that this pottery belonged to the site and was not imported from anywhere. The occurrence of the NBP in the upper level of Period I and the lower level of Period II has chronological implications for the dating of both Period I and Period II. Four radiocarbon dates have been obtained from the trench number AGM-2 at varying depths between 1.4 m and 2.8 m. These are reported as associated with black-and-red-ware. Considering that the total occupational depth of this trench was 4.85 m, it is logical to believe that all the radiocarbon samples were derived from Period II. The dates are consistent in the sense that the central point of their calibrated versions hovers between c. 400 and c. 200 BC. From this point of view, the excavators' date for the beginning of Period II at c. 300 BC is not particularly off the mark. This also tallies with the occurrence of a few sherds of NBP in the lower level of Period II. However, the NBP also occurs in the upper level of Period I at the site, and considering that the NBP is found to date from the central Ganga valley sites from c. 800 BC and earlier, there is no reason at all to date the Period I NBP from Alagankulam at anything less than 500 BC. In fact, considering the golden lustre of the NBP sherds found at Alagankulam, it was observed by Rakesh Tewari (personal information) that they resembled the NBP pieces found in the early NBP levels of Uttar Pradesh. One need not be surprised if the Alagunkalam NBP pre-dates

500 BC. The beginning of Alagankulam Period I should certainly go back to the beginning of the first millennium BC.

There seems to be some confusion about the position of punch-marked silver and copper coins and Pandyan square copper coins at Alagankulam. In the first paragraph of p. 82 of Sridhar's Alagankulam excavation report it is mentioned that these coins were obtained from Period II, whereas 'no coins were recovered from Period-I'. However, further down the text, punch-marked coins are shown against Period I. Their dates are obviously uncertain; Natana Kasinathan has ascribed one of these two punch-marked coins to the 4th century BC. In any case, this corroborates the early dating for the beginning of the site and also our inference of the opening of some major routes by the 4th century BC.

We know less about Korkai, although its pre-eminence in the Classical sources ('Colchis' in the *Periplus* and 'Kolkhoi' in Ptolemy) and the Sangam literature is well understood. Ptolemy goes to the extent of naming the Gulf of Mannar 'Kolkhic/Colchic Gulf'. The Sangam literature describes Korkai as 'far-famed port' which was reputed for its pearls. There were also salt-pans in its neighbouring area of Kayal (Champakalakshmi 1996: 124). The location of Korkai has been studied with the help of satellite imagery by Arunachalam, Sukumar and Sukumar (2006).

> Korkai is located 7.5 km away from the sea, close to Eral. It is on the northern left bank of Tamiraparani river close to the apex of the bird-foot delta. The agriculturally productive delta of the river known for abruptly rising flash floods is dynamic and fast growing out into the sea, due to heavy sedimentation of the river alluvium in a relatively tideless sea. Palaeo-channels traced from the satellite imagery scenes all around Korkai indicate that the river has shifted its course progressively east and south. As can be seen from a scrutiny of the topographic sheets and satellite imagery and tracking of palaeo-channels, Korkai, once on the sea has receded away from the shore. The nature of the birdfoot delta, lobes, lagoons, marine terraces, beach ridges and bars on the sea front, newly formed and old islands have all helped in tracing the probable stages in the evolution of the delta, as the river course progressively shifted south, and the distributaries elaborated. The Korkai Bay in the advancing front of the delta lobe got silted, and the port had to decline. The siltation is so rapid that in the last 2000 years of the historic past, land has advanced into the sea over a distance of about 8 km. After the decline of Korkai, Palayakayal emerged as a new port, but never rose to the prominence of Korkai. The replacement of Korkai by Kayal might have commenced around the 6th century AD. But its importance as a major port did not take effect till the 12th century AD. The port site is at a location called Palayakayal on a northern distributary of the delta, about 5 km northeast of Korkai. Interpretation of

> satellite imagery indicates that in the 1st and 2nd century AD, the Tamiraparani river might have flowed towards northeast from Eral, parallel to the coast and joined the sea south of Tuttukudi town ... The ancient port Korkai might have been situated on one of the distributaries of the Tamiraparani close to the sea coast. About 1 km southwest of Korkai there is a settlement called Kanavisamudram, indicating presence of sea or extensive water body nearby. There must have been a bay close to Korkai in the Gulf of Mannar, which would have allowed more ships to anchor.

Apart from yielding urn burials, the meagre excavations at the site have yielded NBP, rouletted ware of local origin, black-and-red ware of the megalithic type, red-slipped ware and plain red ware. A brick platform of nine courses of large bricks was excavated, and below it, a soakage pit made of three terracotta ring-wells. A number of potsherds inscribed in Tamil-Brahmi were found along with innumerable pearl oysters at various levels of the site (*IAR* 1968-69, pp. 32-33).

A single radiocarbon date puts the NBP from the site in the 8th century BC, if not in the ninth or tenth. The find of a large quantity of pearl oysters at the site even in a minor excavation supports the traditional association of the site with pearl fishery.

The combined evidence from Alagunkalam and Korkai, both Pandya ports, puts the beginning of their early historic context squarely in the first half of the first millennium BC. Whether the NBP at these sites reached them overland or by the sea is uncertain, but considering the virtual absence of the NBP at other Tamil Nadu sites and also a rather limited distribution of the NBP at sites in Andhra where the southernmost NBP-bearing sites seem to be Amaravati and Vaddamanu, we would put more emphasis on the probability that their presence at Alagankulam and Korkai was the result of maritime contact with the Andhra/Orissa/Bengal coasts.

R. Champakalakshmi (1996, p. 134) points out that the ancient name of Alagunkulam was possibly Marungur Pattinam in the Sangam literary text *Akananuru*. It was supposed to be divided into two parts, one part (*Nelin Unur*) agricultural, and the other commercial (*Marungur*). The *Maduraikkanchi*, another text of possibly the same period, refers to a place called Nellin Ur as a busy port with ships from different countries. According to Champakalakshmi, Nellin Unur and Nellin Ur stood for the same place. She also notes that there is still a village called Marungur near the coast in the same area.

Little is known of the third major Pandyan port site, Tondi. Whether *Tyndis* mentioned by the *Periplus* in the context of the Kerala coast can be Tondi of the Pandya territory on the east coast is doubtful. Champakalakshmi (1996: 134) mentions Tondi "as another Pandya port known from the early mediaeval sources" but cites at the same time (Champalakshmi 1996, p. 187) a reference to it in the *Silappadikaram,* which says that "the rulers of Tondi dispatch vessels loaded with *akhil* wood (eaglewood), silk, sandal and spices and all sorts of camphor". As far as one is aware, no archaeological work has been done at Tondi. On the basis of the comparatively recent but pre-modern documents, S. Arasaratnam (1986, pp. 29-30) has pointed out that it lay on the eastern side of the Pamban passage, the passage which separates Rameshwaram from the mainland. In the seventeenth century, the port fell in the principality of Ramnad and was a place of coastal trade within the sheltered waters of the Madura and Tinnevelly coasts, which could cater to trade both with Sri Lanka and the Kerala coasts. Although the shipping here during that period was small-sized (less than 100 tons), the total traffic in the exports of textiles, rice and chanks and the imports of arecanuts, pepper and timber was considerable, gathering a good number of one- to three-masted small-sized boats. Finally, Champakalakshmi (1996, p. 225) cites a 13th century inscription from *Tittandatanapuram* or Tondi, which records an agreement reached by several merchant groups on some levies to be imposed on the sale and purchase of goods for the rebuilding of a local Siva temple. Inscriptions of this kind are known from various parts of the subcontinent, but this one shows that Tondi was a commercial centre even in the 13th century.

VIII.2. The Chola Territory

The core of the Chola territory is the Kaveri delta. This is where the dynasty surfaces in the Sangam literature, and of its early kings, two names – Kocengannan who fought the Chera king Irumporai, and Karikala – stand out. That there was an early nucleus of Chola power is evidenced by the find of early Chola coins with tiger as the distinguishing Chola symbol. The area immediately to the south of the Chola territory is Pudukottai where at Sittanavasal the Jaina monks had their abode with donors' inscriptions in Tamil-Brahmi. One is not sure how this region figured in the early Chola political scheme, but it is doubtful that as long as the Pandyas of Madura remained powerful, the Cholas could bring Pudukottai directly within their fold. The Pudukottai territory has traditional political association with the Vellalar chieftains.

Throughout the long early historic period, the Cholas did not play any substantive role but that did not seriously impair their apparently dormant political ambition. In the ninth century AD, the Chola Vijayalaya, who was a feudatory of the Pallavas with their centre at Kanchipuram in the Tondaiman territory, set up his own political power around Thanjavur. The Pallava control was overthrown soon afterwards, and the Kongu territory or the Coimbatore-Salem belt was wrested from the Pandyas and Western Gangas. The latter's capital, Talakkad, fell to the Cholas. The Pudukottai territory was annexed too, and the Chola territory now extended from the Tirupati area to Pudukottai. The Cheras were an ally of the Cholas at this stage. Early in the 10th century, the Chola king, Parantaka I, successfully attacked the Pandya territory and later defeated the combined forces of the Pandyas and Sri Lanka at Vellur near Madurai in AD 915. In the next stage he exerted supremacy in the territory of the Western Gangas, and by defeating a Rashtrakuta-Pallava alliance advanced up to Nellore, thus carving out a kingdom from the North Penner River to Cape Comorin, which had the Cheras and Western Gangas as its westerly neighbours. Parantaka was subsequently defeated by an alliance of the Rashtrakutas and Western Gangas in AD 949, which led to the loss of both Pallava and Pandya domains. The Rashtrakutas came to control Kanchipuram. Parantaka II (AD 957-973) campaigned unsuccessfully against the Pandyas and Sri Lanka.

The Cholas regained their power under Rajaraja I (AD 985-1014). He defeated the Cheras and Pandyas and also took possession of Coorg. His successful expedition to Sri Lanka saw the establishment of Chola capital at Polonnoruva, with the Chola control firmly established in northern Sri Lanka. The area of the Western Gangas was possessed in AD 991. His ambition against the Western Chalukyas further north was not successful and the Cholas came to be confined to the south of the Tungabhadra. The eastern Chalukyas of Vengi, however, were brought under control and paved the way for his conquest of Kalinga. The Maldives also were successfully attacked. The Chola power at this stage spread over northern Sri Lanka, Maldives, the whole of South India up to the Tungabhadra and the eastern coast up to Kalinga.

Building on this power, Rajendra I (c. AD 1012-1044), the successor of Rajaraja I, conquered the Raichur doab, Banavasi, Kulpak near Hyderabad, Manyakheta in north Karnataka, Sri Lanka, Maldives, an island called Sandimattivu in the Arabian Sea, the Western Chalukyan territory, Maski, places in Bastar, Madura, Orissa, South Kosala, Jajnagar in Orissa, Dandabhukti in Midnapore in West Bengal, and the territories of the kings Dharmapala, Ranasura and Govindachandra of West Bengal, and the territory of the Pala king Mahipala I. In 1018 Sri Lanka was completely conquered and ruled as a province. He also captured the Pandya territory in 1018 and converted the Pandya territory into a Chola province in AD 1018. Another newly added province was the Chera kingdom. The Western Chalukyas, despite their earlier defeat, kept the Cholas confined to the south of the Tungabhadra. A Chola naval expedition was successfully undertaken against Sumatra and the Malayan peninsula in AD 1025. In AD 1029 there was unrest in Sri Lanka, which was followed by the unrest in the Pandya and Chera areas too. The Western Chalukyas were attacked again towards the end of his reign. The Western Chalukyan capital Badami was conquered.

The Western Chalukyas killed his successor Rajadhiraja in the battle of Koppam, but earlier Rajadhiraja could subdue Sri Lanka. His successor Rajendra II became victorious against the Western Chalukyas and moved as far north as Kolhapur. The Western Chalukyas, however, continued to be a thorn in the Chola ambition, and their territory could not be subjugated totally, though they were defeated again by Rajendra II's successor Virarajendra I (AD 1063-1070) who also defeated a rebellion in Sri Lanka and sent in AD 1069 an expedition to Kadaram/Keddah to install a ruler of his choice on its throne. In AD 1070, the Chola throne went to Kulottunga I (AD 1070-1120) of the Eastern Chalukyas of Vengi, who as a great- grandson of Rajaraja I established a Chola-Eastern Vengi line. Vengi was unsuccessfully attacked by the Kalachuris of South Kosala in AD 1073, but in about this period Sri Lanka fell to the power of Vijayavahu, a Sri Lankan.

In the Pandya and Chera areas, the Cholas established military colonies leaving the internal administration to the local powers. Kadaram seems to have been attacked again under Kulottunga who also attacked Kalinga twice (AD 1096, AD 1110), although without any territorial annexation. A friendly relation was maintained with the Gahadavalas of Kanauj, although their territory was away in the north. Towards the end of Kulottunga's reign, the Western Ganga area was captured by the Hoyasalas who raided the Chola territory up to Rameshwaram, and the Western Chalukyas captured Vengi.

After Kulottunga, his successor Vikrama Chola gained some success against the Western Chalukyas, capturing the Kolar area from them. Rajaraja II (AD 1146-1173) and his successor Rajadhiraja II reigned till AD 1179. The period was dominated by a tussle with the Pandyas, a faction of whom was helped by Sri Lankan king Parakramabahu. The Cholas intervened in favour of the rival Pandya faction. The issue was resolved only during the reign of Rajadhiraja II whose successor Kulottunga III (AD 1178-1216) had to face the Pandya-Sri Lankan problem again.

Kulottunga III (c. AD 1178-1216) succeeded Rajadhiraja II. The Pandya problem re-surfaced during his reign, with one of the Pandya factions seeking help from Sri Lanka. The Pandya ambition was curtailed but Sri Lanka repeatedly attacked the Pandya land, and seiged Rameshwaram. The Chola authority was restored in the Kongu area between AD 1190 and AD 1194. Kanchipuram was captured in AD 1196 from the Telegu-Chola feudatory kings who controlled the area between North Arcot and Nellore. In c. AD 1205 an expedition was sent against the Pandyas, and in 1208 AD, there was an expedition to Andhra.

The Chola power lasted up to AD 1279, but precariously. The Pandyas captured the Chola capital and the Chola king was imprisoned by one of his feudatories at Sendamandalam in South Arcot. The Hoyasalas at this stage helped the Cholas but established a foothold in the Chola territory. Kanchipuram was captured by the Kakatiyas. The subsequent attempt to increase the Chola power was defeated by the Pandya king, Jatavarmana Sundara Pandya.

After the Cholas, the Kaveri delta was controlled in various stages by the Muslims, the Vijayanagara kings and their successors in the area, and finally by the British.

The maritime exploits of the Chola power are well-known, but in the peninsula, its main thrust was towards both south Deccan and the coast of Andhra. At one point they succeeded in venturing as far north as Kolhapur in the Deccan, and with their base in the Andhra coast they could exert their influence in Orissa and beyond.

The Chola capital, Urayur in the city of Trichinopaly or Tiruchirapalli, was perfunctorily dug, with virtually no light on the chronology of its early phase. Period I shows megalithic black-and-red ware, rouletted ware, russet-coated painted ware, plain red, and plain black wares. Inscribed sherds have been placed by Champakalakshmi (1996: 125) in the first and second centuries AD. There is no C-14 date, but a date well in the first half of the first millennium BC for the beginning of Urayur, a city well described in the Sangam literature, is probable, especially in view of an uncalibrated radiocarbon date of 315 BC from the wharf area of Kaveripattinam or ancient Puhar, the major early Chola port. The Chola ancestry is also clear from the references to them in the Asokan edicts and Katyayana's *Varttika* (the latter related to Panini and dated in the 3rd century BC). Period II shows a transition to the use of red-slipped pottery. What this may mean in chronological terms is unknown. Period III apparently carries the occupational sequence down to the 9th-13th centuries AD.

As Champakalakshmi (1996: 126-129) argues, more detailed literary and archaeological data are available on Kaveripattinam, with one of the Sangam literary pieces (*Pattinappalai*) being devoted exclusively to its description. Besides, the *Silappadikaram* and the *Manimekalai,* which are generally viewed as post-Sangam texts, include the details of the Buddhist and Jaina establishments and shrines of the Brahmanical and folk deities. Known variously as Puhar, Kakandi and Sampapati, the last one still preserved in the name of the modern temple dedicated to Sampapati, the tutelary goddess of the city, the site of Kaveripattinam (or, Champakalakshmi puts it, *Kaverippumpattinam*) denotes in literature a big town or city (*Perur* and *Managar*). The site is said to cover about 40 distinct archaeological localities where inadequate diggings have brought to light a sequence from c. 3rd century BC to the 5th century AD. Considering that the wharf area has yielded an uncalibrated radiocarbon date of 315 BC, the date of its beginning is likely to be earlier. Archaeologically, the substantive features include a brick structure identified as a wharf, where boats were anchored with the help of wooden pegs, at the locality of Kilaiyur, a semi-circular brick structure (internal diameter: 8 m), which was possibly a water reservoir fed by a 83-m wide inlet channel from the Kaveri, at the locality of Vanagiri, and the remains of a Buddhist monastery and *Chaitya* at the locality of Pallavanesvaram. The last-mentioned remains have been put in the 4th-5th century AD, with evidence of their continuation in later periods.

According to Champakalakshmi's textual analysis, the city was divided into two parts, one residential and the other commercial, by an open ground which was the venue of its morning and evening markets. In the list of imports she mentions horses, bags of black pepper (brought overland by carts), gems and gold from the 'northern mountain', sandal and *akil* wood from the 'western mountain', pearls of the 'southern sea', corals of the 'eastern sea', the produce of the Ganga valley and Kaveri valley, foodstuffs from Sri Lanka, and luxuries from Kadaram (Malayan peninsula).

According to Champakalakshmi, the importance of Puhar was replaced by that of Nagapattinam in the early mediaeval period.

In the case of the ports of the Pandya territory, it was easy to pinpoint them with reference to their locations in relation to the Bay of Madura and the Pamban passage. The coastline of the Chola territory had a larger number of ports in the 17th century, the cut-off point of Arasaratnam's analysis (Arasaratnam 1986). It is unlikely that all of them had a considerably earlier ancestry, but Arasaratnam's discussion on the basic character of these ports suggests that even in the early historic and later historic periods there could be more comparatively minor ports catering to the needs of the Kaveri-Coleroon delta.

The southernmost of Arasaratnam's ports, which can be related to the Chola territory, is Adirampatnam, about 28 miles west of Point Calimere and the nearest port of any significance south of Nagapatnam or Nagapattinam. This belonged to the kingdom of Tanjore and played a role in the trade of the Bay of Madura and the Palk Straits, with voyages from it going to Malabar, Tinnevelly and Sri Lanka. It was a place of small, light crafts and its hinterland produced rice and handloom textiles.

North of Adirampatnam was Nagapatnam, located at the mouth of the Kadavaiyar River which at this point had a constantly shifting bar and prevented large ships from coming in. Nagapatnam in the 17th century was an open roadstead where goods were unloaded from large ships in small boats. The port handled trade in rice and textiles and the import of southeast Asian goods.

Within 3 miles north of Nagapatnam was Nagore, also located at the mouth of the Kadavaiyar, a branch of the Vettar River. The bar of the river here had about 8 feet of water at high tide and the port could shelter boats up to 300 tons. Its trade, dependent on the exports of rice, textiles, chanks and other sea-produce and the imports of spices, metals, areca-nut, etc., covered the coastal ports of southern Tanjore, Madura and Tinnevelly and went up to Sri Lanka and Malabar. The larger vessels went to Southeast Asia with which the merchants of Nagore are supposed to have had traditional connections.

North of Nagore was Karikal, reputedly an ancient port of the Chola territory and located at the mouth of the Arsalar River which was linked with the Kaveri through irrigation channels. The port was an open roadstead, used basically for the export of paddy and rice of the Kaveri delta and textiles to the other parts of the coast and to Malabar and Sri Lanka. Tranquebar, further north, is noted as an old Danish enclave and located at the mouth of a small river. This too was an open roadstead with links to Southeast Asia. It was ceded to the Danes by the king of Tanjore. North of Tranquebar, Arasaratnam refers to two ports of the 17th century: Thirumulavasal, located at the mouth of a river of the same name and having direct access to the inland town of Sirkali and the rice and textiles of the area; and Kodiapaleam at the mouth of the Coleroon, which was guarded by a small fort – Devicottah.

The point which needs emphasis in this and other contexts is that the historic ports need not have been confined to the places, which are mentioned in our sources or have been traced archaeologically. Depending on the nature of coastal inlets and their hinterlands, there is the possibility of other, possibly comparatively minor, ports.

VIII.3. The Pallava Territory

The Pallavas occupied the Tondaiman territory which in a sense formed a kind of bridge between the Deccan and the Andhra coast and the Kaveri belt. Under Simhavishnu at the end of the sixth century AD they became powerful, pushing as far south as the Chola territory on the Kaveri. His successor Mahendravarman I (c. AD 600-630) retained this control but faced the hostility of Pulakesin II of the Chalukyas of Badami in the north. The first of the many Pallava-Chalukya battles took place at Pullalur or Palur near Kanchipuram. Under Narasimhavarman I (c. AD 630-668) the Pallavas defeated the Chalukyas and had the possession of Badami, the Chalukyan capital for a number of years. Two naval expeditions were sent to Sri Lanka to support a Sri Lankan prince, with the second one being successful. Narasimhavarman I's grandson, Paramesvaravarman I (c. AD 670-695) continued the struggle with the Chalukyas who intially captured Kanchipuram and moved up to the Kaveri but were eventually defeated. Narasimhavarman II (c. AD 695-722) sent an embassy to China in AD 720. There was another Chalukyan invasion during the reign of his successor Paramesvaravarman II (c. AD 722-730). The Chalukyas wrested Kanchipuram from the Pallavas under Nandivarman II Pallavamalla (c. AD 730-795) who, however, won it back soon. In the south, the Pandya king of the time, Rajasimha I, defeated Nandivarman near Tanjore, but the Pallavas could regain their control of the area. In the north the post-Chalukyan power was the Rashtrakutas, and Dantidurga, the founder of the Rashtrakuta power captured Kanchi but eventually made peace by giving his daughter in marriage to Nandivarman II. There was also a struggle between Nandivarman II and the Western Gangas of Karnataka.

The Pallavas of Kanchipuram remained a strong historical force in the south till the ninth century AD, although losing territory to the Pandyas in the first half of this century during the reign of Dantivarman. Nandivarman III, his son, extended his influence in the Kaveri region and the Coimbatore area. The chief cities of his kingdom were Kanchipuram, Mahabalipuram and Mylapuram (Chennai). The inscriptions of Nripatungavarman, Nandivarman III's successor, have been found as far south as Pudukottai and he won a battle against the Pandyas at Kumbhakonam. Aparajita is the last major king of the Pallava dynasty of Kanchipuram. Soon afterwards, the Pallava territory became the corridor through which the powers further south and further north were moving in various directions.

The Pallava capital was Kanchipuram which, as Champakalaksmi (1996, p. 131) points out, finds elaborate mention in the Sangam literary text of *Perumpanarruppatai,* which describes the palace of Ilamtiraiyan, the chief of the Tondaiyar or Tondainadu in glowing terms. The city stood on the bank of the Veghavati or Vehka. The old town (*Mudur*) comprised a number of possibly separate settlements and was surrounded by a wall. The *Ts'ien han chou,* a text of c. 1st century AD by the Chinese author Pan Kou, refers to the contacts between China and the Indian city of *Houang-tche* which has been identified as Kanchipuram. There was an exchange of presents and goods between the two kings – the Chinese emperor Ping of the Yuan-che period and the king of Houang-tche. Such contacts – pearls, glass and rare stones being exchanged for gold and silk – are said to go back to the period of the emperor Wou (140-86 BC). If there is any truth in the Chinese testimony, it is clear that by the second century BC Kanchipuram was a developed enough city to be known to the Chinese emperor. In that case, the date of its beginning is likely to be considerably earlier than the third century BC, the date Champakalakshmi (1996, p. 152, for the Sangam period and Chinese sources, p. 131) attributes to Period IA of the excavated sequence of the site. Period IB with its assemblage of rouletted and Arretine wares is supposed to date from the first century BC to the third century AD. Period II is put between the third and the seventh centuries AD, and Period III between the eighth and thirteenth centuries AD. Roman contact is clear from the find of Arretine ware, and Champakalakshmi draws attention to the finds of Roman coins in the region around it (cf. Mahabalipuram, Madurantakam/Alamporai, Saidapet and Mambalam). She does not give much credence to the idea of early Buddhist and Jain associations of Kanchipuram.

A place mentioned as Nirppeyarru in the Sangam literature has been said to be Kanchipuram's port (Champakalakshmi 1996, p. 131). This has been identified with Vasavasamudram. Arikamedu and Karaikkadu are two other maritime outlets of Tondainadu. Arikamedu's identification as an Indo-Roman trading station is beyond dispute, and so is its identification as the port of Pouduke of the *Periplus* and Ptolemy. Arretine ware, beads, glass objects (including specimens of Roman glass) and gems mark out the site as a trading place, and the current assessment of its dating puts its beginning in the last three or two centuries BC. Champakalakshmi has clearly emphasized the local character of the place:

> Arikamedu has been identified with Virai, the modern Virampattinam near the site, which was one of the *velar* strongholds known to Sangam literature, In the *Akananuru*, it is described as the harbour of the *velar*, while the *Narrinai* says that it was the centre of the *velar* chieftain Virai Veliyan Venman. Evidence in support of the *velar* association of this centre has been recognized in a BRW sherd with a Brahmi inscription of the first century AD reading Yadu Balabhuti-y or Balabhuti of the Yadu clan. The *velar* claimed descent from the Yadavas. A possible derivation of the Poduca/Podouke of the *Periplus* and Ptolemy is interesting in this connection. Poudouke may be derived from Podikai, a meeting place in a clan settlement. Such Podikais were common among the *velir* settlements of early Tamilakam (Champakalakshmi 1996, p. 135).

Little is known of Karaikkadu, but Vasavasamudram (Champakalakshmi 1996, pp 132-133) near Sadras in Chingleput has a substantial archaeological deposit (1.92 m) which yielded amphorae, Rouletted ware, terracotta ringwells, burnt brick structures, etc. Situated at the mouth of the Palar, this is likely to be the port outlet of Kanchipuram located on the bank of the Veghavati, a tributary of the Palar. Whether Vasavasamudram represents the port of Nirppeyarru mentioned in the Sangam literary text of the *Perumpanarruppatai* or not is not much relevant. A different opinion identifies it with Nirpper in the Madurantakam taluk of the Chingleput district. Some place it even at Mahabalipuram. What is important is that there was a port even in the ancient context near Sadras.

Arasaratnam puts the beginning of the Tanjore coast at the mouth of the Coleroon, about 5 miles south of Porto Novo. What is important is that between Porto Novo in the south and Puleacut/Pulicat in the north, there is a chain of ports in the 17th century, his chosen period. There is no assurance in view of the lack of archaeological explorations that there were ancient ports at all these locations. However, this list clearly highlights the locations where ancient ports could be located. The ancient ports in the southern section of this stretch could belong to the Chola territory, whereas those in the northern section belonged in all likelihood to the Tondaiman or Pallava territory.

The location of Porto Novo on the left bank of the Vellar River flowing into the Killai Bay offers good anchorage. This made it a major centre of international trade in the 17th century, with the English, the Dutch and the other Europeans competing with the Indian traders for its control. It was mainly a Bay of Bengal port, with no westward contact beyond the Kerala coast. Described as the most naturally endowed port on the Coromandel coast, it was named Porto Novo by the Portuguese. The earlier

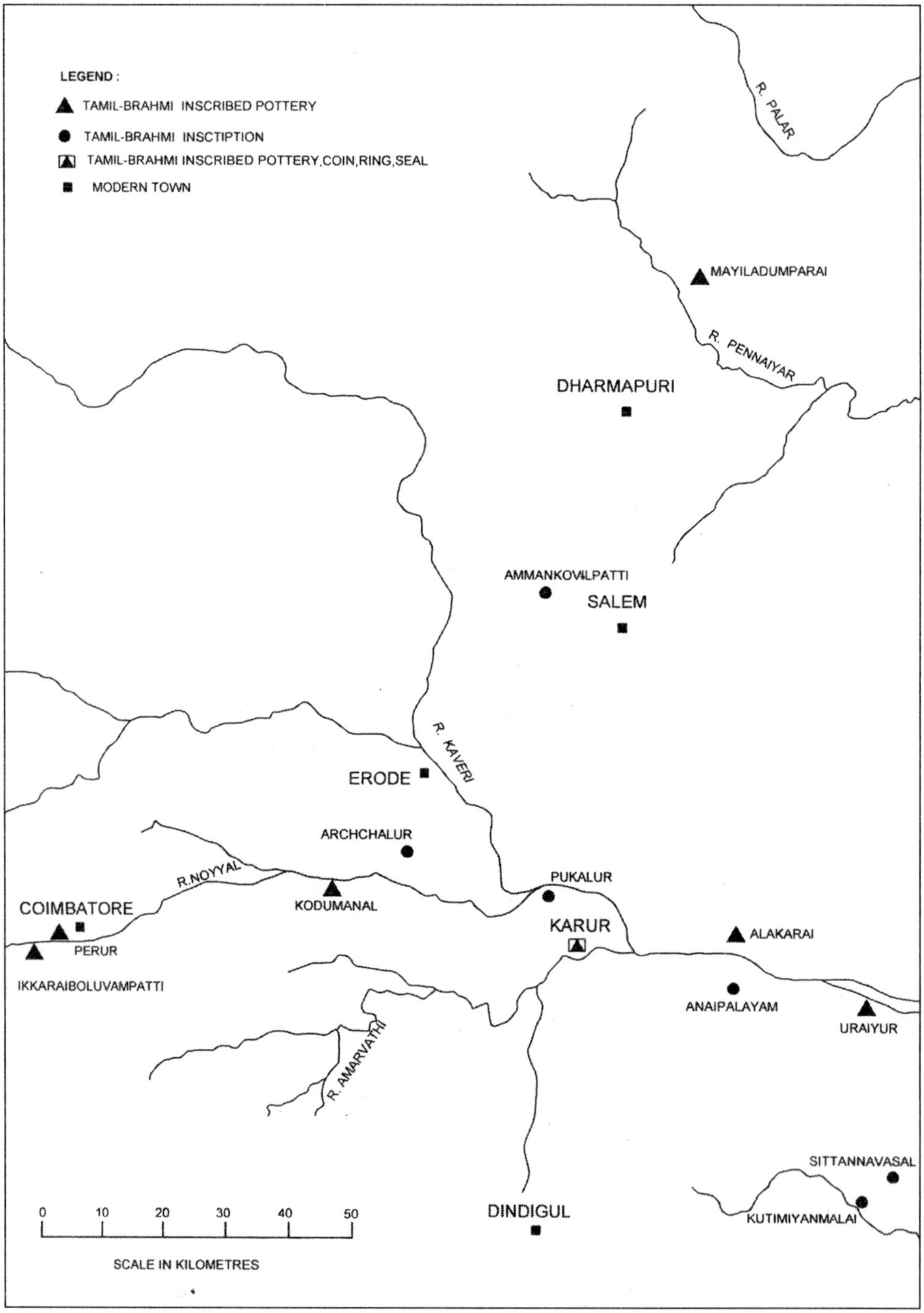

Map 6. Tamil-Brahmi inscriptions in Western Tamil Nadu (after *Catalogue*).

names were Parangi Pettai and Mohammad Bandar. It is possible that this fell in the ancient Chola territory.

The major port north of Porto Novo in the 17th century was Cuddalore, with Devanampatnam two miles to its north. Located at the estuary of the Gudimalam river, which was joined at this point by the Paravanar, Cuddalore had a stretch of backwaters into which the vessels could sail. "Cuddalore was a wintering port for the merchant fleet of the area which could shelter inside the river and the backwaters during the monsoon" (Arasaratnam 1986, p. 24). Devanampatnam is said to have been a port linked to the inland town of Ginjee. The open roadstead of Pondicherry lies about 15 miles to the north of Devanampatnam, and it is interesting to note that in the context of ancient Arikamedu in its southern suburbs, the port developed on the bank of a lagoon. About 10 miles to the north of Pondicherry, is the port of Kunimedu located at the mouth of a small river and having Dutch and English factories in the 17th century. Further 10 miles to the north, is Alambaram, also located at the mouth of a small river and home to a Dutch factory. Twenty miles northward lay Sadurangapatnam or Sadraspatnam, home to an Indian export and import trade across the Bay of Bengal. We have seen how the ancient port of Vasavasamudram was located in the vicinity of Sadras.

> The coastline south of Sadraspatnam was in our period a busy area of trade and traffic. It was littered with a number of ports situated within a few miles of each other, all serving as points of outlet for the rich textile manufacturing hinterland up to several miles deep in the interior. The regions served by these ports were South Arcot, Tanjore, Trichinopoly and Salem, and these were areas of ancient settlement and cultivation. They had commercial links overseas which had developed over centuries and which were continued in our period with varying degrees of intensity (Arasaratnam 1986, p. 23).

Further up along the coast lay Mahabalipuram, reputedly a port of the Pallava period, and the ports clustered around Madras which is primarily associated with the British rule. However, places which are now within the Madras city such as Mylapore and Mambalam have a remote antiquity as centres of trade. Roman coins have been reported from both these localities. According to Arasaratnam (1986, p. 22), "Mylapore occurs as a port of significance in the trade to South East Asia, long before the Portuguese came to San Thome." It was an open roadstead but had the advantage of being located on the Adyar rivulet and linked to a backwater.

About 25 miles to the north of Madras was the port of Paleacut at the southern end of the island of Sriharikotta formed by the sea and a lagoon or backwater known as the Paleacut/Pulicat lake. It was an open roadstead, and as a port it figured prominently in the trade to Southeast Asia long before the Portuguese. It was the outlet of the textiles manufactured in its hinterland of Poneri taluk. It apparently became less significant in the 18th century.

VIII.4. More on the Pre-Modern Ports of the Coromandel Coast

The basic picture is that of a chain of ports right from the Pamban channel in the south and Pulicat in the north. Not all these ports have been proved to be ancient, but a good number of them have the possibility of dating from the early historic to early mediaeval periods. In the context of his period, i.e., AD 1650-1740, Arasaratnam has listed closely juxtaposed centres of handloom manufacture in the whole of this coastal belt. It is possible that these weaving centres have a long history, going back at least to the mediaeval period. Champakalakshmi (1996) accepts the continuity of traditional weaving centres. These must have catered to the trade carried through all these ports and, thus, the routes linking the ports to their hinterlands were an important part of the Tamil Nadu route network, irrespective of its period. The importance of the Coromandel coast ports cannot be over-emphasized in South Indian history. Simon Digby (1982, p. 127) has argued that in the 12th century, the major portion of the export trade from China was not in the Arab boats but in the ships of the merchants of Coromandel and Sri Lanka. In his map of mediaeval ports in the Tamil coast (1280-1500), S.J. Stephen (1998, p. 24) lists the following ports, beginning with those in the Tamraparni mouth: Virapandiyanpattinam, Kayal, Tuticorin (Tamraparni); Kilakkarai (Vaigai), Nagapattinam, Nagore, Thirumalairayanpattinam (Kaveri); Cuddalore, Devanampattinam, Kunimedu, Marakkanam, Sadurangapattinam (Ponnaiyar), and Pulicat. It is claimed that in the inscriptions, Pulicat, Sadras, Marakkanam, Cuddalore, Porto Novo and Tranquebar had all ancient names (Stephen 1998: 25):

Pulicat (Anandarayanpattinam), Sadras (Rajanarayanpattinam), Marakkanam (Eyirpattinam), Cuddalore (Nissakammalanpattinam), Porto Novo (Krishnapattinam) and Tranquebar (Kulasekharapattinam).

Stephen (1998: 26-34) offers some detail on some of these ports on the basis of the primary sources.

The premier port of the Cholas was Nagapattinam (*Na-wu-tan-shan* of the Chinese sources). Trade between China and Nagapattinam flourished between AD 713 and AD 1275, with spices and aromatics coming from the Kerala coast to be shipped to China. Chinese coins have been

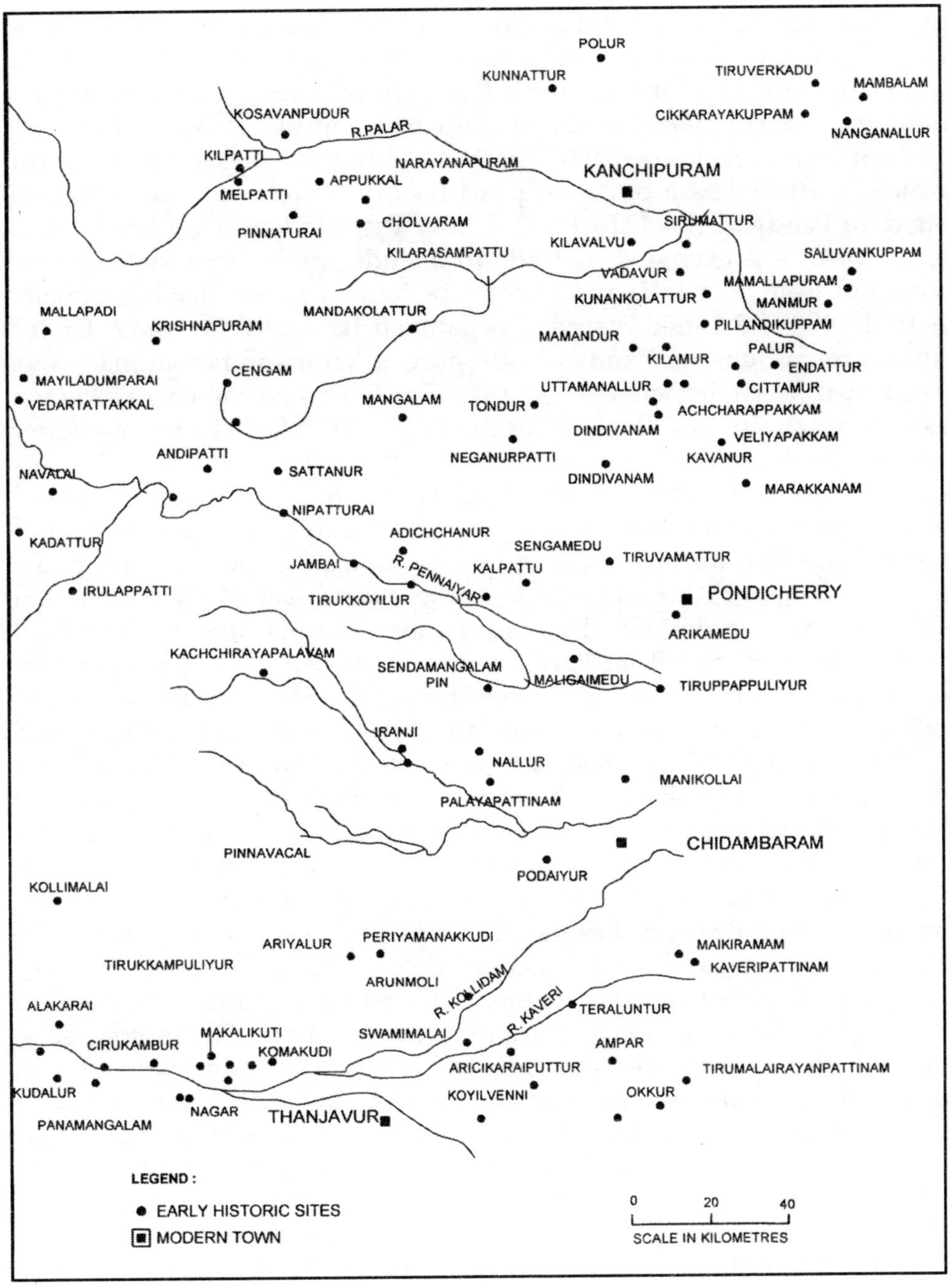

Map 7. Early historical sites in northern Tamil Nadu (after *Catalogue*).

reported profusely in its hinterland. An inscription, dated AD 1018-19, of Rajendra Chola mentions that a merchant from Keda in the Malayan peninsula – the chief merchant Sri Kuruttan Kesavan (alias Agralekai) – donated a particular amount of gold to a temple at Nagapattinam. Devipattinam, also known as Ulagamadevipattinam, was a Pandyan port which flourished as a centre of pearl fishery trade under Maravarman Sundara Pandya I (AD 1216-1241). Under the Pandyan king Srivallabha (c. AD 1348) this extended its trade to include spices from Malabar and areca-nut from Sri Lanka and came to be known as Srivallabhapattinam. A traders' guild called *Nanadesi* organized its maritime trade. Under Maravarman Sundara Pandya I, the port of Virapanditanpattinam was frequented by Arab merchants and the Tamil Muslim merchants, known as *marakkayars*. In 1387, the Muslim chief of the port levied a tax of quarter per cent on the sale of commodities in this port for the maintenance of its Jumma mosque. Another Muslim-dominated port nearby – Kayal – offered better anchorage and developed under the Pandyas as a port to import horses from Hormuz and Aden and export silk, aromatic roots and pearls to Syria, Iraq and Khorasan. Between the second half of the 13th and at least the 15th centuries, Kayal was a stopping place of Chinese ships bound for the Malabar coast. Kilakkarai, which lies closer to the Vaigai mouth, developed as a centre of pearl trade from an earlier coastal settlement called Anuthogaimangalam. It was an important trading centre visited by the Arab and Chinese merchants towards the end of the 15th century. Periyapattinam lay about 6 km south of Rameshwaram in the Gulf of Mannar. The Chinese celadon ware found in this area testifies to its Chinese contact in the 13th and 14th centuries. Modern Cuddalore was mediaeval Devanampattinam, whose origin can be epigraphically traced to the 13th century when it developed as the port of Kopperunjingan, the chief of the Kadavaraya lineage who then ruled the delta region of the South Penner/ Ponnaiyar. This developed close links with Sri Lanka. Under the Pandyas in the 14th century, it was a centre of salt production. The Portuguese in the 16th century recorded this port as *Tevanapatao*. Sadurangapattinam or Rajanarayananpattinam (modern Sadras) was in the 14th century a centre of pearls and textiles. The port also came under the Vijayanagar control and eventually lost its importance to the neighbouring Kunimedu which became a major embarkation point and a famous harbour in the 15th century. Among the 16th century developments, one notes Thirumullaivasal at the mouth of the Upanaar River, with close trade contacts with Sri Lanka. Under the Vijayanagar kings in the 15th century, Pulicat (at the mouth of the Araniyar River south of Nellore) was a major port which was later taken over by the Dutch.

We have put some emphasis on the major political dynasties of Tamil Nadu to highlight the fluidity of their lines of control and interaction. We have drawn attention to some of the excavated places and the chain of ports which dot this coast from early history to virtually the beginning of the modern period. Our aim was not to offer any synopsis of political and commercial history of Tamil Nadu but only to highlight the basic historical context of the major routes of this region. However, as far as the routes of this region are concerned, Tamil Nadu cannot stand alone. We have already drawn attention to how different routes entered Tamil Nadu and Kerala from the Mysore plateau and Andhra and what are the fundamentals of the geographical links between the Coromandel and Malabar coasts. However, it remains for us to discuss in brief the historical trajectory of Kerala or the traditional land of the Cheras.

VIII.5. The Chera Territory

The earliest date of iron-bearing megalithic urn burials of Kerala – c. 900 BC (uncalibrated) – comes from Mangadu north of Trivandrum. The recent excavations at Pattanam, located between Kodungallur and North Paravur in the Ernakulam district of Kerala (about 25 km north of Cochin) and on one of the five branches of the Periyar River, have identified at its base an 'Iron Age' level with a wooden canoe and bollards. The 'error weighted mean date' for the five radiocarbon samples taken from this wood is 500 plus/minus 80 BC (uncalibrated?). Pattanam has been identified with the ancient port of Muziris, which is mentioned in the Classical sources. The canoe and bollards should suggest a place where canoes were tied to wooden bollards and, because of the location of the site, may even indicate some sea-faring activity. Maritime contacts seem to be dominant in the succeeding assemblage of the early centuries AD: Roman amphorae, and generally West Asian pottery of the Parthian-Sassanian and later periods. The site, hidden in the coconut groves of the coastal Kerala, is said to cover 1.5 sq km, of which an area of 600 × 400 m is supposedly core area. It will be some time before the significance of these discoveries, which are as yet only briefly published, is properly analysed and understood. However, in a sense this sheds some background light on the state of Keralaputras of the Asokan edicts. More usually it is known as the territory of the Cheras, "Cherobothra" of the *Periplus* and "Caelobothras" of Pliny, the first century AD Roman historian. The Chera kings loom large in the Tamil Sangam literature. It is doubtful if these references have been worked into a connected history, but the names of the three generations of the Chera kings in the Pugalur inscription near

Karur, which we have mentioned earlier, have certainly settled the question of their historicity. Their traditional capital was at *Vanci Muthur*, of whom one of the identifications proposed is that it was in the Kanthallur-Kizhanthur area of the Idukki district of Kerala and that they shifted to Karur in the Kongu area of Tamil Nadu later. Their 'second dynasty' supposedly ruled from Muziris after the 'first dynasty' ended in the third century AD. There is nothing conclusive, despite the opinion of R. Nagaswamy, that Karur was the only capital of the Cheras. For a kingdom apparently ruling over virtually the whole of the Kerala coast (Venadu in Travancore, and Malabar or Kuttanadu) and a large part of the Kongu territory, Karur was not ideally placed. Although easily linked to the coast by the Palghat gap, it was still too much in the interior to rule the Kerala coast from.

R. Nagaswamy's brief excavations at Karur yielded the following sequence. Period I belonged to the pre-Christian era. The only thing he has written about this period is that it did not yield Roman artefacts. Period II represented the first two centuries AD and contained amphorae fragments, rouletted pottery, black-and-red pottery, and pottery with mat designs. This level also shows sherds inscribed in Tamil-Brahmi. He points out that, as far as Karur is concerned, "the Tamil-Brahmi inscriptions occur from the age of Roman contact only". Period III contained russet-coated pottery, whereas Period IV contained coarse red ware. The only structural remain (not assigned to a particular period in Nagaswamy's publication) is a brick pavement attached to a drain. It is probable that much of ancient Karur has been destroyed by the action of the Amaravati river, on whose bank it stands. All the antiquities which Nagaswamy discusses in his book *Roman Karur* come from the pits dug by the villagers in the sandy bed of the Amaravati and the local antiquity dealers. Apparently, there is a vast number of such antiquities. Nagaswamy has classified them into the following major categories: Roman coins, punch-marked coins, Satavahana coins, Square Chera coins, Square Chola coins, Pallava coins, coin moulds, and various other antiquities including a gold signet ring with the engraving of the lithe and elongated shapes of a female and male standing side by side. The forms are more attenuated than the best of the Amaravati figures and recall the standing royal figure engraved in a low relief from Jagayyapeta. Nagaswamy's opinion notwithstanding, there is no influence of Roman art on it. It predates by several centuries the wonderfully attenuated female and male forms of the Chola bronzes.

With an associated burial site, the 50 hectare occupational site of Kodumanal in the Kongu area itself was primarily a site where various raw materials such as beryl, crystal, carnelian, iron, etc. were processed into shapes and exported. Its earliest phase, already containing potsherds inscribed in Tamil Brahmi, goes back to c. 500 BC. The source of carnelian was Gujarat, and on the whole, the impression is that Kodumanal was the hub of a manufacturing activity with wide inland links. The furnace discovered at the site unmistakably suggests the technique of wootz manufacture. That finely decorated strings of carnelian beads were in good demand is clearly evidenced in the excavations of some megalithic burials at Thandikudi in the Palni hills, one of the home areas of pepper. Apparently, the people who buried their dead in megaliths in the Palni hills apparently supplied pepper to the merchants of the plains and became rich enough to acquire those lovely strings of decorated carnelian beads. The Palni hills are in the Pandya territory but the Thandikudi carnelian finds demonstrate the significance of sites like Kodumanal.

From the point of view of both maritime and associated inland trades, the Kerala coast continues the distribution of the significant number of coastal port sites that we have seen in the case of the Konkan coast up to Mangalore. The chain of port sites that we have seen between Cape Comorin and Pulicat in the case of the Coromandel coast only takes up from what we shall find along the Malabar littoral.

According to Tome Pires, in the beginning of the 16th century the province of Malabar or the coastline of Malabar began at Manjeswaram, nine miles south of Mangalore (between Mangalore and Kumbla) and ends at Cape Comorin. On the distribution of ports along this coast, Pires himself offers a comprehensive list but an early version was offered by the *Periplus* in the mid-first century AD.

> Chapter 53: Then Naoura and Tundis, the first marts of Limurike; and after them Mouziris and Nelkunda, which are now busy places.
> Chapter 54: Tundis is in the kingdom of Keprobotos, and is a well-known village beside the sea. Mouziris, belonging to the same kingdom, is a flourishing (place) with ships from Ariake coming to it, and also Greeks. It stands on a river, and is 500 stades distant from Tundis by river and by sea, and 20 stades from the mouth of the river. Nelkunda is nearly 500 stades from Mouziris, and likewise the same distance by river or by sea. It belongs to another kingdom, that of Pandion, and it too stands on a river, about 120 stades from the sea.
> Chapter 55: At the mouth of this river there lies another village (called) Bakare, to which they send down the ships from Nelkunda before putting out to sea; and they lie in the roadstead for loading cargoes, since the river is full of mud-flats and the channels between them are shallow. The kings of both marts live inland. And to those coming in from the sea a sign of the

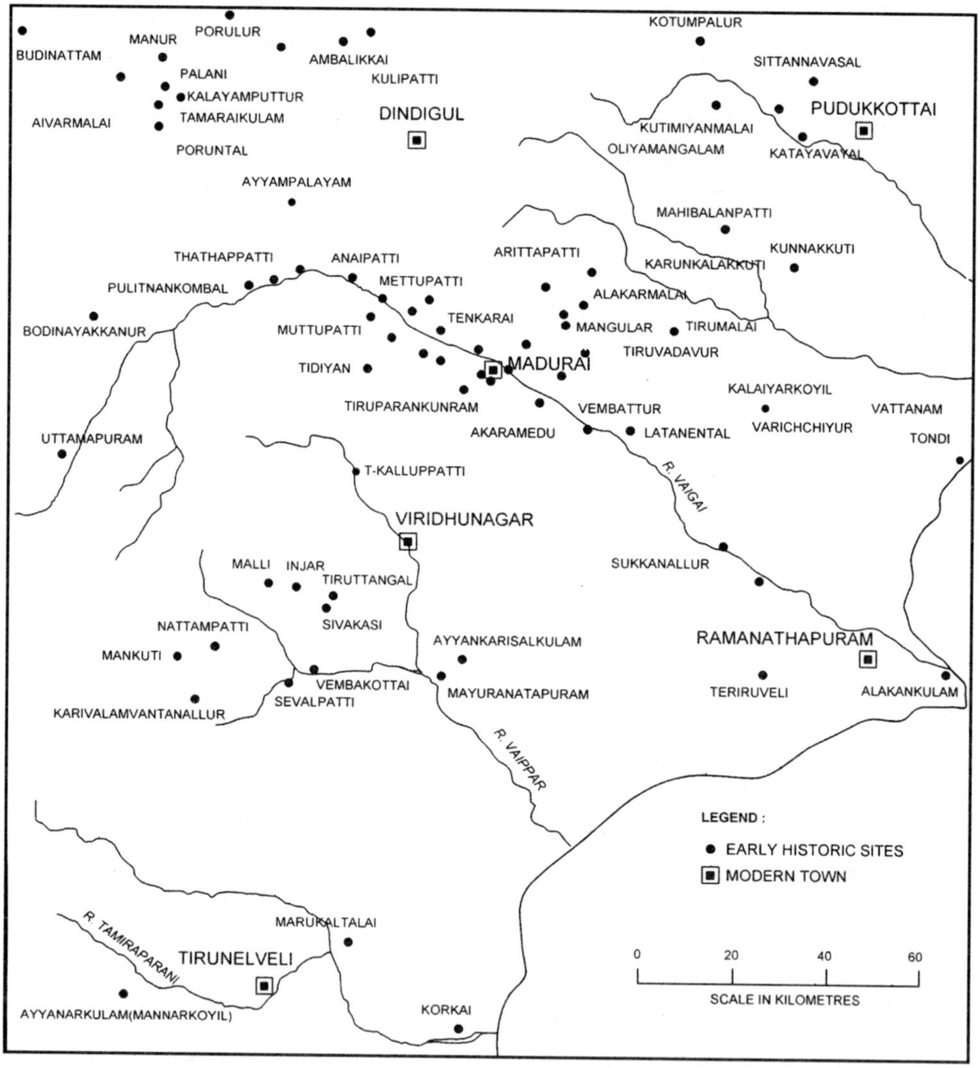

Map 8. Early historical sites in southern Tamil Nadu (after *Catalogue*).

> approach of land is (the sight of) snakes coming out to meet them, black in colour but shorter (than those near Barake), and with dragon-like heads and blood-red eyes.
> Chapter 58: Beyond Bakare is what is called the Red Mountain, and another country extends ... called Paralia towards the south. The first place, called Balita, has a good harbour and a village by the sea. Beyond this is another place called Komar, where are a fort and a harbour, to which come those who, intending to lead dedicated lives, are cleansed and remain celibate; and similarly women. For it is related that the Goddesses abode there at one time, and wasritually cleansed (Huntingford 1980, pp. 50-53)

W.B. Huntingford, who edited this text of the *Periplus*, identified Naoura with Cannanore and Tundis with modern Tanor, about 75 miles south of Cannanore. Limurike, he points out, should be Damirike/ Damurike, the Tamil country, but should include the Chera kingdom. Mouziris, although put by him at Cranganore, is now identified with Pattanam at the mouth of the Periyar. Nelkunda is identified with Kottayam and Bakare is supposed to be modern Vakkarai, the landing place on the sea coast for Nelkunda. Red Mountain may mean Red Cliff, the name given to the steep coast below Quilon. Balita may be Trivandrum or a place called Manpalli, a little northwest of Anjenga, which is about 20 miles to the north of Trivandrum. Komar is Cape Comorin.

According to the *Periplus*, large ships sailed to these ports on account of the large quantity of pepper and malabathrum. The general imports comprised large quantities of coinage, chrysolith, unlined clothing, damasks, antimony, coral, crude glass, copper, tin, lead, wine, red orpiment, yellow orpiment, and wheat for the ships' crew. In addition to pepper and malabathrum, the exports consisted of ivory, Chinese cloth, Gangetic spikenard, precious stones of all kinds, diamonds, sapphires and tortoise shell from Southeast Asia and from the Tamil land itself. From Egypt the ships bound for the Malabar ports sailed in July.

The identifications need not be beyond dispute in all cases, but the chain of ports is clear enough and recalls a similar, although more densely arranged, chain of Malabar ports listed many centuries later by Tome Pires.

> The following are the inhabited seaports in this province where there are ships: Manjeswaram (*Mayceram*), *Mayporam*, Kumbla (*Combula*), Kattakulam (*Coty Coulam*), Nileshweram (*Nijliporam*), *Hyeri*, Baliapatam (*Balea Patanam*), Cannanore, Durmapatan (*Tarmapatan*), Madayid (*Marlarjanj*), Chombakulu (*Combaa*), Puthupattanam (*Pudopatanam*), Tricodi (*Tiricorij*), *Bairacono*, Kollam (*Coulam*), which they call Pantalayini

(*Pamdaranj*), Kappatta (*Capocar*), Calicut, Chaliyam (*Chaliaa*), Parappanangadi (*Para Purancorj*), Tanor (*Tanor*), Ponnani (*Panane*), Velankode (*Bely Ancoro*), Chetwayi (*Chetua*), Kranganur (*Cranganor*), Cochin, Kayankulam (*Caya Coulam*), Quilon (*Coulam*), Vilinjam (*Bilinjao*), Comorin (Cortesao 1944: 74).

Identification does not seem to be a problem with most of these places. Mayporam cannot be identified because the stretch between Manjeshwaram south of Mangalore and Kumbla is a straight coast without any place for a port. The ports of Majeshwaram and Mayporam belong to the northern boundary of Malabar and these two sea ports have a few ships. The Cottayam stretch is said to be devoid of sea ports. The ports of Kumbla, Kattakulam, Nileshweram, Hyeri, Baliapatam (5 miles north of Cannanore and on the bank of a river of the same name), Cannanore, Durmapatam and Madayid belong to the ruler of Cannanore, and except Cannanore, which had a large port and many merchants, these were unimportant ports. The ports of Chombakulu, Puthupattanam, Tricodi, Pantalayini, Kappata, Calicut, Chaliyam and Parappanangadi were all under the Zamorin of Calicut and except Calicut, all were small sea ports. Pires points out that as a port Calicut is not good because the land slopes up from the sea. However, a great deal of trading was done here "by many merchants, natives of Malabar as well as Klings, Chettis and foreigners from all parts, both Moors and heathens. It is a very famous port and is the best thing in all Malabar" (Cortesao 1944: 78). Tanur had many ships, and the ports of Ponnani, Veleankode and Chetwayi were ports with ships and merchants and 'goodly towns'. Kranganur had a great deal of trade. Cochin had many ships. Kayankulam was a minor port but Quilon was "a great port of call where the ships of many merchants from different places" did a great deal of trade. The port of Vilinjam was also in the kingdom of Quilon. The kingdom of Travancore was not rich in ports but the king used to buy many horses for transporting them to Vijayanagar.

One is not sure if the history of the Malabar ports has been as adequately worked out as it has been done in the case of the ports of Coromandel. One is not also sure if the early mediaeval history of Kerala is as rich in the epigraphic sources as Tamil Nadu is. However, there can be no better indication of the richness and complexity of the mediaeval overseas trade pursued through the Malabar coast than the 9th century AD Sthanu Ravi copper-plate inscriptions from Quilon and the 13th century copper-plate inscription of Vira Raghava in the possession of the Syrian Christian church of Kottayam. Among other things, the history of the trade guilds mentioned in these inscriptions – the *Six Hundred*, the *Anjuvannam* and the *Manigramam* – has been brilliantly worked out with great scholarship by Meera Abraham (1988). Our concern here is not the history and workings of these trade guilds but what the Sthanu Ravi and Vira Raghava reveal about Kerala's overseas trade between the 9th and 13th centuries AD.

There are two sets of Sthanu Ravi inscriptions. Sthanu Ravi was the king of the region in the 9th century and, according to the first inscription, the governor of Venadu or the Travancore area authorised the Christian church of Tarisappalli built by Eso da Tapir at Quilon to have certain rights over a few families of toddy-tapper and washerman castes, withdrawing his right to collect some specified taxes from them. The implication was that the church would be able to utilize the services of the families whose taxes were withdrawn by this royal decree. They could also ply their trade within the walls of the city's fort, and it was mentioned that all this was secured through the efforts of Maruvan Sapir Iso mentioned earlier as Eso da Tapir. The second inscription details the grants of lands made to the Tarisapalli church. The boundaries of the gifted land were detailed, and the names of two local families who owned lands on the northern and northeastern boundaries of this land being mentioned. The representative of one of these families was present when the governor of Venadu drew up the agreement with the church, and Abraham infers that this family could be indigenous Christians. The second inscription also grants several trading rights to the Church, including its right to collect a specified amount of cess on the merchandise coming by land or moving in and out of the harbour. What is remarkable is that the signatures appended to the plates of the Sthanu Ravi grants were in three languages and scripts – Arabic, Pahlavi and Hebrew. The presence of Muslim, Jewish and Christian traders in the 9th century Quilon can easily be inferred.

The inscription of Vira Raghava, dated c. AD 1225, states the rights granted to Ravikorran of the Manigramam trading guild in the port of Kodungallur (Cranganore). In the inscription he is called 'lord of the city'. As Abraham (1988, p. 35) puts it,

> Monopoly rights were granted as well as a commission on many commodities including musk, salt and sugar. Unfortunately the other commodities are not named. The Manigramam was also given the right to the customs which could be levied on goods which arrived at the mouth of the river and were then transported to the interior.

Another inscription, dated this time in the 10th-11th century, from a village called Talakkad in the Mukundapuram taluk of Kerala (possibly somewhere in the Cochin area) defines a market area set up with the approval of the prominent villagers or the members of the village assembly and gave them right to levy tax in kind on the stalls put up by the merchants. Otherwise, the merchants were given a free hand to run the market. Two members of the Manigramam guild were granted exemptions from certain specific taxes, although all the merchants had to pay taxes coming in from the sea. It is obvious that in the 10th-11th century, overseas goods were being sold even in village markets of Kerala.

The presence of Jewish traders in the Kerala coast in the 9th and 10th centuries AD, as attested by the Sthanu Ravi copper-plates of the period, is also suggested by the evidence of the Geniza documents found in a synagogue of Old Cairo, although the latter documents seem to be limited only to Mangalore at the top of the Kerala coast. The documents edited and analysed by S.G. Goitein and M.A. Friedman under the title *India Traders of the Middle Ages: Documents from the Cairo Geniza* (Goitein and Friedman 2008) deal with the economic, juridical and family aspects of the 'India trade' conducted principally through Aden during that period. The historical picture which comes through is that of infinitesimal details, which is possible only in the case of very close and easy links between all the relevant regions, principally Egypt, Arabia and the west coast of India. For instance, one letter (dated c.1137-1140) written by Joseph B. Abraham to Ben Yiju, then resident in Mangalore, states the following:

> I am sending you a broken ewer and a dipper that together weigh seven pounds less a quarter. Please make me a ewer of the same measure from its copper, for its copper is good copper. The weight of the ewer should be five pounds exactly. I am sending also eighteen and aquarter pounds of good yellow copper in bars and five pounds of Quali lead in a big mould and a piece of Egyptian lead (in the form of a shell). Please put the bars, the lead, and what remains from the manufacture of the ewer together and have made for me … a lamp, two table jugs for two platters – they should be of good workmanship (Goitein and Friedman 2008, pp. 558-559).

Joseph Abraham goes to specify the exact shape and features of the lamp he ordered. The point is that he sent to Mangalore two of his *broken* copper vessels along with some more copper and lead to be shaped into finished goods of specific weights and features. One letter of the same general period refers to the dispatch of a bag of 'red copper' of specified pieces, weights and price to 'Pandaraina (Fandarayna)', which has been identified with the present day Pantalayini south of Cannanore in the Kerala coast (Goitein and Friedman 2008, p. 332). Interestingly, an Andalusian 'India trader' sent to Tripoly in Libya a shipment of various goods including "two bales of cowrie shells, Indian popular ornaments,

Map 9. Early historical sites in western Tamil Nadu (after *Catalogue*).

which were as avidly sought after in the Mediterranean area, especially in Spain, as corals were in India" (Goitein and Friedman 2008, p. 224).

Examples can be multiplied but the Geniza documents fully substantiate what can be gathered from the copper-plate inscriptions of Sthanu Ravi and Vira Raghava and various other inscriptions and sources analysed by Meera Abraham (1988).

Again, as far as the general alignments of historical routes are concerned, the pictures of Tamil Nadu and Kerala are broadly similar: an array of coastal sites with a number of routes converging on them from the interior, and a limited number of geographically defined lines of movement beyond the boundaries of the State.

IX. THE ISSUE OF LATER ROUTES

The general alignment of early historic movements in Tamil Nadu and Kerala and between Tamil Nadu and Kerala has been discussed in the early sections of this chapter. It was geographically constrained, and we have pointed out how both Andhra and Karnataka were linked with Tamil Nadu by gaps in the northern hills and how Karnataka sent out routes to the Kerala coast through the Wynad plateau and the related areas. The Palghat gap and the Cumbam valley maintained Tamil Nadu's links with Kerala. The issue of the later historic alignments is more difficult to settle. For one thing, the movements between the different internal areas must have considerably increased from the early historic to the early mediaeval and later periods. Among other things, the kings of the relevant internal territories – the Pandyas, Cholas, Pallavas and the Cheras – marched their armies to and fro in search of territorial gains or wealth, and the powers outside the Tamil Nadu and Kerala sections of the southern Peninsula also tried to move far south. There was no perceptible decline in trade after the early historic period. If anything, the quantum of trade, both internal and overseas, possibly increased manifold. Even our admittedly patchy discussion on the distribution of ports in the Coromandel and Malabar coasts is likely to have brought this out. A close geographical examination of the innumerable inscriptions of the later historic periods would have pointed out the basic configurations of the related sites and their linkages. However, the historical geography of the Pandya, Chola, Pallava, Kerala and other related inscriptions has not yet been worked out from this point of view, although there is a vast scope of, and material for, relating the South Indian epigraphic material to elucidate the past historical landscapes of the south. Although the basic style and theme of these inscriptions do not fundamentally differ from the styles and forms of the north Indian inscriptions, the South Indian inscriptions may be said to constitute a separate genre of its own because of their sheer quantity and the details of the mundane life and ground.

The series of maps detailing the urban process of Tamil Nadu from the early historic period to c. AD 1300, which Champakalakshmi has produced on the basis of her grip over the relevant epigraphical sources provides some indirect help in understanding the actual history of links between its different internal areas. Her Map 1, which deals with the early historic period, shows the following early historic routes: (1) Madras > Kanchi > Kovalur > Uraiyur > Kodumbalur > Madurai > Korkai; (2) Takadur > Chengam > Kovalur > the area to the south of Pondicherry/ Arikamedu; (3) Puhar > Uraiyur > Karur > Kodumanal > Muziris; (4) Madurai > Alagankulam.

The other distribution maps of all the major centres of the concerned periods (c. AD 600-850, c. AD 850-985; c. AD 985-1150, c. AD 1150-1250, and around AD 1300) which she lists as 'royal centres' *Brahmadeyas* as large revenue units or *Taniyurs* and also as urban centres, *Nagarams* or urban centres, 'centres of merchant bodies' trade centres, ports, etc. show, taken together, the densest concentration of settlements in the Kaveri delta and along the Kaveri. This concentration is significant also along the Palar, Ponnaiyar, Vaigai and Tamraparni. Elsewhere, including Salem and Coimbatore, it is sporadic.

According to Champakalakshmi, the development of urban process in Tamil Nadu from c. AD 600 to c. AD 1300 depended primarily on an internal process where under the Pallavas and Pandyas between c. 6th and c. 9th centuries AD the creation of *Brahmadeyas* and temples resulted in an intensive agrarian organization which was followed by the emergence of trade centres, although initially only in the key areas. In the next phase the merchant guilds initiated the development of organized trade, and the villages expanded into towns. The temples became land magnets, receiving money and gold as endowments and investing them again in land and occasionally in trade. One need not be surprised that the concentration of all these settlements was primarily in the Kaveri delta and other river valleys and not in the dry and somewhat rocky lands of Coimbatore, Salem and Dharampuri, which marked basically the threads of trade.

It appears from Champakalakshmi's maps that in the later historic periods, the alignment which emerged in the Kanchipuram-Madras zone and led to North and South Arcots, Pudukottai, Trichinopoly, Tanjore and Ramanathapuram and Tinnevely, gained tremendously in significance.

The Coimbatore-Salem-Dharmapuri stretch retained its traditional significance but the routes through it now led to the Kaveri delta and other river valleys, including the ports at their mouths. Champakalakshmi's distribution map of the urban core of the Tinnevelly area shows a distribution oriented from the royal centre Rajendracholapuram (south of modern Tinnevelly) to the west (cf. Ambasamudram, Mannarkoil, etc.), i.e., Kerala. It appears that the route of access to Kerala via Nagarkoil and the Cumbam valley became extra significant during the later historic periods.

When one comes down to the details of the individual routes, one gets a fair amount of detail from the mid-19th century, i.e., from the period before the railway system brought about a substantial change in the whole system (Scott 1853). From Arcot one could move down to Sadras on the coast by Kanchipuram and Chingleput. From Arcot one could also move up to Nellore on the Andhra coast by passing through the Nagar hills and negotiating a pass near Pootoor. The route passed through Kalahasti. Vellore could be accessed from Cuddalore on the coast either through Pondicherry, Wandiwash and Arcot or through Villupuram, Ginjee and Arnee. The route from Cuddalore to Salem was by Chhinna Salem and Attoor. Examples such as these show that the coast was well linked with the interior, and similarly the Andhra coast was not difficult to reach from places like Vellore and Arcot. Bangalore, i.e., the Karnataka plateau, was within easy rich from Madras in at least five ways, using a variety of openings in the Eastern Ghats (cf. the Coorumbarputty pass, the Palmanair pass and the Nykanairy pass). At least four of these routes passed through Kolar. Only in one case the route went through Hosur. From Madras one could go to Bellary by the Naggeri pass, which in the mid-19th century was gentle both in ascent and descent but stony and difficult. In the mid-19th century the coastal route south of Madras was much in use. To reach Trichinopoly from Madras one took the coastal route through Pondicherry up to Cuddalore and move from there to Kumbhakonam to have a direct opening to Trichinopoly. From the Madras area again, the route to Point Calimere was by the coastal route by Sadras, Pondicherry and Negapatnam. Salem was reached from Madras by Arni, Polur, Chengam, Hunur. Kumbhakonam was a major stopping point on the Madras-Tanjore alignment. Palghat was approached from Madras by Arcot, Vellore, Hunur, the Munjewaddy Ghat, Salem, Erode, Avinashi and Coimbatore. This route also went through Dharmapuri. From Trichinopoly the route to Bangalore in the Karnataka plateau went through Salem, the Topoor pass, Ryacottah and Hosur. From Trichinopoly the route to Coimbatore went by Karur.

The Trichinopoly - Srirangapattanam route went by Karur, Erode, the Hassanoor pass and Mysore.

The Kerala tract was well linked with Tamil Nadu and the Karnataka plateau. The routes to Tamil Nadu did not invariably go through the Palghat gap. From Quilon one could reach Madurai by Trivandrum, Aramboli, Palamkottah and Tirumangalam. The Srirangapattanam section was linked with the Cannanore section of Kerala by Manantoddy, the Peria Ghat and Cotianguddy. The route also went through the Pairumbaddy pass. One of the routes from Ootacamund in the Nilgiri hills to Cannanore went through the Neddowuttam pass, Goodaloor, Gunapuddywuttum or Sultan's Battery, Mannantody and the Peria pass. Calicut was connected with Karnataka in two major ways: to Goondalpet south of Chamrajnagar by the Carcoor Ghat, and to Srirangapattanam by the Tamarcherry and Luckricotah passes. Calicut also had links with the Nilgiris by the Sissipara Ghat. There was a route from Cannanore to Mercara in Coorg by the Pairambuddy Ghat. In Tamil Nadu, Dindigul was linked with Gazelhati by Darapooram, Avinashi and Poongar. Gazelhati was a small village with the Moyar River on its left. The pass took one over to the Karnataka plateau. The route to Palghat from Dindigul went via Palni (for the details of the routes mentioned in this section, Scott 1853).

The 'ghats' separating the Kerala coast from Mysore and the Nilgiris were not always easy. For instance, the Carcoor Ghat between Calilut and the Chamrajnagar section of Karnataka drew the following cursory note from F.H. Scott (1853):

> The Ghaut is in very bad order – totally impassable by carts – descents and ascents are considerable – thick jungle and infested by elephants.

Or, one may consider the case of the route from Cannanore to Mercara by the Paireumbaddy Ghat:

> The road in July 1851 totally impracticable by carts – but it is available for Palkee and cattle traffic, though liable to interruption in the monsoon on account of the mountain streams (Scott 1853).

3

Andhra

I. ELEMENTS OF GEOGRAPHY

The two major deltas of the Krishna and the Godavari and a host of lesser estuaries break the long sweep of the Andhra coastline between Nellore in the south and Srikakulam in the north. The long coastline is backed by an equally long sweep of the Eastern Ghats and its outliers, although not all the hill ranges of Andhra may be said to belong to this system. The hills of Adilabad and Karimnagar seem to be an extension of the Central Indian uplands. The two ranges of the Nallamalais and Erramalais in the Anantapur-Cuddapah-Kurnool-Chittoor section in the southwest, and also partly in the Srisailam sector of Guntur produce a dominantly hilly landscape with intervening valleys but do not seriously impair communication between different areas. In the east and the northeast, the hills and jungles of the Bastar-Dandakaranya section of Orissa and Chhattisgarh may be a more difficult terrain to cross, but from the Vizianagram section of Andhra, major routes emanate towards Koraput and Sambalpur in Orissa and Raipur in Chhattisgarh. Compared to the Konkan coast, Tamil Nadu and Kerala, the historical linkages and movements in Andhra have been more easy and open. The contiguous areas of Karnataka and Maharashtra have the same topography and the coastline beyond Srikakulam merges imperceptibly in that of Orissa. It is only to reach Tamil Nadu and the eastern or the Vidarbha section of Maharashtra that one has to follow geographically constricted lines of movements from Andhra. An easy way to approach Tamil Nadu from Andhra is from the direction of Tirupati and then proceed, through

Chittoor, to Vellore. Another way from the same direction is to come to Arakkonam and then to Kanchipuram. The famous Sivalinga site of Gudimallam lies near Papanaiyudu, only a little to the southeast of Tirupati, and seems to be closely linked to the Arakkonam approach to Kanchipuram. The Vidarbha sector of Maharashtra is within easy reach both from Adilabad and Karimnagar. After crossing the Godavari, the route from Karimnagar passes through Asifabad and then takes the Chandrapur-Nagpur alignment. From Adilabad, the Nagpur alignment via Hinganghat is almost straight. Some major historical sites fall on the Karimnagar-Chandrapur alignment. One is not sure of the occurrence of such sites between Adilabad and Nagpur, but that the Adilabad-Karimnagar approach to Vidarbha is historically significant is suggested by the occurrence of such sites as Adam and Pauni in the Vidarbha segment. From Guntur in the heart of the Krishna valley, the route to Bellary and Dharwar in Karnataka is by Vinukonda and the Nandikanama pass in the Nallamalai range. From Nandikanama it goes to the Nandiyal valley and crosses the Erramala range to reach Guntakal and Bellary. The Gulbarga and Bijapur sections of Karnataka are only a little to the west of Hyderabad, and from Gulbarga or Bijapur the area to the east of the Western Ghats up to Pune is open via Kolhapur and Satara. Similarly, the whole of the Raichur doab between the Krishna and the Tungabhadra and the doab between the Bhima and the Tungabhadra are within easy reach from Gulbarga, which is located itself on the bank of the Bhima. Similarly, Bidar and Kalyani of Karnataka lie only at a comparatively short distance to the northwest of Hyderabad, and the Aurangabad-Daulatabad section of Maharashtra can easily be accessed from there. The Aurangabad section can also be easily accessed from Nizamabad via Nanded and Parbhani. The route from the Vizianagram area of Andhra to the Raipur section of Chhattisgarh passes through Bhawanipatna in Orissa and possibly touches the Koraput region on the way. There is no doubt that the historical linkages of Andhra are wide open, dependent primarily on the historical forces of the time and not so much on the restricted geographical alignments.

In fact, in the study of Andhra geography the term 'pass' occurs very rarely. It occurs almost exclusively in the Kurnool-Cudapah-Anantapur-Chittoor section. Two long ranges of hills – the Nallamalais on the east and the Erramalas on the west – cut up the Kurnool district into a number of sections, with the flat, open valley of Nandiyal occupying its central section. The modern Guntakal-Bezwada/Vijaywada section of the railways follows the line taken up by one of the two major cart roads of the district across the Nandikanama pass. There is another pass further north, namely, the Mantralamma pass, but according to the *Imperial Gazetteer of India* (vol. 18, pp. 345-347; hereafter *IGI*), that is 'much less important'. There are also two passes across the Erramalas in Kurnool: the Tammarazupalle pass and the Rampur pass (the *IGI*, vol. 16, p. 41). The importance of these passes lies in the fact that they kept the line of communication between the Raichur doab and Bellary sections of Karnataka and the Andhra coast between the mouth of the Krishna and Nellore open. In the Anantapur district, the Namalguddi pass lies in the Dorigallu stretch of the Palkonda-Sheshachalam range and connects the Kadiri taluk of Anantapur with the Pulivendla taluk of Cuddapah. It has been said to be a 'much-frequented trade-route' (Sankaranarayana 1970, p. 430). Hill paths like the Gaddiakanama near Talaricheruvu links the Tadpatri taluk of Anantapur with the Koilkuntla taluk of Kurnool across the Erramala range and have been said to be important for grain trade of the region. One also hears of passes in the Cuddapah district across the Velikonda range, which separates Nellore on the coast from Cuddapah and Kurnool. The Badvel-Nellore road passes through the Dornala pass. The smaller passes of Pillutlakanuma and Somasila also helped to maintain the links between the interior and the coast (Sankaranarayana 1967). Sankaranarayana has pointed out in his Cuddapah district gazetteer (Sankaranarayana 1967) that the term Cuddapah in Telugu means 'threshold', which is supposed to mean in this case the 'threshold to Tirupati' – a camping ground for the pilgrims from the north to Tirupati. He further points out that of all the passes or *kanumas* in the Pulivendla stretch of the Seshachalam hills, the most important is the Namakgudi pass, which has cliffs rising to a height of c. 300 feet. N. Ramesan in his Chittoor district gazetteer (Ramesan 1979) refers to the Tirupati area as a pass which was used, among others, by Shivaji in his march to Gingee in Tamil Nadu. Gudimallam falls on the route coming from the side of Nellore and beyond. From Nayudipet on the Nellore side, one comes to Srikalahasti and from there the road leads to Pananaidupet and Tirupati. Gudimallam lies near Pananaidupet. From Tirupati to Vellore via Chittoor is almost a straight line. More straight is the line from Tirupati to Arakkonam in Chingleput. Tirupati thus maintains an important position in the route system passing through the Rayalseema section of Andhra.

There is also no dearth of hill ranges and isolated hills in the Telengana section of Andhra, but one does not come across any allusion to the presence of historically significant passes in them. The Satmala range traverses the Adilabad district from the northwest to the southeast for about 175 miles, and there are also hills of minor importance in the east. The *Imperial Gazetteer of India* (vol. 5, pp. 22-23) describes this district as "very sparsely populated, containing extensive uncultivated wastes". However, there are two routes to Vidarbha through Adilabad – one straight from Adilabad to Nagpur, and another coming from Karimnagar and going towards Chandrapur through the eastern part of the district. There does not seem to be any evidence of the early historic antiquity of the Adilabad-Nagpur alignment except that early historical sites have been reported from Adialabad, but of the early historic antiquity of the Karimnagar-Chandrapur alignment there is ample evidence, as we shall see later. Karimnagar also is not lacking in hills, of which three separate ranges are known to exist. The eastern part of the district is reasonably free of them, and the Karimnagar-Mancherial road follows a northeastern alignment and reaches Mancherial after crossing the Godavari.

Sporadically, hills occur in many Andhra districts, both in and out of the Eastern Ghats system. One is not sure if those in Warangal, Hyderabad, Nalgonda and Mahbubnagar can be related to the Eastern Ghats. The hills of the districts towards, and along, the coast certainly belong to this system. The juxtaposition of the hills and fertile deltaic soil has been brought out rather clearly in the case of the Kistna/Krishna district of British India:

> On the extreme west the District consists of stony uplands, dotted with rocky hills or crossed by low ridges; the centre and north are a level plain of black cotton soil; but the eastern portion is made up of the wide alluvial delta of the Kistna river, an almost flat expanse, covered with irrigated rice fields, and containing some of the most fertile land in the Presidency (the *IGI*, vol. 15, p. 319).

The Godavari delta or the Konasamudram delta has a feature of its own. Below Rajamahndry where the Godavari is about 3 km wide, at Dowleshwaram where an anicut or dam has been put up, it divides into two branches and flows through a wide and irrigated delta.

> ... from this point to the sea the country is a vast expanse of rice fields dotted with gardens and villages. During the rains the greater part of this tract becomes one sheet of water, only village sites, canal banks, roads and field boundaries appearing above it. Later in the year, as the rice grows higher, the dividing boundaries are hidden; and the whole country looks like a single rice field, only the palm trees along the edges of the fields, the groves round the villages, the road avenues, and the white sails of the boats gliding along the main canals breaking the uniform sea of waving green crops ... (the *IGI*, vol. 12, pp. 281-282).

The Visakhapatnam district abuts this delta on the east and northeast, with the rocky hills overlooking, if not coming down to, the sea. Vizianagram in this district is an important communication point.

The coastal route goes straight to Srikakulam and enters the Ganjam section of Orissa on the east soon afterwards. The real importance of the Vizianagram area lies in the fact that from here there is a major route to the Jeypore tract of Orissa through the Pottinga ghat, bringing Chhattisgarh and western and northern Orissa within the ambit of the Andhra coast, although this particular section of Andhra fell in the ancient territory of Kalinga. Through this area, Andhra was connected with Chhattisgarh or South Kosala and the Gangetic plain of eastern India.

This cursory review of some elements of Andhra geography was aimed at highlighting the fact that this was easily linked to the historical developments of a very large part of India: the Kanchipuram sector of Tamil Nadu, the Bellary-Gulbarga-Bidar-Bijapur section of Karnataka, and through it, that section of Maharashtra which lies immediately to the east of the Western Ghats, the Aurangabad-Daulatabad area of Maharashtra through Nanded, the eastern or the Vidarbha part of Maharashtra through Karimnagar and Adilabad, the southwestern Orissa and Chhattisgarh from Vizianagram, and finally, the whole of the coastal sweep of eastern India up to the Bhagirathi from Srikakulam. The political forces emanating from all these regions affected the course of Andhra history at one time or another. Economically, the Andhra coast was the terminal point of some trade routes, especially the ones coming from the direction of Paithan in the upper Godavari and from the direction of the Ganga plain through Vidarbha and South Kosala. The importance of the route coming from the direction of Broach and Paithan was pointed out by J.F. Fleet many years ago, and we have seen how the Tirupati gap provided an important line of communication to Tamil Nadu. That the Andhra coast was the terminal point of routes coming in this direction from the Gangetic valley is clearly suggested by the density of its Buddhist religious establishments. It is doubtful if outside the Northwest Frontier, including the mountain valleys to the northeast of Peshawar, the Buddhist establishments were as dense in any other part of the subcontinent as they were in Andhra. All these factors and the fact that Andhra has a long coastline with its chain of pre-modern and in many cases, ancient ports, endow the ancient history of Andhra with an eclectic character of its own.

II. G. JOUVEAU-DUBREUIL'S EXPOSITION (1927) OF THE ANCIENT HISTORICAL ROUTES OF ANDHRA

In his foreword to K.S. Subramanian's *Buddhist Remains in South India and Early Andhra History* (Subramanian 1927), G. Jouveau-Dubreuil offered a section on the 'geographical position of archaeological remains in Andhra' and discussed in that context the different ancient roads which converged upon, and radiated from, the heart of the Andhra country in Vengi. He also produced a map in the light of his ideas. Considering that Jouveau-Dubreuil's opinion extensively figures in the later literature, although not always with acknowledgement, one may take this as a starting-point of the present discussion on the historical routes of Andhra.

Vengi is identified with Peddavegi near Elleru in the West Godavari district. It was the capital of the Eastern Chalukyas for about 500 years between the 7th and 12th centuries and presumably a major political centre even before this period. Jouveau-Dubreuil inferred that it was from the country of Vengi that Indian ships sailed to go to the Far East.

Vengi was considered 'a great meeting place of roads' and five 'great routes' supposedly converged upon that place. These routes are: the road to Kalinga (northeast), the road to Dravida (south), the road to Karnataka (southwest), the road to Maharashtra (northwest), and the road to Kosala (north). All the Buddhist sites were supposedly located along these routes:

> 1. On the road to Kalinga, Vengi, Arugolu, Pithapuram, Kodavali, Ankapalle, Sankaram, Dharapalem, Ramatirtham, Salihundam.
> 2. On the road to the south, Gudivada, Ghantasala, Bhattiprolu, Buddhani, Chinna and Pedda Ganjam and finally Kannuparti.
> 3. On the road to the Karnatic, the sites of Vijayaderpuram (Bezwada), Peddamaddur, Amaravati, Garikipadu, Goli, Nagarjunakonda.
> 4. On the road to Maharashtra are found Alluru, Ramireddipalle, Jaggayyapeta.
> 5. Lastly, at the beginning of the road to Kosala which started from Vengi and followed the Godavari to go to the centre of India via Nagpur, we find the site of Guntupalle. Another road towards the north lay through Korukonda and Yarrampalem. (Jouveau-Dubreuil 1927: vi)

He also added explanatory notes to this list. The road to Kalinga crossed the Godavari probably near Dowleshwaram at the head of the delta and went successively to Pithapuram and Kodavalli, and followed the coastal route from then on through Anakapalle, Sankaram, Dharapalem near Simhachalam and finally, Ramatirtham. The road to the south first led up to Pamarru via Gudivada. The Krishna was supposedly crossed through the island of Potarlanka, the largest island of the Krishna, which was surrounded by three famous Buddhist sites: Srikakulam (a capital of the Satavahanas?), and the two *stupas* of Ghantasala on the left bank of the river and Bhottiprolu on the right. Bhottiprolu is connected with Bapatla by road through Buddhani, and it is on the coastal road from Bapatla that one finds the sites of Chinna and Pedda Ganjam and Kannuparti. The road to Karnataka first crossed the

Krishna between Bezwada and Amaravati and then crossed it again near Goli and Nagarjunakonda. The road to Maharashtra commenced at Ellru/ Alluru and first went to Jaggayyapeta. From there it turned in the direction of Tagara or Ter. Guntupalle is supposedly the only known site on the route from Vengi to Kosala. Another road to the north started from Rajamuhndry and proceeded through the Buddhist sites of Korukonda and Yerrampalem.

Jouveau-Dubreuil's conclusion is that "all the Buddhist sites known at present are found along the grand roads of communication" (Jouveau-Dubreuil 1927: viii).

One cannot be sure of the extent to which Jouveau-Dubreuil was right in focussing only on the present West Godavari area as the heartland of Andhra, ignoring the importance of the Nagarjunakonda-Sri Sailam region. However, when he wrote, the importance of the Nagarjuna-Sri Sailam belt was not as closely understood as it is now. What also weighed strongly in favour of Vengi was his notion that the Indian ships used to sail to Southeast Asia from this area. This idea was first worked out in his *Ancient History of the Deccan* (Jouveau-Dubreuil 1920: 87-88). The starting point was the idea that "the Indo-Chinese civilisation did not come from every place in India, but from a part of the Deccan whence the travellers embarked for Indo-China". This idea was based on the similarity in the palaeography of the inscriptions between the ancient Cambodia and the Deccan. To identify the place where this port was located, he turned to Ptolemy of the second century AD, who mentioned the 'mouth of the river Maisolus' or the mouth of the Krishna, and then successively, 'Kontakassyla, a mart' and Koddura. Kontakassyla is modern Ghantasala and more importantly, from Jouveau-Dubreuil's point of view, is Koddura or Gudur: "the place where ships departed for Indo-China is found near Koddura, a little more to the north of the coast, i.e. not far from the mouth of the Godavari".

There was no reason why ships would embark only from Koddura for Southeast Asia, although this was possibly one such port. Vengi has a long history as an administrative centre in the inscriptions (Mangalam 1986: 93-95), beginning with its status as the headquarter of a division (*Vengo-rashtra*) under the early Pallavas. 'Vengi-1000' figures in a Vishnukundin inscription. *'Vengi-Vishaya'* of the Eastern Chalukyan inscriptions denoted their capital. The Eastern Chalukyan kingdom itself came to be known as *Vengi-nadu* and *Vengi-desa*. Its administrative importance continued, although in a lesser form, till the Kakatiya dynasty in the 13th century AD.

Although we find no reason why Vengi should be the most important point to evaluate the ancient historical routes of Andhra, it must be considered one of the important focal points of Andhra history because of the very fact of persisting as a capital city for about 500 years. Jouveau-Dubreuil fixed his attention only on the distribution of Buddhist sites, ignoring the significance of the distribution of the city sites of the region in this context. In fact, the beginning of the early historic period and the associated major settlements of the period may be a more apt starting point of the study of the major historical routes of Andhra.

III. THE BEGINNING OF THE EARLY HISTORIC PERIOD IN ANDHRA

The problem is directly linked to two issues: were the spread of Buddhism to Andhra and the foundation of the *stupa* of Amaravarti pre-Asokan or even pre-Mauryan? One does not know what to do with the opinion that the Buddha preached *Kalachakratantra* at the *stupa* of Dhanyakakata (cf. Sarma 1988), but there seems to be a sizeable body of opinion in favour of the presence of Buddhism in Andhra in pre-Mauryan times (cf. Sarma 1988, p. 9). There is no firmly dated literary evidence, but the sheer number of sites related to Buddhism in Andhra and the references to a large number of Buddhist sects in the inscriptions found in them suggest that the Andhra coastal tract had a special significance in the history of Buddhism. The first wave of the spread of Buddhism was possibly tied to the movement of monks along the well-known trade routes of the time, and there is no reason why this had to wait till the period of Asoka.

More directly relevant is the question of archaeology. Amaravati is the primary focus here. The Amaravati museum houses a fragmentary stone railing which is inscribed in clear Mauryan characters of the third-second century BC. Towards the left of the surface of this piece of inscribed stone, the Bodhi tree is shown encircled by a railing. The Bodhi tree itself carries decorative features at the top, and there are decorative devices at the four corners of the railing enclosure as well. To the right, the main *stupa* is shown. Of the main *stupa*, the outer enclosure of railings at the ground level is clearly depicted. One can also detect the upper circumambulatory path. At the base of the drum, one can see a row of lamps. One can also detect a flag-like ornamental device projecting from the base of the drum on the left side. Also on the left side, there is a motif which can be interpreted as a decorative umbrella motif. Among other things, the row of lamps brings to mind the name by which the Amaravati *stupa* mound was known locally, namely, 'the mound of lamps' (personal information from I.K. Sarma). Most importantly, it shows the existence of a simpler *Mahastupa* before the third-second century BC, the date of the inscribed characters on this piece of railing. This also offers almost a sure proof in favour of the opinion that the spread of Buddhism to the Krishna valley is pre-Asokan.

The evidence furnished by the inscribed stone fragment in the Amaravati museum is basically borne out by I.K. Sarma's excavations at the *Mahastupa* site in 1973-75. In the first phase of occupation at the site there are traces of thatched huts supported by wooden posts and the *stupa* was a low mound of mud. This phase yielded a large number of NBP sherds. The second phase also yielded a large number of NBP sherds and witnessed the addition of a granite railing to the *stupa* and an inscribed pillar at its threshold (Sarma 1988: 8). The second phase has to be put in the Asokan period in the third century BC, but Sarma takes the first phase back only a hundred years earlier and dates it in the 4th century BC. One suspects that this dating is based on a comparatively lower dating of the NBP in the Krishna valley than its date in North India where it is found to go back to c. 800 BC, if not earlier. What is generally ignored is that the NBP spread outside the Ganga plain not with the expansion of the Mauryan kingdom but with the expansion of trade, which is graphically suggested by the *Jataka* stories among other categories of evidence. Even on a conservative estimate there is no reason why the date of the appearance of the NBP at Amaravati should be later than c. 500 BC. Sarma himself (1988: 8-9) points out that the NBP at Amaravati belongs to a variety of colours and hue and is reminiscent of the specimens from the classic Ganga plain sites. For this reason, our date of the beginning of the early historic period in Andhra is c. 500 BC.

Further evidence of the Mauryan period *stupa* sites comes from Bhottiprolu and Vaddamanu. Sarma's detailed analysis of the inscribed stone relic caskets inside the main *stupa* of Bhottiprolu (Sarma 1988: 30-56) brings out their Mauryan character.

> There are, in all, six granitic stones, belonging to three containers, massive and roughly worked on the exteriors. Each comprised of a lower stone block having a central groove, deeply cut with a raised rim on top to receive the lid of the upper block of slightly bigger dimensions. The inner faces of the lower container as well as the upper lid were smoothly finished, the inscriptions mostly engraved around the ridged socket of the lower Box stone and correspondingly on the lid part of the upper stone. It is at once clear from the letters and highly polished surface thereon, that after engraving the letters (text), the rock face was subjected to the typical Mauryan Polish, exactly as obtained in the case of Asokan edicts. This fact has not been noticed by the earlier writers (Sarma 1988: 38-39).

Pl. 1. Position of Narttamalai temple on the hill at Narttamalai.

Pl. 2. Sittanavasal hill.

Pl. 3. General view of Adichanallur.

Pl. 4. Another view of Adichanallur with the Tamraparni in the background.

Pl. 5. A view in the vicinity of Pattinam.

Pl. 6. Ruined megaliths at Thandikudi, Palni hills.

Pl. 7. General view of a reconstructed Andhra stupa.

Pl. 8. Part of a reconstructed Andhra stupa.

Pl. 9. A section of Guntupalle caves.

Pl. 10. A stupa complex at Guntupalle.

Pl. 11. A stupa at Salihundam overlooking the river and the plains.

Pl. 13. The dwarf supporting the Gudimallam Siva.

Pl. 12. Gudimallam Siva image.

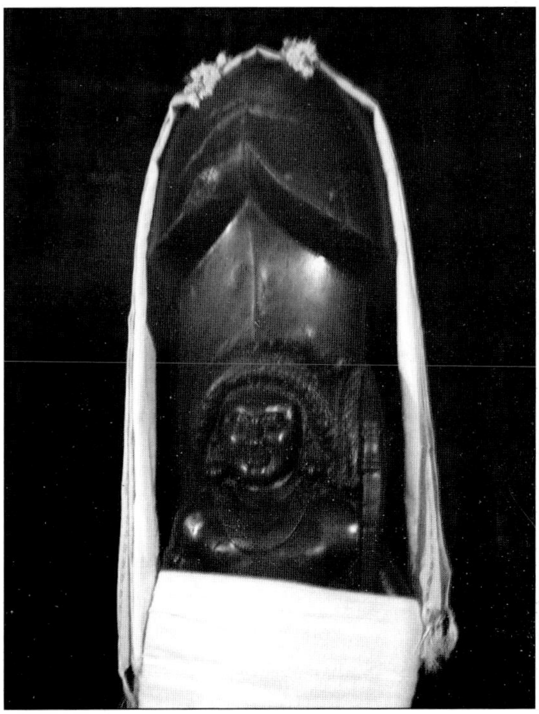

Pl. 14. The face of the Gudimallam linga.

Pl. 15. Railing enclosing Gudimallam Siva image.

Pl. 16. The temple which contains Gudimallam Sivalinga.

Sarma has argued that the Bhottiprolu relic casket inscriptions denote certain palaeographical and linguistic features which can be understood by referring to the Telegu-Kannada script, just as the Tamil-Brahmi inscriptions of Tamil Nadu carry some features of the Tamil language. The date of these inscriptions is also not beyond dispute. Sarma cites the opinion of as competent a palaeographer as K.V. Ramesh, according to whom the Bhottiprolu relic casket inscriptions are "among the earliest known Brahmi writings of the Indo-Aryan dialect" (Sarma 1988: 51). Sarma (*ibid.*) adds that "the Buddhist base at Bhotttiprolu, if not the *stupa*, is quite older and as at Amaravati, might be of pre-Mauryan date".

It is difficult to argue in favour of the pre-Mauryan antiquity of any other Buddhist place in Andhra. The earliest phase of the *stupa* at the top of a hill at Vaddamanu near Amaravati has yielded NBP, but as Sarma (1988: 37) points out, there is lack of clarity regarding the details of the basal level.

However, there does not seem to be any doubt about the pre-Mauryan antiquity of Buddhism in Andhra, with corresponding implication for the beginning of its early historic period.

An indirect light on the problem of the beginning of the early historic period in Andhra is also thrown by the question of the location of *Asmaka Janapada* or one of the sixteen *Mahajanapadas* of the sixth century BC India. The location of the Asmaka/Assaka territory is not beyond doubt. The central point here is the story of the sage Bavari who, according to the Buddhist *Suttanipata,* was living on the bank of the Godavari near the territory of Alaka and in the midst of the territory of Asmaka/Assaka. B.S. Upadhyay (1991: 372-373) has pointed out that one of the relevant sources categorically associates Pratisthana or Paithan on the Godavari with the territory of Alaka. Further, both these territories were supposed to be in the *Andhaka* territory. The fact that Alaka was in the Andhaka territory with Pratisthana as its capital suggests that the ancient Andhaka territory does not necessarily mean some area in modern Andhra. However, it is probable that some parts of modern Andhra may fall within it. A little more positive clue is provided by the journey of Bavari's disciples who first went to Pratisthana and thence successively to Mahishmati and Ujjayini. This fact rules out the ancient cities of Adam and Pauni in Vidarbha being within the Asmaka territory. To go to Sravasti from the Adam or Pauni area in Vidarbha, nobody in the ancient times is likely to have taken the Paithan-Mahishmati-Ujjayini alignment. The route through Balaghat from Pauni would have been a far more direct route. The fact that Bavari's disciplies went first to Pratisthana makes me feel that the attempt of some scholars to identify the area of Kotilingala (Karimnagar) and Bodhan (Nizamabad), the two major ancient cities of northern Andhra, with the ancient Asmaka territory has to be taken seriously. The general alignment of the Godavari can easily be followed from the general area of these two places to Pratisthana via modern Nander. If we accept that the Asmaka/Assaka territory of the *Suttanipata* includes, at least partly, the modern Nizamabad and Karimnagar sections of modern Andhra, there is no difficulty in assuming that Andhra had witnessed the process of a major state formation by the sixth century BC. Thus, from all points of view, it makes sense to infer that the early historic period began in Andhra by c. 500 BC.

IV. THE POLITICAL REALITIES

The two minor rock edicts (Minor Rock Edict I and Minor Rock Edict II) and the fourteen rock edicts (Rock Edicts I to XIV) at Erragudi, Minor Rock Edict I at Rajulamandagiri, and a fragment of a pillar edict at Amaravati clearly suggest Andhra being a part of the Mauryan kingdom, a fact also testified by the reference to the Andhras being a part of Asokan dominions in Rock Edict XIII. Both Erragudi and Rajulamandagiri are in the Kurnool district. Amaravati is in the Krishna valley.

Attention may also be drawn to the reported find of an Asokan record in the Vidarbha area, to which A.M. Sastri drew attention some years ago. In addition, when one takes into consideration the location of Minor Rock Edict I at Jaugada in the Ganjam district of Orissa across the Andhra border from Srikakulam, one realizes that the Mauryan control of the Andhra territory is likely to have extended to all its areas. The coins of a number of kings, who are all post-Mauryan but pre-Satavahana, have been obtained, reputedly from stratified contexts at Kotilingala on the bank of the Godavari in the Nizamabad district. These kings are 'Gobhada', 'Kamavayasiri', 'Narana' and 'Samagopa' but nothing is known about them except their coins. Of roughly similar date is the reference to the king 'Kuberaka' in an inscription from Bhottiprolu, which is located lower down the Krishna valley from Amaravati. Even in the Amaravati area – Vaddamanu and Amaravati itself – there are inscriptional references to two kings: Somaka (Vaddamanu) and Kumariyya Sammliya (Amaravati). Whether all these references to the local kings suggest a political fragmentation of the Andhra area after the Mauryas is a difficult issue to settle. For instance, in the Krishna valley itself, between Amaravati and Bhottiprolu, there were apparently three local kings – Somaka (Vaddamanu), Kumariyya Sammliya (Amaravati) and Kuberaka

(Bhottiprolu). They were more likely to represent mere local powers who were tied probably to a broader political framework, the nature of which is still uncertain.

The find of a first-second century BC inscription, four copies of which were found inscribed on limestone pillars belonging to a *mandapa* or pavilion at Guntupalle, which is located in a hill range in the northern part of the West Godavari district, seems to throw some light on this political frame. The gist of the inscription is that *Cula Goma*, the scribe of *Maharaja Siri Sada* who bore the title 'the king of Kalinga and Mahisaka' donated this pavilion. There are different opinions regarding the date and even the reading of the inscription but there does not seem to be much disagreement about the suggestion that the Mahisaka territory may be placed in the lower Krishna valley. This would mean that at some point in the late centuries BC, the kings of Kalinga wielded some power in the lower Krishna valley. As Hanumantha Rao *et al.* (1998: 110) point out, several other 'Sada' rulers are known, apparently from the numismatic sources, in the Krishna valley. Their explanation is the following:

> Taking advantage of the political uncertainty in coastal Andhra, other members of the dynasty (following Kharavela's repeated expeditions) carved out for themselves small principalities and ruled till the Satavahanas took the region under their effective control.

The Satavahanas came in focus in the first century BC, if we accept the current preference for a late chronology for them. The issue, in fact, is by no means clear. If one ascribes the beginning of the Satavahanas towards the end of the first century BC, one has to postulate a long political vacuum in the Deccan after the Mauryas for about a hundred years. In any case, the coins of the first Satavahana king, Simuka, are said to occur at Kotilingala. Other Satavahana coins also occur in some abundance in many areas of Andhra including the Krishna-Godavari valley. The number of the inscriptions of their reign in Andhra seems to be rather limited, one of Vashisthiputra Pulumavi, son of Gautamiputra Satakarni from Amaravati, and another of Gautamiputra Vijaya Satakarni himself from Nagarjunakonda. The Nagarjunakonda inscription records the gift of a pillar in the king's sixth regnal year. The Amaravati inscription was not issued by the king but records 'the meritorious gift of a dharmachakra' at the western gate of the great *stupa* or *mahachaitya* by some householders. Whatever may be the direct epigraphic evidence of the Satavahana rule of Andhra, there is no reason to doubt the strength and consolidation of their rule in the region as far south as its coastline. It does not seem to be clear if the term *Satavahana-ahara*, which is supposed to denote a major administrative division of the Satavahana kingdom, was applied to a specific part or the whole of Andhra (cf. Prasad 1997: 26), or even denoted Andhra at all.

In the Krishna-Godavari valley, the power of the Satavahanas was replaced by that of the Ikshvaku dynasty in about AD 220/225. Several kings of this dynasty find mention in the inscriptions obtained from Nagarjunakonda or the ancient Vijayapuri, their capital. Sri Chantamula I, the founder of the dynasty, had the following successors till the end of the third century AD: Sri Virapurushadatta, Chantamula II and Virapurushadatta II. The decline of the Ikshvakus possibly began from about the end of the third or the early part of the fourth centuries AD. The immediate cause was the defeat of Virapurushadatta II by Simhavarman of the Pallava dynasty, which later became famous as the Pallava dynasty of Kanchipuram in northern Tamil Nadu. Based in the heart of the Krishna valley at Nagarjunakonda, the Ikshvakus are epigraphically proved to run an organized administrative system, which was based on the posts of *Mahadandanayakas* and *Mahasenapatis* in the army and the post of *Mahatalavarulu* dealing with the issue of law and order. Groups of villages were known under the terms of *Mahapanchika* and *Mahagrama*. The Ikshvakus have carved out a niche for themselves in Indian history for the magnificence of the excavated remains of their capital and the donations made principally by the ladies of the royal household to the cause of Buddhism. The gist of one such inscription is the following:

> The record is issued during the 6th regnal year of king Madhariputra Siri Virapurisadatta on the 10th day in the 6th fortnight of the rainy season. It registers the erection of a pillar by *Mahatalavari* Adavi Chamtisiri who was the daughter of Vashishtiputra Ikshvaku Siri Chamtamula, sister of Madhariputra Siri Virapurisadatta, wife of *Mahatalavara, Mahadandanayaka* Khamdavisakhamnaka of the Dhanaka family. The grant was made with due regard for both the families to which she belonged and for the attainment of herself, welfare and happiness in both the worlds (Hanumantha Rao *et al.* 1998: 138).

The kings performed Hindu rituals, including *Asvamedha* sacrifice.

The political situation of Andhra became more diverse after the Ikshvakus. The *Brihatphalayanas,* who are known principally from a single inscription, seem to have Koduru in the coastal section of the Krishna as their capital. The name of only one king – Jayavarman – is known. The *Salankayana* dynasty established itself in the Vengi area of West Godavari, and although they left behind several inscriptions, the dynasty died out by the early part of the 5th century AD. The dynasty of the *Ananda Gotrins,* who seem to be associated principally with the Guntur area, survived up to the 6th century AD or possibly later. The Pallavas, who ousted the Ikshvakus, established a kingdom in the Nagarjunakonda area and survived in the area till at least the invasion by Samudragupta in the mid-4th century AD. These developments were followed by the advent of a major dynasty – the Vishnukundin dynasty – in the early part of the 5th century AD. It continued to be powerful till the 7th century AD. Their main foes seem to be the Pallavas and the Vakatakas, against both of whom they were not wholly successful. In the map of the territorial boundaries of ancient Andhra, Mangalam (1986, map 1, p. 96) shows the Salankayana territory as around Vengi and Amaravati. In the same map, the Vishnukundin territory is shown spanning a much larger area covering both the Krishna-Godavari deltas, the Nagarjunakonda area, Vengi and the area as far east as Srikakulam. The early Pallava domain, as sketched in this map, covered the area from the south of the Pennar to the area of Amaravati.

Rising to power in the sixth century AD and remaining powerful till the last quarter of the 8th century, when their power was usurped by the Rashtrakutas, the Chalukyas of Badami with their centre at Aihole in modern Karnataka, exercised powerful influence on the political history of the period in Andhra. The most important Chalukyan invasion came from Pulakesin II in the early 7th century, establishing the Chalukyan control over the Vengi area. The governor appointed by Pulakesin II in Vengi set up, after Pulakesin II's death, a new house of the Chalukyas called the Eastern Chalukyas or the Chalukyas of Vengi, who remained the most powerful dynasty of Andhra till the 11th century. The link with the Badami area could not, however, be completely severed, because the successors of the Chalukyas of Badami, the Rashtrakutas, inherited the earlier ambition of the Badami Chalukyas to control Vengi. Towards the end of the Eastern Chalukyan dynasty, the Vengi area also bore the brunt of the Chola ambitions in the Andhra coast. The Chalukyas of Vengi operated within the orbits of the Pallavas of Kanchi, the Western Gangas of the Talakkad area of the Mysore plateau and the Rashtrakutas of the Deccan. They did not directly confront the Cholas of the Kaveri delta but from the late 10th century onward, they had to bear the brunt of the Chola pressure, till in about AD 1070 the Vengi Chalukyan and the Chola kingdoms were united in the person of the Chola king Kulottunga I. The Kakatiyas of Warangal rose to power in Andhra soon afterwards.

Originally the feudatories of the Rashtrakutas, the Kakatiyas became independent under Rudradeva in the mid-12th century AD. He established his capital at Warangal and extended his control over the coastal area, trying his power at the same time with the Yadavas of Devagiri near Aurangabad. Under Ganapatideva, who ruled from 1199 to AD 1262, the Kakatiyas annexed the coastal area to their kingdom and successfully launched an invasion against the Nellore area where a dynasty called the Telegu-Cholas, apparently a relic of the earlier Chola movements through the area, was ruling. His repeated invasions of Kalinga did not meet success. He was also defeated by the Pandyan king Jatavarman Sundara Pandya in the Nellore sector. Even under his successors, the Yadavas of Devagiri continued to remain an enemy. The feudatories of the Cuddapah region began to turn hostile, but success looked at the Kakatiyas in the area of Nellore, which was annexed to the Kakatiya kingdom. The fourteenth century began with the Muslim inroads under Alauddin Khalji from the direction of Devagiri, and by the end of the first quarter of this century, the Kakatiya rule in Andhra was over and gave way to a number of smaller states such as those of the Reddis of Kondavidu and other local powers. Such states were closely involved in the political struggles with the major Muslim powers of the general region – the Bahamanis of the Deccan, for instance. Once the Vijayanagara kingdom became paramount in the Bellary section of the Deccan and successfully developed territorial ambitions in all directions including the Andhra coast, Andhra fell under the Vijayanagara influence, but after its fall in the battle of Talikota in AD 1565, the Andhra region came to be controlled by the Qutub Shahi rulers of Golconda. Early in the 18th century, the Asif Jahis established a state with its centre in Hyderabad on the ruins of the Mughal rule in the Deccan.

Historically, Andhra thus was subject to the political forces emanating from a host of areas, beginning with the Ganga valley from where the Mauryas came. Andhra's interaction with the wider Deccan including both Maharashtra and Karnataka was constant, beginning with the Mauryas and ending with the Qutub Shahis. Kalinga was very much an integral part of the Andhra political universe. Among the ancient states of Tamil Nadu, the Pallavas of Kanchi were never far away, and in the course of fulfilling their ambition in the Deccan, the Pallavas cast their eyes, often successfully, on the riches of the Andhra coastal plain, especially the Krishna valley. The Pandyas of Madurai appeared rather late in the Andhra history, and although the Cholas also were somewhat late in the Andhra sequence of historical events, they left behind a more lasting impact in the sense that there was a joint Chalukya-Chola power which eventually gave way to the presence of a Chola group called the Velanadu Cholas as a local power in the coastal region. From our point of view, what is important to remember is that the ancient routes of Andhra had to conform to the political realities that we here have outlined.

The element of interaction between the different internal political boundaries of Andhra may also be a pointer in the direction in which the routes were likely to be aligned. We have already referred to the Map 1 of Mangalam's work, which outlines the territorial boundaries of the Salankayanas, Vishnukundins, and the early Pallavas.

The Eastern Chalukyan boundary does not extend to the west much beyond the Krishna delta but includes the Nagarjunakonda area and stretches in the east roughly up to the Visakhapatnam zone. In Mangalam's Map 2, the boundary of the Eastern Gangas of Orissa comes up to the borders of the Godavari delta but is oriented more towards Kalinga and beyond in Orissa. The Chalukyas of Kalyani in the Deccan pushed up to Pithapuram at the eastern border of the Godavari delta, but the most comprehensive boundary area in Andhra is that of the Kakatiyas. From an area considerably to the south of the Pennar and encompassing some parts of Madhya Pradesh, the Kakatiya boundary extends a little beyond Pithapuram. An interesting aspect of these political boundary lines drawn by Mangalam on the basis of the relevant historical sources is that these are all interacting lines. Only the smallest of these areas, the one represented by the Salankayanas, lies within the fold of the larger boundary lines. In all other cases the lines cut through the lines of the other boundaries, suggesting that the political boundary lines of Andhra had been interacting and fluid. However, all these boundaries at some point tried to incorporate the two deltas. The Salankayanas do not seem to have been successful in controlling the Godavari delta but they were in clear occupation of the Krishna delta, including Amaravati. The Vishnukundin area incorporated the Krishna as far upstream as Nagarjunakonda, and apart from controlling both the deltas, stretched as far east as Srikakulam. The Nagarjunakonda area was within the target of virtually all the political powers involved. Even the area covered by the early Pallavas whose orientation was to the west and the south, had the Nagarjunakonda area within their control. Except the two deltas of the Krishna and the Godavari and some area to the east of the Godavari, the Eastern Chalukyas could not ignore Nagarjunakonda either. The expansion of the Chalukyas of Kalyan or Kalyani was short-lived, although successful in its thrust up to the eastern border of the Godavari delta. The Eastern Gangas were clearly oriented towards the east. The only all-encompassing 'Andhra' state, comprising almost the whole of modern Andhra except its eastern part, was the domain of the Kakatiyas. The Mauryas and possibly the

Map 10. Some early historical sites in Andhra.

Satavahanas controlled the whole of it, and among the early dynasties, the Ikshvakus seem to be mostly focussed in the Krishna belt.

The maps 1 and 2 published in Mangalam's study of the historical geography of Andhra clearly suggest that the routes which came to Andhra had as their targets the Nagarjunakonda area, the Krishna-Godavari delta and the associated long coastline.

V. THE DISTRIBUTION OF HISTORICAL SITES

V.1. Adilabad-Karimnagar – Warangal-Khammam

Early historical sites seem to be well distributed in the Karimnagar district. Three of them have been excavated: Kotilingala, Dhulikottah and Peddavankur. There are also a number of explored early historical sites in this district: Bharatmunipetapadu, Kasipet, Rebbaladevapalli and Rayapatnam, the last of them located to the right of the bridge at the Godavari crossing on the Karimnagar-Nagpur road (Babu 1999: 20-22). V.V. Krishna Sastry (1983: 126-128) reported a few more explored sites in the Karimnagar district, including a fortified site (mud fortification) called Budigapalli. Its exact location is unreported but it is said to be near a hill range known as Valasagattu. Two fortified early historical sites of Karimnagar (Kotilingala and Dhulikattah) have been excavated, both by the Andhra Pradesh State Department of Archaeology. Lying within a rectangular mud fortification wall, Kotilingala (18-41N/79-47 E) measures more than 100 acres in extent, is c. 6 m high, and stands close to the south bank of the Godavari, not far to the left of the present Karimnagar-Mancherial alignment. The site is encircled on the east and the south by the Kapparaopetvagu, and on the Godavari front the fortification wall is said to be c. 300 m long. The brick structures disposed in a long row on the river-bank have been interpreted as a wharf. There are bastions at the four corners of the rampart and there are several gates in the cardinal directions. The burnt bricks used in the ancient structures of the site form the material of a large number of houses in the modern village. Iron slag and ore have been found in plenty in and around the site. A stone slab currently used in the fence wall of an agricultural field on the way to Manulagutta from Kotilingala carries a few second century BC label inscriptions in Brahmi. Another stone slab or pillar found in a field about a kilometre away carries the inscribed label *Nagagopiniyaka* in Brahmi of c. first century AD. It is apparent that there was a *stupa* near this site at Kotilingala. Krishna Sastry's map of the proto- and early historical sites of Andhra (Krishna Sastry 1983: frontispiece) shows a Buddhist *stupa* at

Pashigam, a little to the west of Kotilingala. Its position on the map does not suggest that it was associated with Kotilingala, although B. Subrahmanyam (1999: 4) refers to it as "a Buddhist monastic complex lying near Pashigaon, outside the fortified city of Kotilingala". In this context he mentions the find of "an apsidal *Chaityagriha* and *stupas*, belonging to the Theravada sect of Buddhism of 3rd century BC" at Pashigam. According to I.K. Sarma (1988: 116), the site is 5 km west of Kotilingala. V.V. Krishna Sastry's map also plots two Satavahana period sites in the Adilabad district which is to the north of the Karimnagar district. Interestingly, the alignment of these two sites, Pochampad and Kadambapur, falls more or less in a straight line to the north from Kotilingala. Another early historic site, Karnamamidi, has been noticed in the Adilabad district.

The Kotilingala excavations, basically unpublished, are supposed to have yielded, apart from a large number of coins, "fine black-and-red ware, red-slipped ware, tan ware, terracotta figurines, iron objects, beads and bangles" in the habitational complex. Four layers have been reputedly identified, and from the bottom upward, they show the following sequence:

1. pottery, silver punch-marked coins, uninscribed cast copper (rarely lead) coins with 'bull and flower' motif, and gold beads. This is pre-Satavahana and taken to date from the 6th century BC.
2. the successive occurrence of pre-Satavahana and Satavahana coins. This supposedly dates from the second century BC. The inscribed coins of the pre-Satavahana kings who are known only from this area belong to the kings Gobhada, Narana, Kamvayasa and Samagopa. These coins were succeeded by the Satavahana dynastic coins of Simuka.
3. the evidence of destroyed brick structures. No other category of evidence has been reported.
4. the coins of Gautamiputra Satakarni and Vashisthiputra Pulumavi Satakarni, and a silver Roman coin.

Dhulikatta, the second excavated major site of the Karimnagar belt and about 45/50 acres in extent, is also fortified by a mud rampart and stands on the bank of the Husainivagu nala. There was a gate in each cardinal direction. Excavations inside the fortification were conducted at the site of the southern gateway and in the centre. The gateway complex comprised a gate-house which was backed by guard-rooms The plan of the gate-house was broad on the outside, constricted in the middle, and broad again towards the guard-rooms. The central part had 'ambush niches', only one of which – the one on the west – has survived. It measured 1.2 m × 0.9 m, was dug into the wall and had a flight of steps leading to its floor. The guard-room complex comprised two rectangular halls separated by a 4.4 m wide pathway. The height of the mud rampart was about 5 m and it is possible that on the inside, it had a supporting brick wall with battlements built over it.

Five phases of building activity were traced in the centre, all these being followed by a single phase of hutments. There was a brick-built enclosure wall (26 m × 30.5 m and 2.6 m high and 0.8 m wide) laid over a rubble foundation. A doorway has been traced but very little else as the deposit is covered by the later structures. In the second phase, a structure was raised over a rammed earth foundation and showed a complex with rooms and a 50 cm wide entrance to the east. There were vertical chutes in the wall outside a room to hold wooden posts for possibly a terrace. The structures of the third phase comprised "spacious halls, with floors paved with brick", granaries, wells and multi-storeyed buildings. The plan of the buildings of this phase comprised four rectangular halls on four sides with an open courtyard in the middle. There was a square brick-built well in the compound which had also two brick-built granaries in the shape of inverted cones dug in the ground. The buildings were plastered smooth with lime in the fourth phase. The fifth phase was marked by structures made of reused bricks. This gave way to apparently artisan's quarters (makers of beads and bangles), which were rectangular or oval hutments.

The excavated *stupa* at Dhulikatta lies across a nala, close to the fortified mound. At the base, it was initially a 2 m high solid drum encasing the circular dome. The dome rose 5 m above it and had a *harmika* and *chhatra* on top. The drum was enclosed by walls on four sides and the space between the circular drum and the walls was filled with earth and paved with bricks at the top, thus creating an upper circumambulatory path or *pradakshinapatha*. The dome was constructed in alternate levels of brick and grit (*moorum*) and made hemispherical without the use of any wedge-shaped brick. The fragments of the *chhatri* (umbrella) have been found in the excavations, and the inscribed fragments of a sandstone circular box found near the *harmika* might have contained the *stupa* relics. In the second phase, which has been ascribed to the second century BC, the drum circle was enlarged and the *ayaka* platform was raised at the four cardinal points. The diameter of the enlarged *stupa* was 36 m. Forty-seven carved *ayaka* slabs of marble adorned the dome, a common motif being that of *Muchulinda* snake protecting the Buddha who is symbolised by two feet. Among the other motifs, one notes two devotee couples sitting with folded hands on either side of *dharmachakra* or 'wheel of law'. Donors' records occur on some slabs. The beginning of this *stupa* is not later than the Mauryan period; it may even be somewhat earlier.

At a distance of only 2 m from the *stupa* to its northeast, there is a row of monastic cells (3.3 m × 3.5 m), whose 90 cm wide doors open on to a verandah running along the entire length of the row. The verandah and the floors of the cells were brick-paved and the roof was covered by tiles.

Dhulikatta is a remarkably neat and an almost archetypal early historic fortified city with a *stupa* not far from the rampart walls. The beginning of the complex has been traced to the third century BC. The Satavahana coins appear to have been abundant at the site. A road paved with rubble and veneered with grit and sand has been traced through the excavated southern gateway of the site. The walls of the monastic cells comprised two single-brick rows of walls, with a gap of about 42 cm between them. This gap was filled with brickbats and grit. Apart from achieving an economic use of bricks, this possibly was intended to keep the inside of the rooms a little cool in summer.

The third major excavated site in Karimnagar is Peddabankur, although it measures a little more than 10 acres and has no fortification. Its importance lies in the fact that it has yielded three large walled enclosures with traces of houses of burnt brick or mud over rubble foundation, cisterns, wells and a covered drainage arrangement. Enclosure-I (16.8 m × 15.8 m) was enclosed within 0.65 m wide walls, with an entrance in the middle of the southern wall. This has been dated in the first-second century BC. There was a terracotta ring-well outside the south-western corner of this enclosure. Enclosure-II (30 m × 40 m) was found to have a 2.5 m wide entrance at the north-eastern corner. Enclosure-III (30.89 m × 30.8 m) had a 2 m wide surrounding wall. Enclosure-II yielded several thousand Satavahana coins. Except the terracotta ring-well outside Enclosure-I, the number of brick-built wells excavated in Peddabankur is twenty-two, one of them being square in plan and the rest round. The round wells were made of wedge-shaped bricks. A covered drain, made of three courses of bricks on either side with a space of 12 cm on a brick-laid floor between them, was excavated for the length of 11.5 m. The drain was covered by bricks throughout and had side-vents on both sides at regular intervals. Brick-built cisterns (0.8 m × 0.8 m with floors paved by bricks and/or grit) seem to be another feature of Peddabankur.

Interestingly, two brick-built structures, one (5.3 m × 4.9 m) about 100 m away to the west of Enclosure-III and the other (2 m × 2.5 m) about 50 m away to the east of the same enclosure, have been advocated as temples. The second structure had a flight of steps to its west, and while clearing these steps, a Neolithic axe made of dolerite came to light. It does not necessarily follow, as the excavator suggests (Krishna Sastry 1983: 144), that this axe was placed inside and worshipped.

Peddabankur yielded a large number of antiquities, including two inscribed terracotta seals, a hoard of silver punch-marked coins, many Satavahana coins, and several silver Roman coins. A seated female figure made of kaolin clay and holding a bunch of fruits is a major find among the terracotta figurines obtained from the site.

Krishna Sastry's map shows a Buddhist site called Hanumakonda near the modern town of Warangal, the headquarter of the district of the same name. However, he does not discuss the site, nor is any information available on this site in the other relevant publications. The only early historic site mentioned in Warangal seems to be Polakonda in the Jangoan taluk. This covers about 25 acres and has three phases of occupation: pre-Satavahana, Satavahana and mediaeval. A brick-built cistern has been located in the Satavahana level and in the pre-Satavahana level dated to the second century BC, if not earlier, there is an inscribed coin in potin, on which the inscription reads *Mahatalavarasa Vijasamikasa Seva Sabha*. The same legend occurs on a terracotta seal from Peddabankur. One is not sure if Krishna Sastry's ascription of this coin to the pre-Satavahana level (Krishna Sastry 1983: 129-130), and not to the Satavahana level, is right.

On the whole, it appears that the Adilabad-Karimnagar-Warangal districts of Andhra had a fair number of early historic sites including Buddhist remains. There is a comparative lack of them in Warangal but that may be due to the lack of exploration in this sector. Slightly southward, in the Khammam district, a Buddhist religious site has been reported at Nelakondapalli (Sarma 1988: 116; Babu 1999: map of the Satavahana-Ikshvaku sites in Andhra Pradesh, site no. 20). The site, 20 km south-west of Khammam, lies on the highway between Khammam and Bezwada. Excavations here (Babu 1999: 46-47) have brought to light a three-tiered spoked *stupa* with *ayaka* platform and *pradakshinapatha*. Completed in the Ikshvaku period, the *stupa* was enlarged in the Vishnukundin period. The remains of two structures with drains and soak-pits were found in the habitational mound. The *mahastupa* of Nelakondapalli (17-06.678 N/ 80-04.106 E) is 189 m in circumference and built on a wheel-shaped plan. Next to Amaravati, this is the largest *stupa* in Andhra. It has entrances in the four cardinal directions and its components are a lower *pradakshinapatha*, a circular drum with *ayaka* platforms and a dome. The height of the *stupa* is c. 16 m. It was constructed in the third century AD by the Ikshvaku kings and later on patronised by the Vishnukundins. The excavations also revealed a monastic complex with 77 cells, a central hall with nine limestone images of the Buddha in standing posture, a miniature votive *stupa*, a bronze idol of *Padmapani* and several coins of the Ikshvakus and the Vishnukundins. To the northeast of the *stupa* there is a large naturally formed reservoir.

V.2 Nizamabad – Medak – Rangareddi – Hyderabad – Mahboobnagar – Nalgonda

Bodhan (18-39.811 N/77-53.132 E) is known to be a major, though unexcavated, site near Nizamabad. Krishna Sastry (1983: 128) reports the following on the site.

> The entire town is now enclosed by ancient mud ramparts, rising to a height of 9 to 12 m on the west of the village, and a double fortification interned by a deep moat. The inner fortification encloses a high mound, where the historical citadel must have existed. On top of the mud fortification the author has collected early historical potsherds by which it could be surmised that the mud ramparts were raised during the post-Satavahana period or the early ramparts were reinforced during the mediaeval times, digging out early historical habitation in the process. Bodhan was also the earlier capital of the Chalukyas of Vemulavada during the reign of Arikesari II (AD 930-955).

In 2006 we found the site much destroyed. In the lower section of a part of the supposed fortification wall, there were bits of black-and-red ware and red-slipped pottery.

Babu (1999: 22) reports another early historic site, Vadaluru, in the Nizamabad district. Located in the Kamareddi taluk, the site has a mud rampart (6 to 9 m high), yielding inside it early historic pottery and Satavahana period bricks.

In the Medak-Sangareddi belt, the most well-known site is Kondapur (17-32.586N/78-00.815 E). The site, about 60 acres in extent and unfortified, is now seen to lie between the embankment of a tank and a local *nala*. The tank embankment seems to protect the site. The tank itself lies to the southeast of the site. The *nala* seems to encircle the site on the north and the east. The site museum houses black-and-red pottery and the other types of early historic pottery, some with early religious symbols such as *triratna*, fish, *nandipada*, etc. The museum shows a large number of coins and sprinklers of red polished ware. The site has also yielded a large number of terracotta figures including *lajja-gouri* images. It is basically an undisturbed site at the foot of a low rocky hill, on the top of which the site museum is located. Another low ridge can be seen at some distance.

The whole area between the site and the distant hill is open, verdant, and undulates into the distance. In the excavations conducted in the 1940s, the most important category of excavated structures was a group of brick-built underground chambers with brick-paved floors. These yielded coins and their moulds, inscribed seals, semi-precious stone beads and gold objects. Figures made of kaolin clay are an important feature of the antiquities from the site. An ivory comb and a clay 'Roman' bullae are among its other antiquities.

In the Medak district, Rekulapadu (150 m × 489 m) in the Sadasivapet taluk is another early historic site (Babu 1999: 52). This is located in the valley of the Manjeri River.

Three successive phases of occupation from the first century BC to the second century AD have been found here. Sarma (1988: 115) reports a Buddhist site called Chaitanyapuri in the Hyderabad district without giving the details. Among the early historic sites of Mahboobnagar, Yapaladevipadu (c. 20/25 acres) near Peddamarpur seems to have yielded circular and rectangular brick-built platforms for pounding grain, evidence of the manufacture of tiles, wells, and possibly the evidence of a fortification (Babu 1999: 57). Another relevant site of this district is Kyathur near Alampur (Babu 1999: 42-43)

The most important Buddhist site excavated in the Nalgonda district is Phanigiri (17-25.640 N/79-28.343 E), about 35 km from Suryapet on the Hyderabad-Vijaywada highway. The site lies on the top of a somewhat flat and undulating low hill about 150 m high from the level of the surrounding fields. The excavated features that one could observe in 2006 were a monastic complex associated with at least two *stupa* remains and an apsidal *chaitya*. In the *mahastupa*, the circular dome is encased by decorated marble slabs. The decoration consists principally of medallions. There are many fragments of sculptural pieces of the Amaravati style, and in the small modern store-room on the hill-top, one can observe regular panels of sculptural reliefs which were parts of the *stupa* embellishment. More sculptures are said to lie in a store-room below the hill. The site was also used in the later periods and the villagers point out the ruins of a Shiva temple. The complex as a whole overlooks a fertile plain dotted with similar hills on the horizon.

The published technical details are the following: the *mahastupa* (18 m diameter) has the plan of a spoked wheel and erected possibly over a brick platform. Each of the four *ayaka* platforms measures 4 m × 1.5 m and the one on the west shows the stumps of five lime-stone *ayaka* pillars. The drum and the *ayaka* platforms were plastered with lime and decorated with sculptured panels. The remains of a stone-pillared congregration hall with entrance on the northern side have been traced to the south of the *stupa*. Some of the sculptured panels found in the debris of this hall bear inscriptions in Brahmi of the first to the third centuries AD. There are also remains of monasteries in this complex. Three such monasteries have been identified. Many Satavahana and Ikshvaku coins have been found in the monastic cells, each of which measures 2.7 m square. One of the label inscriptions refers to the founder of the Ikshvaku dynasty, Chantamula. Further excavations at the site dated its earliest phase to the first century BC. It continued to flourish till the Vishnukundin times in the fourth-fifth century AD. Two apsidal *chaityas* to the north of the great *stupa* were possibly covered with tiled roof supported by wooden pillars. A room (3 m × 7 m) between these two *chaityas*, which yielded stone idols, has been supposed to be the room of the chief priest of the complex. Some large inscriptions and many sculptured reliefs have been found in the excavations at Phanigiri and are awaiting detailed studies (*IAR* 2001-2002).

The site of Gajulabanda, which is about 5 km away from Phanigiri, goes back to the first-second century BC and shows a *stupa* and monastery complex with two phases of constructional activity. Sarma (1988: 118-119) reports a few more Buddhist sites in the Nalgonda district: Kokireni, Thirumalgiri (in the Phanigiri area?) and Vardamankot.

Yeleswaram in the Nalgonda district is located on the bank of the Krishna. The most significant excavated remains of the Satavahana period at the site are a bathing *ghat* on the Krishna and a *mandapa* or pavilion. In the case of the bathing *ghat*, a flight of steps (each step 0.465 m wide) went down to the Krishna. The *mandapa* (148.8 m × 40.3 m) was a huge structure supported by limestone columns. This is Period II of the site, Period I being megalithic. The excavated coins and terracottas put Period II in the first and second centuries AD. Period III has been placed in the period of the Ikshvakus in the third century AD. The excavated religious structures include a *chaitya* hall and two *stupas*, one having *ayaka* platforms. Covered drains seem to be a feature of the residential complex of this period.

V.3. Kurnool – Anantapur – Cuddapah – Chittoor – Nellore – Prakasham

The most important excavated settlement site of the Kurnool region is Satanikota (Ghosh 1986) on the bank of the Tungabhadra, dated between the middle of the first century BC and the middle of the third century AD.

The rampart, gate and moat of this fortified settlement came up during its first structural phase. As it followed the natural contours, the fort was irregular in shape. The 3.2 m wide main wall of the rampart used stone blocks set in mud mortar and was fronted by a 1.45 m wide facing of burnt brick. There was a 3 m wide burnt brick pavement on the inner side of the main rampart wall. The moat (3.2 m deep and 4.25 m wide) was dug into the bed rock with embankments of boulder and Cuddapah stone slabs at its outer edge. There was possibly a drawbridge over the moat, and the structural complexes inside showed rectangular halls.

The Asokan Minor Rock Edict I site of Rajula Mandagiri is located in the Pattikonda taluk of the Kurnool district, on the Pattikonda-Adoni road. The edict has been engraved on a rocky open surface on the top of a low, rocky hill. It lies beside what seems to be a well hewn into the rock. The edict is open to the sky, without any protective cover. The well is partly overlooked by a *Pipul* tree which now almost covers the mouth of the well. There are two modern Shiva temples on the same hill (*Ramalingeshwara* and *Bhimalingeshwara* temples). In the dry months, the so-called well dries up, and, according to the villagers, one can see the opening of a horizontally cave. It appears that this was a cult spot where people used to congregrate, and the inscription was engraved on the bedrock open to the sky above the mouth of this cave. There are fragments of mediaeval sculptures in the area, testifying to a long tradition of sacredness of the spot.

The Asokan Minor Rock Edicts I and II and the set of 14 rock edicts at Erragudi (15-12.600N/77-34.616 E) are engraved on a series of boulders on the top of a c. 100 m high rocky hill, itself part of a low range of hills. The place is marked on the Archaeological Survey of India board on the Gooty-Pattikonda road as Jonnagiri (15-14 N/77-35 E). The place falls in the Kurnool district and is not far from Rajula Mandagiri. There is no trace of habitational mounds in the vicinity of these two locations of Asokan edicts. It is, however, possible that the local agricultural operations have razed such mounds, if any, to the plain level fields and that only an intensive surface survey in the area can yield results.

Veerapuram in the Nadikoktur taluk of Kurnool lies in the Tungabhadra belt. Its early historic period follows the earlier neolithic-chalcolithic phase and is noted for the excavated remains of a number of temples which have been divided into two structural phases. The earlier phase, made entirely of bricks, is placed in the third century AD. The temple group lay within a wall and the individual temple plan was square, approached by a step and stood on a simple basement.

There is report of a Buddhist site at Ketavaram in Kurnool (Sarma 1988: 118). Babu (1999: 27-28) reports the find of a square brick temple in the excavations at Chabole on the bank of the Bhavanasi in the Nandikoktur taluk of Kurnool. The site also yielded an inscription of the second century AD.

Sarma (1988: 111) refers to three such sites in the Cuddapah district: Adapur, Peddachepalle and Pushpagiri. In addition, Babu (1999) refers to the excavations at Nandalur and the explored site of Dommarandiyal. The Nandalur excavations (Babu 1999: 46) brought to light miniature votive *stupas*, an apsidal *chaityagriha* and a monastery. About 1650 Satavahana coins were found along with two inscribed potsherds of the first-second century AD. Hanumantha Rao *et al.* (1998: 125) refers to an inscription engraved on a *Buddhapada* slab from the site. This donatory inscription of a certain Vinayadhara also belongs to the first-second century AD. The site (14-15.834 N/79-07.889 E) is located on the northern bank of the non-perennial Cheayyeru River, which it overlooks from the slope of a hill. There are also many hills on the other side of the river.

The lone early historic site excavated so far in the Anantapur district is Sasenikota in the Pargi area where, on the basis of pottery, the site has been placed in the post-Satavahana period of c. third century AD (*IAR* 2001-2002: 2). Babu (1999: 21) refers to Peddavadugu in the Gooti taluk of the district, which has yielded both coins and pottery of the early historic period.

In the Chittoor district the most important early historic site seems to be Gudimallam (13-36.191 N/79-34.596 E). On the basis of his excavations, Sarma (1994) distinguishes two phases in the history of this *Shivalinga*. The first phase is dated to the Mauryan period with the help of stratigraphy and associated objects like pottery and punch-marked coin.

> It was found fixed within two circular *pithas* at the centre of a square *vastumandala* drawn on the levelled ground.... A closely set three-barred rail, *vedika*, segregated the deity from the habitation (Sarma 1994: 50).

In the second phase, dated c. first-second century AD, a brick-built apsidal temple was raised at the place without disturbing the railing. This arrangement continued till the seventh-eighth century AD.

Apart from the image of a *Yaksha* holding up the *linga*, perhaps the only example of the representation of a *Yaksha* in association with a *Shivalinga* anywhere in the sub-continent, a distinctive feature is the presence of a granitic unadorned railing enclosure within which the *linga* is placed. This is remarkably similar to the railing around the Mauryan pillar at Sarnath and almost clinches the issue of its Mauryan date.

It appears that no Buddhist site has yet been reported from the Nellore district, but that this may be due to the lack of exploration is suggested by the discovery of two early historic sites in the coastal area of Nellore by K.P. Rao (personal information, and visit to the sites): Survepalli (14-17.514 N/79-57.934 E) and Puduru (13-53.924 N/79-55.029 E). Survepalli measures roughly 200 m square and has a mud fortification with a c. 10 m wide moat. In K.P. Rao's excavations at the site in 2006, the sequence began with a 50-cm thick layer of neolithic occupation, and it was topped successively by the black-and-red ware level and the early historic level. This is the first occurrence of the neolithic in this part of the coastal Andhra. The black-and-red ware continued to occur in the early historic level, which also saw the use of red-slipped pottery, and plain red and grey wares. The fortification could not be firmly dated but it is likely that it went back to the second century BC. To the north-northeast of the site there is a very large swampy depression. The port of Krishnapatnam is at a distance of about 15 km from the site. The site of Puduru is occupied by the modern village, and thus one can see the cultural debris lying around in the outskirts of the village. Black-and-red ware, red-slipped ware, plain red ware, rouletted ware, conical jars, etc. have been collected from the site by K.P. Rao. There is also report of a Roman gold coin from here. The site is about 20 km from the coast and located on the road which leads to the old port of Durgarajupatnam from the modern Nellore-Chennai highway. Durgarajupatnam is a pre-modern port with historical connection with Dutch traders in the 17th century.

From the point of view of the Buddhist remains, the Prakasam district is a richer area in comparison with the Rayalseema districts of Kurnool, Anantapur, Cuddapah and Chittoor and even in comparison with the coastal district of Nellore. Sarma (1988: 119-120) reports the following sites in Prakasam: Chandavaram, Chhinna Ganjam, Dupadu, Kanuparti, Konidena, Kukutapalle, Malekonda, Peddaganjam, Ramatirtham and Vellacheruvu. Of these, some data are available on Chandavaram, Chhinna Ganjam, Dupadu, Ramathirtha and Malekonda. The excavations at Chandavaram in the Podili taluk revealed three monastic complexes, a 'great *stupa*' and a few rock-cut caves, among others. There was also possibly a pillared *mandapa*. The site dates from the second century BC to the second century AD, and there are donatory inscriptions. Chhinna Ganjam has yielded early historic pottery, brickbats and limestone fragments, and a fragmentary inscription of c. second century AD (Hanumantha Rao *et al.* 1998: 128), which mentions the Satavahana king Gautamiputra. Dupadu is located near Chandavaram and limited excavations have led to the finds of *stupa* panels and other early historic material. A donor's record is found engraved in the script of the first century AD (Hanumantha Rao *et al.* 1998: 124). The Buddhist remains at Ramatirtham are located on the Durgakonda and Gurubhaktakonda hills and have been found associated with clay sealings and a Satavahana lead coin. The Brahmi legend mentioning the king *Sivamaka Vijaya* is inscribed in the script of the first century AD (Hanumantha Rao *et al.* 1998: 128). Malekonda is a series of rock-cut caves in the Kandukuru taluk.

> The high hills (offshoots of Eastern Ghats) are of weathered Khondalite. The hillock is peculiar and almost unique in this area. It is full of big and lofty crags affording extensive shelters in many places. Frontages and stepped approaches, etc. indicated temporary occupation perhaps seasonally by the wandering ascetics (Sarma 1988: 92).

According to Sarma, a cave locally known as Parvati-guha may contain old rock beds. A Prakrit inscription in the Brahmi script of the third century BC records the gift of a cave by Sri Vira Sresthi, son of Nanda Sresthi of Aravahala or Aruvala lineage. It has been interpreted that the Sresthi or the merchant concerned was somebody of the Tamil lineage. By the side of a small stream called Upputeru, Uppugundur near the coast is another Buddhist site in the Prakasam district (Hanumantha Rao *et al.* 1998: 183). Several images of the Buddha and a large inscribed pillar of c. third century AD have been brought to light. The inscription states that it was dated in the 19th regnal year of the Ikshvaku king Madhariputra Sri Virapurushadatta and recorded the gift of a merchant called Samghila who was joined in this by various members of his family including his mother. The gift was made to the *mahastupa* in an unspecified *pattana* or port town. Although the name of this port is not mentioned, it is probable that Uppugendur was that port town.

V.4. Guntur and Krishna

These two districts form in a sense the core of the early historic Andhra. The sites which have long been parts of our general consciousness regarding early Buddhism and art history of Andhra – Nagarjunakonda, Amaravati, Jagayyapeta, Ghantasala, Goli, Bhottiprolu, and others – mostly fall in this part of the Krishna valley. The Krishna flows between hills from the area around Sri Sailam to the area around Nagarjunakonda, and having come out of the hills, it takes an eastward course, and moves in the direction of the sea after taking a northward loop almost up to Jaggayyapeta. After this, it goes to its delta in a wide curve, and one may say that Vijayawada/ Bezwada is a major point in this curve. The Krishna estuary is not as wide as that of the Godavari, which means that the coastline in this section is less interrupted by river mouths.

Two sites, Nagarjunakonda or ancient Vijayapuri and Amaravati or ancient Dhenukataka, dominate over the rest. Apart from being noted religious and art centres, they are also major cities.

The importance of Nagarjunakonda as an early historic city has been well expressed by K.V. Soundararajan (2006: 3) in the second volume of 'Nagarjunakonda report' edited by him:

> At the height of its prosperity in the middle of the third century AD, the valley had seemingly a monastic community of four thousand strong, besides those of sacerdotal Hinduism and a requisite civic and military population, inhabiting this capital city of Vijayapuri. The fortified citadel area near the river on the west and craft communities and industrial units in sectors SII, SIII and SIV, among which, as in Sector SII, a gold-smith's workshop revealing touch-stones, tong, weights, ornamental moulds, slabs etc. *in situ* were significant; the two citadel gates on the east and west, the latter elaborately planned with guard-rooms, the postern gate on the north and heavy rubble stone as well as plastered brick retainer walls on the river side; temples to a variety of gods like *Ashtabhuja* Vishnu, Pushpabhadrasvami Siva Sarvadeva, Karttikeya and Devasena, Kubera and Buddhist Hariti and many other affiliations ...; the large number of pillared halls on the roadside, for the city gentry to meet and spend their leisure in rest and entertainment, which punctuated various road systems of the city; had all, indeed, after the unprecedented example outside India of the excavations at volcano-smothered Pompeii in Italy, around almost the same era, been the most challenging assignment for Indian archaeology.

What lends further significance to the city, which Soundararajan portrays in the above-mentioned statement, is that it carried within it a history of only about a hundred years, from c. AD 210 to c. 310/c. AD 325. So, the picture of ancient Indian civic life that is portrayed by this site can be appreciated in more or less a compact time-frame.

The citadel of Nagarjunakonda (914.4 m × 609.6 m) was about 16 m high from the level of the plain and partly used the height of a hillock. The mud rampart of the first phase (80 m basal width) was expanded by a burnt brick wall (9 to 14 m thick) in the second phase. The moat around was 12 m deep and 74 to 132 m wide. The main gates were on the east and the west, and there was a smaller and simpler gate on the north. Near the eastern gateway, there were a plastered cistern and barracks and stables. The dwelling complex outside the citadel shows careful and systematic planning, complete with a large number of public places (cf. bathing *ghat*, pavilions on the river-bank, etc. Among more than

30 excavated Buddhist complexes, Site 5 or the monastery of the Bahusrutiya sect (identified by an inscription) offers a good example:

> It was a fairly big monastic unit consisting of a main *stupa*, *stupa-chaitya* and a Buddha-*chaitya* and a three-winged vihara, encasing a pillared *mandapa* in the centre. This was the construction of Bhattidevi, mother of Ehavala Chantamula, in his second regnal year, for the use of Bahusrutiya sect. The main *stupa* was of 49′ diameter, while the *ayaka* platforms on four cardinal directions measure 13′6″ × 4′6″. The inner spokes were eight in number while the outer one were twelve. The thirty-six pillared *mandapa* in the centre measured 53′ 6″ square. The cells of the vihara measured 8′6″ × 6′6″. The entrance of the monastic cell was uniformly 1′9″ (Soundararajan 2006: 166)

The Brahmanical temples numbered about nine. The Sarvadeva temple on the bank of the river has been considered to be "the most magnificent of the buildings excavated at Nagarjunakonda" (Soundararajan 2006: 209) with its three large pillared pavilions. A Sanskrit inscription found inside records its construction by Elisri, the commander of the Ikshvakus in commemoration of a victory and dedicated for the use of gods as *Sarvadevadhivasa* ('abode of all gods').

The publication of the excavation report on the historical structures and other aspects of Nagarjunakonda has been an outstanding event in Indian archaeology, and it will be years before the information contained in this report is properly assimilated and its historical context understood in depth.

Amaravati is a much earlier site, coeval, as we have argued earlier, with the beginning of the early historic period in Andhra. The city-site of Amaravati (Dhenukataka), which lies a little away from the *stupa* site, has not been horizontally excavated, and thus the picture from there is not in any way detailed (cf. Chakrabarti 1997: 239). The arm of the city fortification (16-34.520 N/80-20.595 E – co-ordinates taken at the southwestern corner of the fortification) is still 3-4 m high and more or less well preserved, being covered by thorny bushes. The modern Achampet-Amaravati road cuts through the fortification.

The ancient site of Jaggayyapeta (16-53.225N/80-06.381 E) lies on a hill-top near a large naturally formed reservoir, which is situated roughly to the north of the site. The ridge on the top of which the site is located is a part of a long chain of hills which here have ensconced a fertile and wooded valley. The modern settlement of Jaggayyapeta is located in this valley. The main component of the site, as it stands today, is the drum of a *stupa* which was originally covered with sculptural reliefs of marble slabs, at least on the ground level. There are also traces of a *pradakshinapatha* around the drum at this level. There are four small projections in the four cardinal directions, marking the spots of *ayaka* platforms. There are scatters of displaced marble slabs all over the site and some of them bear the signs of sculptural reliefs. Interestingly, there are signs of burnt brick debris all around. It appears that the *stupa* was associated with a large monastic complex. There are also a few pillar fragments. As far as we could determine, this is the only surviving mound now at Jagayyapeta. The earlier publications suggest the existence of more mounds and structures.

Nagarjunakonda and Amaravati are in the Guntur district, whereas Jaggayyapeta is in the Krishna district. Bhottiprolu (16-05.970 N/80-46.874 E) falls in the Guntur district. The ancient brick drum of the *stupa* is clearly visible, but that is all that survives at the site now. Fragments of marble pillars are scattered around. There is a water body to the south of the site. The local Archaeological Survey of India compound seems to contain some material of the *stupa*. Sarma (1988: 30-56) has undertaken a detailed study of the Bhottiprolu *stupa*, subjecting its construction and the palaeography and content of the relic casket inscriptions. His conclusion is that these inscriptions can securely be dated in the third century BC. Goli is in Guntur and virtually nothing of the site remains, the sculptures having been all removed from this site of c. third century AD. Kesanapalle is also in Guntur, on the bank of the Naguleru River. Excavations have yielded the remains of a *stupa* of the first-second century BC and miscellaneous remains including a *Buddhapada*. Vaddamanu is near Amaravati with the Buddhist ruins located on the top of the two hillocks known as Chinnakonda and Peddakonda. The goes back to the third century BC and possesses NBP. More than 200 inscribed potsherds were found ranging in date from the third century BC to the third century AD. The inscriptions from the site are essentially donors' records. The summit of a hillock at Rentala in Guntur showed the remains of a *stupa* and monastic cells. Apart from the broken limestone slabs once decorating the *stupa* body, the most interesting find here is an inscription of the third century AD. According to this inscription dedicated in the 5th regnal year of Vashisthiputra Siri Chantamula, Samghila, a merchant of the city of Ganjikuta (identified with Peddaganjam in the Prakasam district) who was accompanied by his wife Samgha, son Chutidharasiri (who was also a merchant) and his wife, daughters, cousins and friends erected a stone *ayaka* pillar at the Buddha *samgha* of Upendragirivardhamana in the midst of *viharas* in the village of Tuvara for his own longevity and continued success (Hanumantha Rao *et al.* 1998: 187). Nanduru is another site in Guntur district (Hanumantha Rao *et al.* 1998: 188-189). It has yielded a pot in a brick casement. The pot is inscribed in the script of the third century AD and contains the corporeal relics of possibly a husband and a wife. More sites occur in the Guntur district. Sites such as Takkellapadu (broken pillar, first century BC inscription) and Buddham and Nandayapalem (two contiguous sites of c. first century AD) underscore the possibility of the discovery of many more Buddhist sites in the Guntur region.

Ghantasala (16-10.195 N/80-56.934) or the ancient Kantakasaila (Ptolemy's Kantakossyla) is a famous site of the Krishna district, not far from Masulipatnam. That it was an important port is suggested by the local finds of Roman gold coins and ship-marked coins of the Satavahanas. The donors' records from the place mention, among others, the gift of an *ayaka* pillar by "Uttaradata, wife of *Mahanavika* Sivaka". That it continued as a port is suggested by the name of a local temple as the temple of *jaladhiswara* (lord of the seas). In the mediaeval period, Ghantasala was known as *Chola-Pandya-Pattana* (Hanumantha Rao *et al.* 1998: 130; Subrahmanyam 1999: 53-55)). The sculptured slabs and *stupa* railings kept in the local museum show that there was a major *stupa* here in the early centuries AD. However, the sculptural relief of a *mithuna* couple on a pillar suggests that this particular sculptural piece dates from the first century BC. The *stupa* site which we found covered by tarpaulin is situated inside the modern museum compound.

Outside the modern settlement of Ghantasala is Ernamadudibba (16-10.298N/80-56.054 E). Recent excavations here have revealed a large structural complex which included, apart from an assortment of walls, at least three structures in a row, the one in the centre being the largest. There is a brick-built enclosure in the centre of each of these structures. It appears that here we are faced with a temple complex where the figure of the Buddha or *stupa* was kept in the centre of each of the three structures. There are also scatters of marble slab fragments at the site.

About 9 km to the east of Jaggayyapeta, Gumadidurru has revealed a *mahastupa*, votive *stupas*, an apsidal *chaityagriha*, Buddha images, seals with Buddhist creed and other inscribed material ranging in date from the second century AD to the mediaeval period (Hanumantha Rao *et al.* 1998: 131; Subrahmanyam 1999: 55-56)). Near Yerupalem, Alluru in the Krishna district had a large monastery of the Purvasaila sect of the Buddhists. Of the two inscriptions of c. third century AD found at the place, one records some gifts to the Buddhist monastery of the place by a number of persons including an unspecified king and an unspecified *mahatalavara*. Apart from some specified measures of land, the gift comprised "500 cows, 64 bullock carts, 40 servants, some cauldrons, especially brass cauldrons, 4 bronze vessels, some hand lamps of the vadala fish shape, some yenak lamps, a tank in the vicinity of *Ataragiri* and one thousand *purana* and *kahapanas* as a permanent endowment" (Hanumantha Rao 1998: 184-186). Gudivada yielded four relic caskets, suggesting the existence of a *stupa* site (Babu 1999: 38; Subrahmanyam 1999: 55).

V.5. West Godavari – East Godavari

Peddavegi (16-48.849 N/81-06.367 E) or the ancient Vengi, the capital of the Salankayanas and the Vishnukundins, is an important site of the West Godavari district. The site is about 10 km to the north of Elluru. A part of the fortification of the site seems to have survived. The excavated and conserved features that one can observe today comprised two large structural complexes. One of them seems to be a *stupa* built on a platform of burnt bricks. This complex has four subsidiary shrines at four corners. The second complex is apparently a shrine built on a platform with four off-sets on the larger side and three off-sets on the smaller side. These off-sets could also have been niches. Here also one notices four subsidiary shrines with a central enclosure, which may be either a temple sanctum or an enclosure meant for the figure of the Buddha. The site is located in the rich, fertile tract of coastal Andhra to the north of Elluru. There are three stratigraphic phases of the site: fourth-fifth century AD, mid-fifth to end sixth century AD, and end sixth to early seventh century AD. Over an area of 6 sq km, there are extensive ruins including a fortified township. An area of 1 sq km is encircled by the gravel fortification known locally as Kotadibbalu, and an associated moat. That the occupational remains of the area may be earlier than the fourth-fifth century AD is suggested by a few donors' records found at the site. They belong to the second-third century AD (Hanumantha Rao *et al.* 1999: 190-191).

The Patagandigudem copper-plates of Sri Ehavala Chantamula, the Ikshvaku king of the third century AD, which were recovered from the Kallacheruvu village of the West Godavari district, is an important historical document. This recorded the royal gifts to the *mahavhara* of Pithunda, generally identified with Pithapuram in the East Godavari district (Hanumantha Rao *et al.* 1999: 191-193).

Guntupalle (17-01.108 N/81-07.757 E) is situated in a hill range about 65 km to the north of Elluru. It is known primarily for its rock-cut Buddhist cave complex. Sarma (1988: 57-91) has discussed in detail the various structural, epigraphical and ancient geographical aspects of the site. The caves are located in the upper half of a ridge near the village of Guntupalle. The first complete cave from the left is the famous one showing a domed ceiling with stone replicas of wooden rafters over the rock-hewn *stupa,* which shows the dome on the top of a high circular platform (also rock-hewn). The cave is fronted by an ogee arch, again showing stone replicas of wooden rafters. Outside the cave there are post-holes and there are slots on the wall, possibly for inserting wooden beams. The parallel with the Lomas Rishi cave of the third century BC is unmistakable. The rock-cut chaityas of Guntupalle show rectangular halls with cells at the back or on the sides. In some cases the cells have rock-cut beds and niches for monks. Sarma assigns the date of second century BC to them, but there are later caves as well. Sarma's 'new vihara cave' dates from the first century AD, and a bronze figure of *Bodhisattva Padmapani* from the debris at the same spot dates from the ninth century AD. There is also extensive evidence of structural *stupas,* monasteries and votive *stupas* on the top of the ridge. Among the large number of donors' records from the site, an interesting one of the first-second century AD records the gift of a 'master mariner; or *mahanavika* who is said to be a resident of Mahanagaparvata, the ancient name of Guntupalle. An inscription of the first-second century BC is important in the political history of the region. It records the gift of a *mandapa* by the great king Sri Sata or Sada, lord of the Kalinga-Mahisaka country and belonging to the Mahameghavahana dynasty, i.e., the dynasty of the Orissan king Kharavela. Sarma puts the Mahisaka country in the Masulipatnam area and infers that at some point in the first-second century BC, the Krishna delta was under the rule of the Kalinga kings.

In the East Godavari district, Adurru, Kapavaram, Timmavaram and Erravaram are noted sites. At Adurru (16-28.736 N/81-57.296) a central *stupa* is surrounded by a number of subsidiary *stupas*. The central *stupa* has *ayaka* platforms in the four cardinal directions, and the dome on the top of the sloping body of the supporting drum has a mud core and is supported by rows of brick walls. One of the subsidiary *stupas* is in the shape of a spoked wheel while others have central positions marked for the Buddha image. Both to the north and the south of the main *stupa,* there is a large apsidal structure with the place of the *chaitya* clearly marked. The entrance to the complex seems to lie on the west and is flanked by a number of subsidiary shrines.

The monastic complex of Kapavaram (17-10.54N/81-48.792 E) is located on the top of c. 100 m high, somewhat flat-topped, hill. It has a row of open rock-cut caves on a ledge below the top. The dominating feature is the monastic complex on the top, which overlooks the Godavari plain with a broad sweep of view. The site is approachable from Korukonda on the Rajamuhndry-Visakhapatnam section of the highway along the east coast. The complex comprises a fairly large monastery with rows of cells along the longer axis. There is an open courtyard in the middle with a wall and a shrine with space for three Buddha images. There is also a circular *stupa* at the edge of the hill-top. Close to the monastery is a complex with four small circular votive *stupas* and an apsidal hall with space for the *chaitya*. Its entrance is marked by a half-moon-shaped platform. The rest of the site is strewn with a number of circular *stupas* and an apsidal hall (without space for *chaitya*). The main *stupa* of the complex now shows only its drum and the platform on which it is built.

At Timmavaram near Pithapuram some relic caskets were discovered from a *stupa* demolished in the mid-nineteenth century. These have been studied by B. Subrahmanyam (1999: 74-75) who assigns them a date ranging from the second century BC to the first century AD. B. Subrahmanyam (1999: 79-80) also reports the site of Erravaram located on the top of a hillock in this area. Apart from two rock-cut caves, the site comprises a *mahastupa* overlooking the plain and a habitational area comprising early historic pottery and some inscribed material. Subrahmanyam infers that the site can be dated between the second century BC and the second century AD. A relic casket was also reported from the site.

V.6. Visakhapatnam – Vizianagram – Srikakulam

There is a chain of major Buddhist sites in this belt. There is also a major city site. Gopalapatnam (17-20.62 N/82-36.840 E) in the Visakhapatnam district has its Buddhist remains (votive *stupas*, monolithic remains, etc.) scattered around three hills, with traces of habitation found in the neighbouring village. These hills overlook a lush coastal plain, which is cut by a small river joining the sea. The local tradition says that this river once used to flow close by. The sea is not far from this place (Babu 1999: 133). Near Ankapalle there are two hills (Lingalakonda and Bajjanakonda) with Buddhist remains. The site is known as Sankaram. The Lingalakonda hill (17-42.529 N/83-00.825 E) features a large number of rock-hewn votive *stupas*, which are replicas in rock of the *stupas* which have their drums placed on high circular bases. The westernmost edge of the hill has a massive rock-hewn *stupa* with a comparatively smaller *stupa* beside it and about three rows of votive *stupas*. There are also two or three rock-cut caves (Subrahmanyam 1999: 73-74). On the basis of the epigraphic, numismatic and the sculptural evidence, Subrahmanyam dates the complex between the second-third century AD and the ninth-tenth century AD.

The Bajjanikonda hill (17-42. 594 N/83-00.937 E) has a rock-cut cave with a verandah and a *mandapa* in front at the lower level of a two-level cave complex. The *mandapa* has a seated Buddha image flanked by flying *Vidyadharas* and devotees. The sanctum shows a large seated Buddha image. The façade of this twin cave complex has a number of seated Buddhas. The style is reminiscent of the immediately post-Gupta style of the Deccan. At the lower level there is also a large pillared cave with a rock-hewn *chaitya*. The entrance is flanked by a giant standing Buddha (or a large *Yaksha*-like figure). The façade has *chaitya* and *stupa* motifs.

Thotlakonda (17-49.708 N/83-24.558 E) is 15 km from the Visakhapatnam city. It overlooks a bay which lies to its north-east. The site is basically a conglomeration of a large *stupa*, about 18 or 20 smaller *stupas* and scattered monastic complexes (for a detailed discussion on the area, Fogelin 2008). Offering, as it does, an unhindered and panoramic view of the bay, the site is certainly among the most beautifully located archaeological sites of the sub-continent. Among some interesting features of the site, one may note a refectory, a 64-pillared hall and a stone-paved pathway leading to the refectory. It has been dated to the period from the first century BC to the second century AD (Babu 1999: 55, 134-147) but Hanumantha Rao *et al.* (1998: 94-95) put it between the third century BC and the third-fourth century AD. Palaeographically, the latter dating is correct. The ancient name of the Thotlakonda hill (and possibly the Bavikonda hill as well) was *Senakagiri*.

In comparison with Thotlakonda, Bavikonda (17-49.077 N/83-23.463 E) offers a more distant view of the bay. It shows a large *stupa* with *ayaka* platforms, a number of subsidiary *stupas*, scattered monastic complexes and apsidal *chaitya* halls. Pavuralakonda (17-53.362 N/83-26.287 E) is located near Bhimunipatnam (a port near Visakhapatnam on the way to Vizianagram) and the remains are spread on two hill terraces. This also overlooks the bay and a range of hills on one side. The complex is dominated by a monastery which had one main *stupa*, many brick-built votive *stupas* and some structural remains. At a lower level there are some rock-cut cisterns bearing donors' records dated between the third century BC and the first-second century AD (Hanumantha Rao *et al.* 1998: 95). Ramatirtham (18-10.594 N/83-28.573 E) in the Vizianagram district is basically a rock-shelter, which was modified by the Buddhist monks for living within it. One can also detect scattered microlithic tools.

Salihundam (18-20.26 N/84-2.589 E) in the Srikakulam district lies on the top of an eminence overlooking the Vamsadhara river. The highest point is occupied by a circular *chaityagriha* which has a circular paving

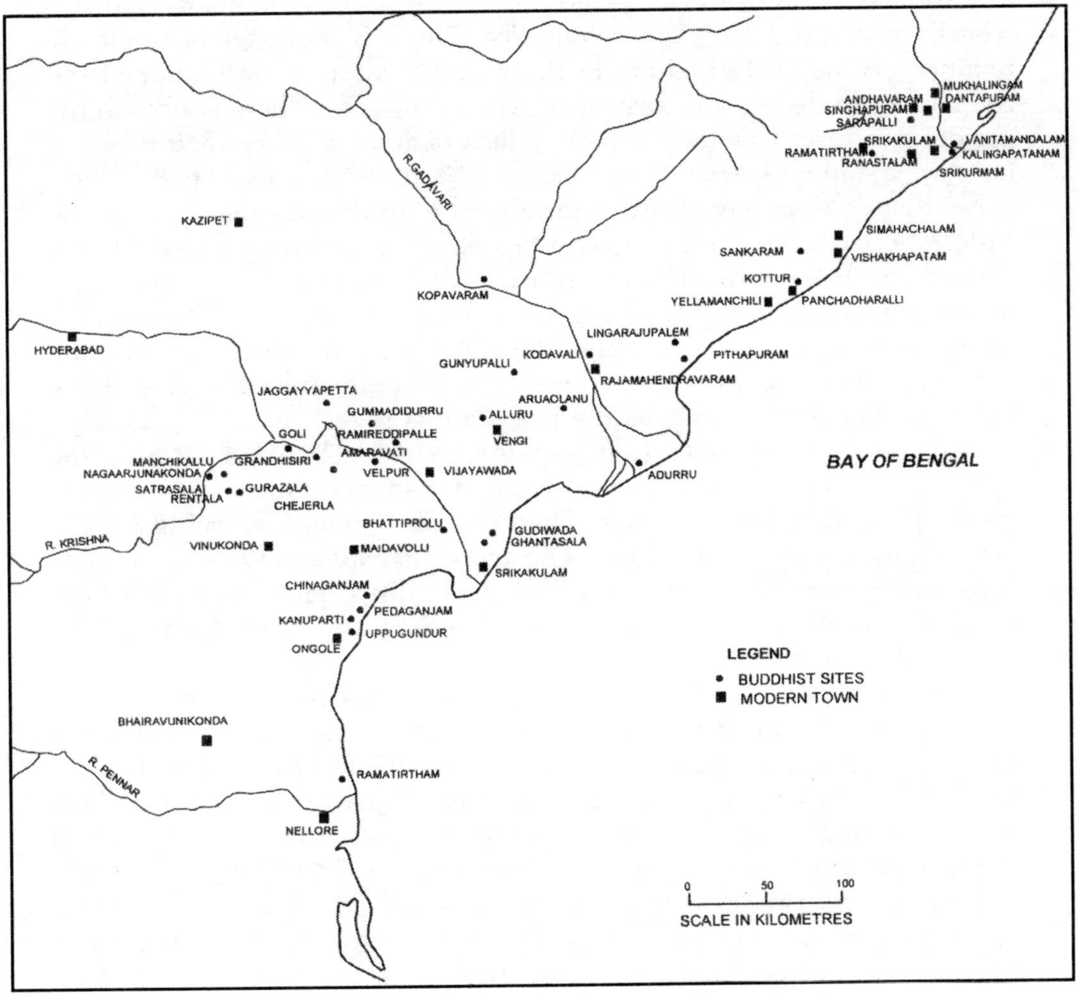

Map 11. Some major Buddhist sites in Andhra.

for the installation of the Buddha image. It is encircled by a high wall with a long entrance corridor coming from the east. There are traces of a proper double doorway whose sockets can still be observed at the ground-level lintel. The entrance corridor beyond the gateway is also flanked by two niches, possibly for the installation of sacred images. As the hill slopes towards the east, one notes on the northern side a large circular spoked-wheel *stupa* and a circular *chaityagriha*. There is a cluster of monastic remains on the eastern slope of the hill. The eastern perimeter of the complex is fronted by a securely laid walled entrance. There is also a large apsidal structure. The hill overlooks a lush plain on all sides, and the river has carved some gorgeous loops around its base, offering one of the loveliest views that one can have from a Buddhist site in the sub-continent. In the eastern horizon, one can make out the area where the river meets the sea. Coming up the river, this *stupa* must have formed a very distinct and towering landmark for the sailors. On the basis of the inscribed material, which also includes conch-shells, the site has been placed between the first century BC and the eighth century AD (Hanumantha Rao *et al.* 1998: 117-122). Its ancient name, as the inscriptions reveal, was Salipataka.

The Buddhist *stupa* at Kalingapatnam (18-19.828 N/84-6.628 E), the port site of Salihundam, is in the shape of a spoked wheel. The drum is partially preserved on all sides. There are also spoked wheel-like walls between the drum and the dome. The *stupa* currently overlooks a desolate area which is used for making salt these days. However, there are occupational debris in the area as a whole, hiding the remains of the ancient port of Kalingapatnam.

Dantapuri (18-28.615 N/83-55.34 E) is a fortified city site, the east-west distance between the fortifications being more than 1 km. On the eastern side, there is a tower-like formation in the fortification wall. It is a large site, covering, according to the villagers, 500 acres. Even a mere look at the site suggests that this is one of the major early historic city sites of the sub-continent. The pottery that one can see on the surface is mostly red-slipped and a blackish grey pottery. The site is more or less undisturbed, although there is a modern village within its periphery. There is a range of hills in the northern horizon, and a line of tanks marks the course of the former moat. There is no doubt that this site, whatever its identification, holds a very important position in the archaeology of the region. The sea is about 20-25 km from the site and the Vamsadhara river lies some kilometres away to the east. Recent excavations (unpublished) here have revealed the remains of a brick-built *stupa*. Three votive *stupas* in brick are visible in the excavated trench, and in the same area one could collect black-and-red ware sherds.

Even the foregoing sketchy outline of the distribution of historical sites in Andhra should be enough to underscore the importance of this region in the historical period. One of the problems of Andhra archaeology is that here the neolithic-chalcolithic base of the beginning of early history is not as closely visible as it is in various other parts of the country. The plethora of megalithic sites (Rao 1988) should in all cases have habitational sites nearby, and excavations of such habitational sites should provide important insights into the process of early historical beginning in the Andhra region. It is not that the neolithic-chalcolithic base does not exist in Andhra. Singanapalli, Ramapuram and Patpadu are only three such sites among perhaps many more neolithic-chalcolithic Andhra sites. The neolithic core of development seems, however, to be quite strong as it is in the neighbouring Karnataka. What is striking about the distribution of the early historic sites of Andhra is their spread all over the region, with varying densities. The density and significance of sites in the deltaic and the coastal regions, however, stand out and may have to do something with the historical significance of the Andhra coastline.

VI. PRE-MODERN PORTS

In the Andhra section of the coast in Ptolemy's description of the Indian coast, the following names occur: Manarpha, "a mart" at the mouth of a river called the Manara; Kottis, which is said to lie to the north of Manarpha; Maisolia at the mouth of the river Maisolos; Kontakossyla; Koddoura; Allosygne, "a mart" which is said to be the point of departure for the ships bound for Khryse or the Malayan peninsula. Of these, the identification seems to be positive in the following cases: Maisolia, whose name and position suggest Masulipatnam; Kontakossyla, which is convincingly Kantakasaila; Koddoura identified with Gudru or Koduru, perhaps a similarly convincing identification because of the similarity in the names; and finally, Allosygne which has been identified with Koringa, a port a little beyond Point Godavari, perhaps on the basis of Ptolemy's statement that it was the point of departure for the ships sailing to the Malayan peninsula. Kantakasaila, Masulipatnam and Koduru lie in the general area of the Krishna mouth, while Coringa, near modern Kadinada, lies in the Godavari delta, a little to the north of the eastern mouth of the Godavari. The two ports which seemingly lie up the coast from Pulicat – Manarpha and Kottis – could be any two of the several known small ports which lie between Pulicat and Masulipatnam. K.P. Rao (1999) identifies Kottis with Kottapatnam near the mouth of the Svarnamukhi River in the Nellore district. This place has yielded rouletted ware and stamped pottery of the type found at Arikamedu. Rao thinks that some of the designs on this stamped pottery compare well with the designs found in Schezuan in southern China. In view of the hypothesis that Kanchipuram had contacts with China as early as the second century BC, Rao assumes that the Kottapatnam pottery also belongs to this period and had contacts with China. He also assumes that the Svarnamukhi river, which is now about 8 km to the south of the site, was once near the site. An irregular creek was initially used for the berthing of ships, but later, a 1.25 km long and 200 m wide channel was dug. Large quantity of pottery, including what has been assumed to be 'foreign pottery', has been found all along this supposed channel.

A convenient reference point for the pre-modern ports of the Andhra coastline is W. Milburn's reference to these ports in his *Oriental Commerce* which, although published in 1813, essentially represents the eighteenth century situation.

The first port after Pulicat in Milburn's list is Armagon or Duvaspatam, 12 'leagues' (a 'league' is roughly equal to 5.5 km) north-northwest of Pulicat and the site of an old English 'factory' (1625). Interestingly, Milburn (1813: 84) observes that "the appellation of Coromandel is often applied to the whole extent of coast from Cape Comorin to Balasore". Although Milburn ignores them, one notes that even some modern maps show several places with 'patnam' at the end of their names in the Andhra coast above Pulicat. Serially, they are, from Pulicat upwards, Durgarajupatnam, Kottapatnam, Krishnapatnam, Ramaypatnam and Alluru Kottapatnam. Further, places like Utukuru (on the north bank of the mouth of the Penner), Karudu, etc., which are all shown located at the mouths of small rivers in this section, have also the possibility of being minor ports in pre-modern times. That the listing of the modern maps is not off the mark is clearly pointed out by the testimony of the *Imperial Gazetteer* on the Nellore district:

> Several small ports had a considerable coasting trade in former times ... of these places, the most important, beginning from the north, were Kottapatnam, Itamukkula, Ramayapatnam, Iskapalli, Kistnapatam, and Durgarajupatnam or Armagon. At none of them is access possible to boats of heavy tonnage (the *IGI*, vol. 19: 7).

Still, more names are added by the Nellore district gazetteer of 1977 (Rajagopal 1977: 116): Dugarajupatnam (Svarnamukhi river), Krishnapatnam (Upputeru river) and Iskapalle (not river, but a lagoon), and "smaller ports like Pakala, Ramapatnam, Maipadu, and Tummalapenta were important ports of this district exporting chiefly salt and grain".

This multiplicity of small ports in the Nellore section suggests that this was probably a significant maritime area in the ancient context too. From this point of view, the identification of Ptolemy's Kottis with Kottapatnam in this area by K.P. Rao makes sense, although except the presence of rouletted ware, the archaeological basis of this identification seems to be somewhat insecure.

The port which figures in Milburn's list after Armagon is Mootapilly, 8 'leagues; north-northeast of Pedda Ganjam (or 'Great Ganjam', as Milburn puts it). The town is about a half-a-mile inland, and large ships lie about a mile from the shore, "with Mootapilly pagoda bearing Northwest by North". In terms of the modern map, Motupalle lies about 3 miles to the northeast of Chhinnaganjam and its ancient name has been supposed to be Bisyuyyakondapattana (Rao 1999). The Guntur district gazetteer (Rajagopal 1977) lists Motupalle, Aluru-Kothapatnam, Nizampatnam and Vadarevu as ports along the district coastline. What is important is that Motupalle is also said to possess Buddhist relics, which are also said to occur in the general area. The idea that Motupalle was an ancient port (personal information from K.P. Rao) makes sense. In fact, there should be more ancient ports in this sector. For instance, both Kanuparti and Chhinna Ganjam are on the sea-coast or close to it, and Buddhist relics have been reported, as we have noticed before, from both these places.

In the history of early mediaeval Indian trade and commerce, Motupalle has a distinct position because of its stone pillar inscription of the Kakatiya king Ganapati Deva (AD 1244-45). In the language of this inscription it was an edict assuring freedom from fear, and this assurance was given to the traders who came from foreign lands (both islands and different lands) and whose cargoes, if ship-wrecked, used to be forcibly possessed by the earlier kings (*sakala-dvipantariya-desantara-pattanesu gatagatam kurvanebhyah samyatrikebhya evamabhaya-sasanam dattam*). Interesting too is the description of the ship-wrecked merchandise: gold, elephants, horses, gems, etc. (*kanaka-kari-turaga-ratnadini vastuni sakalani valadapaharanti*). Such merchants were assured that henceforth nothing but the specified custom duties would be levied on their goods, even if ship-wrecked:

> (1) One in thirty on all exports and imports; (2) on one *tula* (400,500 or 800 *tulas*) of sandalwood – 1 *Gadyana* (*Varaha* or pagoda, a gold coin of 48 Ratis or 87.81 grains) and ¼ *Pana* (*Fanam*, a gold coin of 4 or 5 grains); (3) on 1 *Gadyana* worth of camphor, Chinese camphor (*Chini-karpura*) or pearls ¾ + 3/8 *Pana;* (4) on 1 *Gadyana* worth of rose-water, ivory, civet, camphor oil, copper, zinc, lead, silk-threads, corals and perfumes –

1 ¼ *Panas* + 1/8 *Pana*; (5) on 1 *Gadyana* worth of pepper – ¾ + 1/8 *Pana*; (6) on 1 measure of silk of all kinds – 5 ½ *Panas*; and (7) on one lakh areca-nuts – 1 *Gadyana* and 3-1/4 *Panas* (Sircar 1983, pp. 550-559).

The nature of the organized trade under Ganapati Deva is also clear from the details of taxes given by native and foreign traders in what is called his 'Warangal inscription at Khan Saheb Gardens' (beginning of the 14th century AD). The goods on which the taxes were levied have been listed as areca-nuts, betel-leaves, vegetables, coconuts, different varieties of fruits, pickles, sesamum, grains, oil and ghee, salt, rice, mustard, pepper, honey, tin, lead, copper, sandal, camphor, silk yarn, ivory, pearl, rosaries, glass beads, turmeric, ginger, etc. (Sreenivasachar 1940, pp. 57-61).

From Mootapilly to Point Divy, the west side of the Bay of Masulipatam (a modern map shows this western point as "False Point Divy" whereas the eastern point of the Masulipatam bay has been called 'Divy Point'; the relevant map of the *Imperial Gazetteer* puts 'Point Divy' to the east of Masulipatam), two port sites are reported: Nizamapatam and Pettapollee (modern name Palaipatti?). Masulipatam figures next. The area in Milburn's time produced salt, tobacco, 'teak timber of the best sort', and cloth of different kinds. The shore is said to be very flat all round the Masulipatam bay, and "ships in the fair season generally anchor abreast the town, in four or five fathoms". Yanan where the French had a 'factory' lies at the confluence of the Coringa with one of the principal branches of the Godavari River. The Coringa Bay had good repairing facilities for large ships. The following comment by Milburn is significant:

> To all these advantages, add the vicinity of Coringa Bay to Pegu river, for the supply of large teak timber of all ports, and other naval stores, not being more than 10 days' sail from it in either monsoon; also the port of Rhio in the southern part of the straits of Malacca (Milburn 1813: 89).

In fact, this seems to be the basis of Jouveau-Dubreuil's opinion that ships used to sail for Southeast Asia from the Vengi ('West Godavari') region. The port of Jaggernautporam lies 7 miles north of Coringa. Kakinada ('Cocenara' of Milburn) further up the coast lies in a deep bay. The anchorage is in five-and-a-half fathoms. Ships and vessels are well-built here and cheap. For instance, ships of 65 feet keel and 24 feet beam, which could carry 9000 Bengali *maunds* (a *maund* equals a little more than 37 kg), could cost 4000/5000 rupees. The next port up the coast is Vizagapatam or Visakhapatnam, which could admit vessels of 300 tons and where "the safest and most convenient berth for large ships to anchor is in nine fathoms" (Milburn 1813: 90). The English had a 'factory' here in 1688. Bimlipatam, 5 'leagues' from Vizagapatam, was the site of a Dutch 'factory', and "between Bimlipatam and Ganjam are the rivers of Chicacole and Calingapatam, places of little trade, and seldom frequented".

Milburn attached considerable significance to the Godavari mouth as a suitable centre for ship-building:

> ... the facility, convenience and cheapness with which ships of war, or of burthen, not exceeding 500 tons have been and might in greater number be constructed in the ports of Coringa and Narsipore, two of the principal branches of the Godavari, are consideration of utmost importance to a maritime state (Milburn 1813: 86).

What is striking is that both Ptolemy and Milburn emphasize the role of the ports at the Godavari mouth in sending ships to the Malayan peninsula. Milburn's map showing the Andhra ports in the second volume of his book includes the following in the south-north orientation: Armagon, Kistapatnam, Divelan, Mootapilly, Nizamapatam, Masulipatam, Narsipore Point, Yanon, Coringa, Jaggernautporam, Waltara, Vizagapatam, Bimlipatam, Chicacole and Calingapatam. This particular map adds about four names – Kistapatam, Divelan, Narsipore Point and Waltara – to his textual description.

There are some extra notes on Nizampatam, Coringa, Cocenada and Bimlipatam in the different volumes of the *Imperial Gazetteer of India*. Coringa (the *IGI*, vol. 11, p. 51) lay at the mouth of the northernmost branch of the Godavari and was 8 miles by road from Cocenada (Kakinada). It was formerly the principal sea-port on this coast and reputedly the only place between Trincomalee and Calcutta where large vessels used to be berthed (Yule 1903: 256). The Godavari in this section silted up and not a single vessel entered the port in 1900-1901. Cocenada (the *IGI*, vol. 10, pp. 338-340) rose in importance after the decline of Coringa, especially during the American Civil War when it was a place of shipment for cotton produced in Guntur. At Nizampatam (the *IGI*, vol. 19, pp. 127-128), the English set up a 'factory' in 1621 and called it Pettipollee after the name of the neighbouring village of Peddapalle. Bimlipatam (the *IGI*, vol. 8, p. 238) was the site of a Dutch 'factory' in the seventeenth century and although the port is an open roadstead, it is said to be well protected by the Uppada and Sugaloaf headlands. The *Imperial Gazetteer* (vol. 10, pp. 217-218) does not attach any importance to Chicacole as a port.

Among all the ports on the Andhra coast, Masulipatam is given the highest importance by the seventeenth century European travellers. For instance, J-B Tavernier found Masulipatam to be a straggling town with wooden and detached houses.

> This place, which is on the sea-shore, is renowned for its anchorage, which is the best in the Bay of Bengal, and it is the sole place from which vessels sail for Pegu, Siam, Arakan, Bengal, Cochin, China, Mecca and Hormuz, as also for the islands of Madagascar, Sumatra, and the Manillas (Crooke 1925: 141).

Masulipatam was also visited by Thevenot (Sen 1949: 147-148):

> The coast is excellent, and therefore ships come thither from all nations and go from thence into all countries. I saw there Cochin Chinese, men of Siam, Pegu and of many other kingdoms of the East.
>
> ... The traffic of these parts consists in rice, fine clothes, iron, wax and lacre which is as good as Pegu, and from abroad they import copper, tin, lead and pepper.

An important point regarding the early mediaeval trade of the Andhra coast was the presence of the Tamil merchants in this area. The point has been highlighted by B. Hemalatha:

> The most important community which carried both overseas and inland trade on a large scale in mediaeval Andhra was the Balanja merchant community. They are described as Tamil merchants who carried their trade with foreign countries like Burma, Sumatra and other countries of Far and Middle East. The evidence relating to this particular community is available from the inscriptions issued from 13th century during the times of the Kakatiyas down to the fall of the Vijayanagara empire.... Most of the merchants of this community carried overseas trade to Sumatra and Burma from the town of Nangegadda near Talagadadiv of the present Krishna district and they paid Sulka collected in the form of custom and octroi duties at the ports. On the inland trade, they paid a tax called Peta Sunkamu as informed by an inscription dated 1308 AD. The Tamil merchants' trading activities in northern Andhra are further substantiated by two inscriptions available from Visakhapatnam, dated AD 1090 and AD 1200 respectively. The merchants with the support of Kulottunga Chola (AD 1070-1118) were described to have carried large scale business in this region. Some of the inscriptions from Simhachalam temple, belonging to this period (11th and 12th centuries) also mention Tamil merchants (Hemalatha 1991, pp. 63-64).

In the context of this period, Ranavir Chakravarti (paper in Mathew 1995) has highlighted the trading links between the Andhra coast and Myanmar, with Myanmar acting as an intermediary of the Andhra coast's links with China. What is also clear from Hemalatha's reference to the significance of the Tamil merchants' business activities in this region is that the entire length of the Tamil Nadu and Andhra coasts had got integrated as one commercial unit by this period.

VII. ROUTE ALIGNMENTS

The alignments of several routes can be made out on the basis of the distribution of early historic settlement sites and Buddhist relics in Andhra. First, the location of such sites in Karimnagar and Adilabad clearly suggests an orientation towards Vidarbha or the ancient Nagpur region where one can draw attention to such major sites as Adam and Pauni. The importance of this alignment has already been pointed out by us in the wider context of the routes coming from the Ganga valley towards the Deccan and the Andhra coast.

> From Pauni the Wainganga-Pranhita valley can be followed southward, through the modern Chandrapur area, to the Karimnagar sector of Andhra, which has a number of early historic settlements. In the Chandrapur area itself an extensive early historical and later site has been found at Nandori (20-11 N/79-02 E). The mound rises about 8 m high from the level of the plains and has in its vicinity some architectural and sculptural remains. The site lies in the southern direction from Pauni. Before one reaches the Godavari valley from the Chandrapur side, one comes across a hilly tract. It is not particularly a case of high hills, and unlikely to have offered a major obstacle to the movement of people. To the west of the place where the modern road crosses the Godavari is the site of Kotilingala (Chakrabarti 2005: 61).

The importance of Adam also has to be considered in this context. Like Pauni, this also is a fortified city-site but smaller. However, Adam also is likely to be related to the Andhra-Vidarbha alignment of routes. First, it has yielded an inscribed terracotta sealing bearing the term *Asika* or *Asmaka*. This sealing comes from Period V or the Satavahana period of the site. Whether the occurrence of this term in the Satavahana context at Adam means that it was the capital of, or even within, the territory of the old *Asmaka janapada* of the sixth century BC is debatable. However, if Kotilingala is supposed to be the capital of the Asmaka territory, it is likely that this territory included the area of Adam to its north as well. Secondly, Adam has yielded Roman silver coins and terracotta bullae. A hoard of Roman gold coins was also found accidentally outside the periphery of the site. As we commented earlier,

> As is well-known, Roman coins served as bullion, and there is also no doubt that Adam was a centre through which this bullion moved from the south to the north. The Wainganga valley leads straight to eastern Deccan or Andhra through Karimnagar district of Andhra (Chakrabarti 2005: 58)

Equally interestingly, Adam has yielded NBP and stone objects with Mauryan polish showing clear links with the Ganga valley. The excavator has also pointed out the occurrence of "cast copper coins of Taxila origin of the three-arched hill and hollow cross type" in the pre-Satavahana phase of the site. Thus, the route, of which the Roman coins at Adam were a part, certainly went up to the Ganga valley in the first instance, and from there to the Potwar plateau where Taxila is located. That this route also went up to the Northwestern Frontier is suggested by the report of two Amaravati-type sculptural slabs at Birkot Ghundai in Swat and Ching Patali in Dir by M. Taddei (2000), a distinguished art historian. Thus, the route which began in the Andhra coast went a long way, passing through Karimnagar, Adilabad and Vidarbha.

There is, of course, no geographical difficulty in reaching the Andhra coast from Karimnagar. Before the route goes to the Krishna and the Godavari valleys, it has to go through the modern districts of Warangal and Khammam. On the Karimnagar-Warangal modern road itself, an early historic site has been reported from near Hanamkonda and the alignment is straight in the direction of the districts of Khammam and Krishna. Another early historic site has been reported from near Jangoan, which lies to the southwest of Warangal. From this sector also, there is a straight alignment to the Guntur and Krishna districts through Nalgonda. There seems to be another branch of all these alignments linked to the Karimnagar sites. The rock-cut and open-air cave and structural complex of Guntupalle lies about 65 km north of Elluru in the West Godavari district. It may be important to realise that the location of Guntupalle is not a part of any alignment towards Orissa from Andhra. It lies considerably to the north of this eastern alignment. There is an inscription of a king of the Mahameghavahana dynasty at Guntupalle, and so an eastern link cannot be denied outright for the site. However, it is possible that from Guntupalle one could also move through the bordering Khammam and Warangal towards Karimnagar. Or, from Khammam one could also brave the jungle of Bastar to reach Chhattisgarh. However, this stretch remains unstudied by us, and the hypothesis of a route from the direction of Guntupalle to the Karimnagar area or to Chhattisgarh through Bastar is nothing more than a speculation. It is, of course, possible that the route coming from the direction of Karimnagar could reach the West Godavari sector and thus the Godavari delta directly through Khammam. That would have been a much more direct route for the Godavari delta from the northern parts of Andhra. The role of the Khammam area in the ancient network of routes in Andhra is also emphasized by the position of the major Buddhist site of Nellakondapalle on the Khammam-Vijayawada road.

The same role can be postulated for the Nalgonda region which has, on the modern Hyderabad-Vijayawada alignment, the Buddhist sites of

Phanigiri and Gazulabanda. In fact, on the same alignment lies the site of Jaggayyapeta in the Krishna district. Yelleswaram and Nagarjunakonda lie in the bordering area of Nalgonda with Guntur, Yelleswaram on the Nalgonda side of the border and Nagarjunakonda on the Guntur side.

The sites of Bodhan and Kondapur cannot be understood in the context of Vidarbha links. The Nizamabad area where Bodhan is located is almost directly linked, through Nanded and Parbhani, with the Aurangabad sector in the heart of the Maharashtra Deccan. Paithan or ancient Pratisthana, the generally recognized capital of the Satavahanas, is also located in this sector. Early in the fourteenth century, the Muslim invasion which had Devagiri or Daulatabad near Aurangabad as its base, came to subdue the Kakatiyas of Warangal by this route. This was almost precisely the route adopted by J. de Thevenot in 1666-67 to reach Golconda from Aurangabad/Daulatabad. This journey (Sen 1949: 321ff) took him through Ambad, Ashti, Lasina, Nander, Lisa, Dentapur, or Nizamabad, Kondalwadi, Indalwai, Chhinna Mallareddi, Biknur, Mellur, Jidpalli, and Medchal before he reached Bhagnagar or Hyderabad. On his return journey, he travelled through Bidar and Pathri.

J-B Tavernier, who extensively travelled in India in the 1640s and 1650s, also followed the same broad alignment to reach Hyderabad or Golconda from Aurangabad. The route which he accepted first was the following (Crooke 1925: 119 ff): Aurangabad > Pipeli > Aubar > Guisemner > Asti > Saruer > Lesona > Nadour > Patonta > Kakeri > Satapour > Sitanaga > Satanagar > Meluari > Girbalti > Golconda. Like Thevenot, the starting point of his journey was Surat, and to travel the whole length to Golconda, it took him 27 days. William Crooke, Tavernier's modern editor, identified this route as through Nander, Patanta, Karkheri, Santapur, Satulanagar and Shankarpalli before arriving at Golconda.

In his second journey from Aurangabad to Golconda, Tavernier followed roughly the same orientation but asset of different places: Aurangabad > Pipelgan > Ember > Deogan > Patris > Bargan > Palam > Candear > Gargan > Nagouri > Indore > Indelvai > Regivali > Masapkipet > Mirelmolakipet > Golconda.

The position of Bodhan is clear. It lies on the route between the Andhra sea-board and the heart of the Maharashtra Deccan where sites like Paithan and Bhokardan are located. The position of Kondapur near Sangareddi is also equally clear. We followed this route from Paithan to Ter near Osmanabad and from Ter to Sangareddi near which Kondapur is located. These two routes, the one from Bodhan and the one from Kondapur, both reach the Paithan sector, and the location of these two city sites on them underlines the importance of the link between the Andhra coast and the upper reaches of the Godavari valley. The Ter-Kondapur alignment is the southern route whereas the alignment through Bodhan is the northern one. As early as 1901, J.F. Fleet outlined the significance of this combination of two great routes from the Andhra coast to the west coast port of Broach. From the coastal terminal point of Masulipatam or basically the mouth of the Krishna and the imaginary (imagined by Fleet) inland terminal point of Vinukonda, where the produce of the region could be collected, the lines of movement, met somewhere near modern Hyderabad,

> And from that point the single road ran in the most natural manner, througth easy country, via Haiderabad, Kalyani, Ter, Paithan, and Daulatabad to 'Chandore' and Markinda in the west of the Nasik district (Fleet 1901: 548).

In the next stage, the way was found through the gaps in the Western Ghats north of Nasik for Broach on the Gujarat sea-board.

It is difficult to guess which area served as central point in the communication system of ancient Andhra. One would tentatively suggest that the Nagarjunakonda area served that purpose. It is well protected both by the river and the range of hills around it, but at the same time, the movement out of it was not difficult, the river being an important help in this direction. It gave ready access to the Krishna delta. If the Ikshvakus set up their capital in the hilly recess of the Nagarjunakonda valley, defence must have played an important role in their site-selection, but they would not have lavished so much effort in making their capital such a magnificent city if it had been somewhat cut off from the other areas. In fact, its position north of the Krishna delta made it able to cast its eyes in all directions, including the area further down the Krishna. The position of Amaravati is at the head of the Krishna delta, and roughly similar is the position of Vijayawada. The Godavari delta is not separated from the Krishna delta by a great distance. It is perfectly possible to control the Godavari system by being based at the head of the Krishna delta. The road from Vijayawada to Rajamuhndry at the head of the Godavari delta does not actually pass through the delta. It skirts it in the north. Peddavegi, or ancient Vengi, is located to the north of Elluru, giving it a central position between the two deltas. This possibly is the reason why Vengi had been important in Andhra history for so long, beginning with the Salankayanas in the fourth century and later during the long rule of the Eastern Chalukyas.

A general idea of the broad line of movement from central Andhra to the mouth of the Krishna can be understood by referring to the journeys of both Tavernier and Thevenot from Hyderabad/Golconda to Masulipatam. Tavernier (Crooke 1925: 139-141) went by the following way: Golconda > Tenara (modern Sarurnagar) > Iatenagar (modern Hayatnagar) > Patengi (Pantangi in Nalgonda district) > Penguel (Pangal near Nalgonda town) > Nagelpar (Nagalpad on the bank of the Musi River) > Lakabaron (Lacuarion) > Coulor (Kollur in Guntur district) > Kah Kally (Kakani, 4 miles northeast of Kolluru) > Bezouar (Vijayawada) > Vouchir > Vyyuru > Pamarru > Nilmol (Nidomulu) and Masulipatam. The halting places of Thevenot in his Hyderabad-Masulipatam journey were different up to Vyyuru, but the orientation was about the same (Sen 1949: 334). In fact, one would follow the same general alignment if one sets out on a journey from Nagarjunakonda or Amaravati to Machilipatnam today.

How would one have travelled from the Krishna delta to the Bellary area of Karnataka and Kanchipuram in Tamil Nadu? From the area of Guntur one would move in the direction of Vinukonda and Giddalur, cross the Nandikanama pass to the Nandiyal valley, and cross the Erramala to reach the Pattikonda area and thus Guntakal at the doorstep of Bellary. Interestingly, Roman coins have been reported from Nandiyal, testifying to its long-standing importance in the line of movements in Andhra. From the Guntur area again, there would have been a route parallel with the coast right up to Nellore. From Nellore the route would move in the direction of Kalahasti and Tirupati, and from there both Vellore and Kanchipuram are within easy rich. The most important early evidence of this route is Gudimallam Siva.

The configuration of ancient routes in the Rayalseema area of Kurnool, Anantapur, Cuddapah and Chittoor is important because it is the area through which communication was maintained between the Gulbarga area (the location of Sannati in Karnataka) and the Mysore plateau and Tamil Nadu. From Sannati on the bank of the Bhima near Yadgir, one would follow the alignment of the river till it met with the Krishna and proceed further along the Krishna till near its confluence with the Tungabhadra, crossing the latter in the area of Satanikota of Kurnool. It is possible that this Satavahana period fort was built to exercise control over the area of this crossing and the confluence of the Krishna and the Tungabhadra. From this crossing one would possibly move in the direction of the two Asokan edict sites, Erragudi and Rajula Mandagiri, both located in the southwest section of the Kurnool district. Once across this part of Kurnool, one would arrive in the Anantapur area which abuts the Chitaldurg area of Karnataka on the east, and through Chittoor the Kolar area of the Mysore plateau is also within reach from Anantapur. One could also move from the southwestern Kurnool, where the Asokan edicts are located, to Cuddapah and Chittoor to reach Tamil Nadu through Tirupati and Gudimallam.

The chain of Buddhist sites which command beautiful views of the plain, the rivers and the sea and continue eastward from Vengi falls possibly in the orbit of the fortified site of Dantapuri, the capital of Kalinga in the Srikakulam area. From Srikakula eastward, one can easily travel across the coastal plain which must have been the major line of movements of the Orissan kings to Andhra. However, from the general area of Vizianagram, before one reaches Srikakulam, one can easily travel to the Koraput or Jeypur area and through that, to the Raipur sector of Chhattisgarh or the area of South Kosala, a rich early historic area by itself.

Our discussion of the route alignments of early Andhra will be incomplete unless we draw attention to the term *Andhra-patha,* which occurs in the 4th century AD Mayidavolu copper-plates of the Pallava king Sivaskandavarman (Hultzsch 1900-01). The inscription, issued from Kanchipuram, carried an order for the governor at Dhenukataka, and the gifted village is mentioned as Viripara in *Andhra-patha (Andhrapathiyah gramah*). The term also occurs in the inscriptions of the Bana kings (8th-9th century AD and later) from Gudimallam (Venkayya 1911). Here, the Bana territory is said to be the 'land to the west of the Andhra road'. Venkayya writes that "we have to suppose, at least provisionally, either that there was a road leading to the Andhra country (perhaps from Dravida) or that the country which lay between Andhra and Dravida was called Vadugavalli, as the road to the Andhra country lay through it, and it was the country to the west of this road or the western portion of it that was ruled by the Banas" (Venkayya 1911, p. 231). As we have seen, the road to Andhra from Tamil Nadu and even the Mysore plateau goes through the Rayalseema districts where Gudimallam is located, and from that point of view the road may rightfully be called *Andhra-patha*. But whether the term can be applied in this sense to the Viripara village in the Amaravati (Dhenukataka) area is uncertain. Interestingly, an inscription (Sreenivasachar 1940, p. 196) dated AD 1277 at the Lingappa temple of Bothpur in the Bothpur taluk of the Mahbubnagar district mentions that two persons – Bacaya and Boppoa – were sent to "Varanasi in the name of his grandmother" (apparently to offer *Pinda* – ablutions and offerings – in the memory of their dead grandmother).

4

Summary and Conclusions

Those who have tried to familiarise themselves, however roughly, with the Indian coastline from Daman to Srikakulam and its hinterland in Maharashtra, Karnataka, Tamil Nadu, Kerala and Andhra are likely to be bewildered, if not awe-struck, by the historical and geographical details and complexities which lie rooted in this land. To break these details and complexities down to a few geographical lines along which the historical movements may be said to have taken place in this vast region can never be an easy task and would take, in any case, many more years of ground research than we have been able to devote to it. However, an understanding of the broad pattern was considered possible, and this is what we have tried to achieve in the preceding three chapters.

I. THE KONKAN COAST: PORTS, PASSES AND THE HINTERLAND

I.1. The Connotation of Konkan in Epigraphy

While trying to delimit the Konkan coast, we put it between the area south of Daman in the north and Mangalore in the south. Epigraphically, the term *Konkana* is not earlier than the Nerur grant of the Western Chalukyan king Mangalesa (c. AD 579-609). Seven copper-plate grants were accidentally discovered in April 1848 at Nerur in the Kudal division of the old Sawantwadi state near Ratnagiri. The third of these grants was the earliest in the series and issued by Mangalesa. It is not dated but was inferred to be later than AD 578. Konkan here is mentioned as an administrative division – *Vishaya*. The village Kundivataka which was donated by Mangalesa lay in Konkana-Vishaya. The Aihole inscription (c. AD 634) of Pulaksin II of the same dynasty refers to Konkan in plural – *Konkaneshu* where 'the imperious waves' of his forces 'swept away' the Mauryas. He also "besieged Puri, the fortune of the western sea, with hundreds of ships in appearance like arrays of rutting elephants" (Kielhorn 1900-1901). Although this reference to a vast number of ships at Puri is a literary hyperbole, Puri is possibly best identified with Elephanta and not with Thana, as Raychaudhuri (1960, p. 60) hypothesized. This inscription establishes Elephanta's identity as a major port in the 7th century AD. It must be understood that *Revati-dvipa* or the island of Revati, which is mentioned as one of the places attacked by Pulakesin II, does not figure in the Aihole inscription specifically as a part of Konkan but the context shows that it was an island somewhere off the Konkan coast. In the language of the inscription, Pulakesin II's army, as it ascended the ramparts of the island of Revati (our note: and was reflected in the sea-water), looked like the forces of Varuna, the sea-god. The identification of Revati-dvipa is uncertain, but it can denote the position of any of the island forts off the Ratnagiri coast, Sindhudurg, Vijayadurg, Vengurla or even Janjira and Kolaba. The fact that these forts, as they stand today, date from the Maratha period does not necessarily imply that they did not have any early ancestry. According to Raychaudhuri (1960, p. 30), by AD 888 Konkan, as testified by an inscription, came to include the area around Surat. In AD 1112, another inscription used the term *Konkana-rashtra* or Konkan state, whose king styled himself 'the lord of Gokarna', a holy place in North Kanara. Thus, epigraphically, the term Konkana is not earlier than the 6th century AD and by the 12th century AD it could mean the area from Surat to North Kanara. We have extended the applicability of the term to include South Kanara as well, because there is hardly any difference in the terrain between North and South Kanara.

I.2. Comments on the State of Indian Archaeological Research on the Coastal Sites

In the case of this long coastline between Umbergaon-Sanjan and Mangalore, we have tried to outline the following. First, we have enumerated all the pre-modern ports of this section, which find mention in the Thana, Ratnagiri and Kolaba volumes of the late 19th century *Gazetteer of the Bombay Presidency* and in the later publications of this type on Goa, North and South Kanara. We have observed how the major ports of the different segments of this long section were accompanied in each case by a large number of minor ports, many of which were in use in the

19th century. The basic history of most of them does not stretch beyond the 16th and 17th centuries, the period when the European records on them began. Notices before the 16th century are available in only a limited number of cases and confined mostly to the writings of the Arab geographers. The records which are still earlier comprise only a handful of inscriptions, a few well-known Indian and classical textual references, and bits and pieces of archaeological evidence. We have briefly discussed this evidence in all the relevant cases.

But for the availability of European records of pre-modern times, it would, in fact, have been impossible to appreciate the real richness and complexity of the long-distance and coastal trade which characterised the entire length of the Indian coastline. Besides, as the truly ancient record is limited to only disjointed fragments of archaeological and ancient historical data, the pre-modern European writers offer detailed insights into the pattern of, and commodities involved in, this trade.

Archaeological research in this domain has suffered from the long-standing pre-occupation to locate 'foreign' pottery at the Indian coastal sites. There is no doubt a fair amount of imported pottery along the coast and occasionally even in the hinterland. Such pottery and other bits of related evidence cover a great length of time – Roman, West Asiatic, Chinese, Southeast Asiatic and East African. However, these cannot lead to a complete picture of India's maritime trade on their own unless they are firmly tied to the indigenous Indian framework. Research along this line has already begun, and although it is difficult to apply the term 'marine archaeology' to most of this endeavour, the point is that there is now a better awareness of the archaeological significance of the Indian coastal sites.

One of the basic ingredients of research on the coastal sites is, of course, an understanding of how such sites were geographically and historically related to their hinterlands. This is where the question of the focal points of the hinterland and the routes linking them to the coast becomes significant.

I.3. From the South of Daman to Elephanta

In the northern segment of the Konkan coast, which may be said to stretch roughly from the south of Daman to the Elephanta island in Mumbai, the ancient historical focus is on Sopara and Elephanta itself. The presence of the Asokan edicts (fragments of Rock Edicts VIII, IX and XI) at Sopara and its mention as Surparaka in the *Jatakas* and other early textual sources raise the question of its antecedence, if any, in the region. That its beginning is pre-Asokan cannot be doubted and the fact that its earliest ceramic sequence is a phase marked by black-and-red ware and NBP seems to push it back considerably further. Whether there was an earlier proto-historic phase in the history of the site is still unknown but its possibility is there, as Ghate's find of microliths (dated c. 1500 BC) in the area suggests. Regarding the continuity of the maritime significance of the Sopara area down to the pre-modern period, there does not seem to be much doubt, although the presently available evidence is admittedly fragmentary. That it finds place as a major mart in the writings of the Arab geographers of the 10th-12th centuries strengthens this conviction. There is also nothing in the historical records to assume that maritime trade of this sector had declined since the ancient period and was revived only in the 9th century AD and later. As we have seen in a different context (Chakrabarti 2003), the maritime significance of India's west coast remained basically unimpaired in the post-Roman context because of its position in the Sassanid and early Arab frameworks of trade. Sopara does not seem to have figured in any 6th century foreign record but Kalyan or Calliana in the same north segment of the Konkan coast was mentioned as a major mart in the account of Kosmas Indikopleustes of this period.

No archaeological sequence has been obtained from Elephanta or the ancient city of Puri, but surface studies seem to have assured that it was a major maritime trading centre in the 1st-7th centuries AD. Between the 6th and 10th centuries AD, its significance as a capital of the Konkan Mauryas and the Silaharas is indisputable and has been highlighted by Pulakesin II's invasion of the place as recorded in his inscription of 634 AD. Kalyan remains archaeologically uninvestigated but its mention as Calliana in the *Periplus* puts it squarely among the ports of the early historic period in the northern segment of the Konkan coast. Of all the references to the ports of the region (Kalyan, Sopara and Chaul) in the inscriptions of Kanheri, those to Kalyan are the most frequent (Luders' inscriptions 986, 998, 1000, 1001, 1013, 1014, 1024, and 1032). If Ptolemy's *Sazantion* means modern Sanjan or Sanjayantinagari of the *Mahabharata* means the same, Sanjan has to be added to the list of early historic ports of the region. This is an inference which is strengthened by the assumption that the first phase of occupation found in the recent excavations at the site can be taken back to the Satavahana period. Regarding its uninterrupted significance in the later historical phases, there is clear epigraphic and other evidence, the Chinchani copper-plates and the mention of Sindan as a supplier of indigo in the Arab geographical records being important in this regard. The other major early mediaeval port of the area was Thana which became a capital of the Silahara kings in the 9th century AD and was mentioned as *Sristhanaka* in a Silahara copper-plate inscription of c. AD 1097. Its mention as a *tirtha* visited by a Kadamba king of Goa in AD 1038 is equally interesting. One is not sure of the beginning of Bassein as early as the early mediaeval period, but lying close to Sopara this seems to be almost its natural successor.

All these ports – Sopara, Elephanta, Sanjan, Kalyan and Thana – seem to be major places, but around them, as we have seen, there was a large chain of small ports: Umbergaon, Dheri, Gholbad, Dahanu, Savta, Navapur, Satpatti, Kelve-Mahim, Sassu Navghar, Ghodbandar, Bhiwndi, Versova, Bandra and Panvel. Their history is uncertain but most of them seem to be mentioned in the Portuguese records, and as the river on the bank of which Dahanu is located is mentioned as *Dahanuka* in a Nasik inscription of the early centuries AD, it is possible that Dahanu itself had an early historic port area. In most cases these small ports were perhaps nothing more than berthing places of small boats, but taken as a whole they highlight a chain of maritime activity which took place not merely in the context of the lands across the seas but also in the context of local and regional coastal trade. They thus add an important depth to the total picture. The same purpose is served by the forts, none of which can presently be dated before the period of the Gujarat Sultans in the 14th-15th century. Most of them belong to the later periods of the Marathas and the Portuguese. They, however, serve the purpose of highlighting the economic significance of this trade network to the political powers of the day and make us aware of the possibility of such scenarios in the earlier contexts too.

When one looks at the list of political powers involved in this sector, one also gets an idea of the general canvas of its hinterland. The Mauryan presence at Sopara indicates their control over northern Konkan and suggests, eventually, close links with the Ganga-Yamuna plain through Central India. The main thrust of the Satavahanas and the Western Kshatrapas in this sector emanated from the Nasik-Junnar sector on the other side of the Western Ghats. In the case of the Western Kshatrapas, the power was geographically rooted both in western Madhya Pradesh (cf. Ujjain) and Gujarat, and in the case of the Satavahanas, Paithan near Aurangabad was an important centre. However, there were links with areas further afield, and when we examine the cases of the Chalukyas and Rashtrakutas, we realize that the power centre of both these groups lay in a specific part of Karnataka. Badami, the centre of the Chalukyan power, and Kalyan and Malkhed in Gulbarga, the centres of the

Rashtrakuta power, all lie in the north-central (Badami) and north-west (Gulbarga) parts of Karnataka. In fact, the Mauryas had also a powerful presence in the form of rock edicts at Sannati near Yadgir, which is near Gulbarga. The link-up of the northern segment of the Konkan coast with north-central and north-west Karnataka is thus clear. The Silaharas and the Maurya dynasty of Konkan were at home in the Konkan coast itself, and so were the Kadambas of Goa. As an example of interaction between the different parts of this coastal region, one may draw attention to an inscription at Karle, which records that this cave-dwelling (*selaghara*), "the most excellent one in Jambudvipa" was caused to be built by the donations of 'the banker (*sethin*) Bhutapala from Vejayanti (*Vaijayanti* or Banavasi in North Canara, (Luders' inscription 1087; Luders 1912, p. 116). Coastal trade must have played a major role in maintaining links between the different sections of the Konkan coast. This is what is clearly suggested by the vast mass of pre-modern European records on this coast, of which only a small portion has been used by us.

When it comes to the question of maintaining links with the hinterland, the passes provide virtually the only geographical avenues between the coast and the interior. We have argued that in the northern sector the Thal, Nana and Bor passes were the most important lines of movement between the Nasik, Junnar and Pune sections of the Maharashtra interior and the northern segment of the Konkan coast up to the Elephanta island in the south. The locations of both settlement sites and the rock-cut cave complexes on both sides of the Western Ghats in this section prove this. Among other things, Nasik, Junnar and Pune have all early historical settlements, and the major Buddhist rock-cut caves are also clustered at both the ends of Thal, Nana and Bor. At the extreme northern end, in the area of Umbergaon-Sanjan and Dahanu, there are possibly other openings, but on the whole, the crucial passes which led from inner Maharashtra to the coast around Mumbai and to its north are these three passes. They need not be the only examples of passes here; we have previously shown the general importance of Malsejghat in travelling from Junnar to the area of Kalyan, but its importance need not be put on the same level with Thal, Nana and Bor.

A major issue in the context of the northern Konkan coast is to find out the general alignments by which communications were maintained with the regions around Aurangabad (cf. Devagiri, Bhokardan, Paithan), Ahmednagar (the Sultans of Ahmednagar) and the central and north-western parts of north Karnataka, i.e., the area from around Badami to the area around Gulbarga. Unless one prefers to approach the Aurangabad area from Nasik in a roundabout way through Manmad or even Chalisgaon, one may easily travel from Nasik to Aurangabad by following the Pravara valley. An important stopping point on this route would be Nevasa. One can also easily reach Paithan from Nevasa down the Godavari. Even from the Aurangabad area, the terrain is easy and open up to Paithan and far beyond. Ahmednagar lies in an open terrain to the east-southeast of Junnar and is easily accessible from there. Pune provides a better area to travel from, for the Gulbarga area. The Pune-Solapur-Gulbarga alignment seems to be a straightforward alignment. Another easy way is to travel from Paithan to Ter in the Osmanabad area and turn from there towards Gulbarga. For the Bijapur-Badami sector, one could come straight down to the Kolhapur area from the mouth of the Bor pass or even the area around Pune and move from there towards Athni to reach Bijapur. For Badami, which lies further to the south, one could come from the area of the Bor mouth to Belgaum and strike east.

A final point may be noted regarding the location of Buddhist rock-cut caves in the section from the Thal to the Bor. The most important site on the coast here seems to be Kanheri. What is striking about Kanheri is not merely its extent and density of caves and cisterns but also the fact that Buddhism survived there in some fashion almost till the Portuguese took over the area.

I.4. From the South of Mumbai to Ratnagiri

The area from the south of Mumbai to Ratnagiri may be said to constitute the second segment of the Konkan coast. Its immediate hinterland is the section from Pune to Kolhapur. Apart from the political powers, which were important in the history of the northern segment of the coast, one has to mention in this context the Sultans of Bijapur and the Bahmanis of Bidar (near Gulbarga). Chaul and Kolhapur are the two major ancient settlement sites of this section, which are backed up by a plethora of passes and Buddhist rock-cut cave complexes of varying importance.

The Kolaba fort which is built on rock and becomes an island in high water is indicative of the significance of the area around Alibag, but there are a few minor landing places to its north and east: Mandva, Avas, Revas, Dharamtar, Antora, Pen, and the islands of Khanderi and Under. Of these, Pen seems to have been significant in the 17th century. The significance of the others, at least in the pre-modern context, was not more than being minor landing places south of Mumbai and possibly acting as strategic places in relation to it. The details of the history of the Kolaba fort seem to be unknown but that it protected the entrances to both Mumbai and Alibag is pretty clear. However, by the 19th century Alibag lost its importance and when the *Gazetteer of the Bombay Presidency* was written, it was nothing more than a centre of coastal trade serving the various needs of Mumbai.

Chaul was the most important ancient port of this segment of the Konkan coast. That it retained its significance till the advent of the Portuguese and the contemporary powers is amply documented by various European travellers. In the early 16th century, it was linked by trade to virtually the entire rim of the Indian Ocean including east Africa. Towards the east, it was linked to China and possibly the whole of the intervening coastlines. The extent to which its significance on this scale was foreshadowed earlier is uncertain. There is no doubt about its Mediterranean links and perhaps links with the Gulf area. One can also take its traditional importance in the coastal trade for granted. Beyond this, it is impossible to make any firm assertion. One cannot be sure that the many glass beads found in Gogte's excavations within a metre of the surface go back to the early historic period or can be clearly dated at all. It appears that the West Asiatic glazed pottery and what has been inferred to be Chinese stoneware are not earlier than the 7th century AD at the site and most of the West Asiatic and Chinese material dates from the uppermost phase of occupation here. The uppermost phase of occupation at Chaul, if the European travel accounts are any indication, need not be earlier than the late mediaeval period. Again, the evidence, if any, of occupation before the Satavahana period is not clear. Black-and-red ware and black-slipped pottery seem to have been found in a pre-Satavahana context, but more evidence is needed to make the beginning of Chaul as a trade centre (both maritime and inland) clear.

The distance from Alibag to Mahad is much less than the distance between Mahad and the southernmost portion of Ratnagiri, but in addition to Chaul, there are several reported ports of varying dimensions and possible significance in the Alibag-Mahad section: Nagothna, Roha, Mandad, Murud, Mhasla, Janjira, Danda-Rajpur and Mahad itself. Of their significance no data are available before the 16th century, and random attempts to identify places with those mentioned in the Classical sources in the context of this particular section of the Konkan coast do not inspire confidence, except, of course, in the case of Chaul. That the trade passing through this sector was significant is highlighted by forts such as Janjira, Raygad and others which looked over the various inlets giving access to this area. The massive fort of Janjira remains in memory, and a fort on this scale of massiveness is unlikely to have been built unless the trade which it was supposed to control was very significant. The same is true of the fort of Raygad.

The passes in this section are directed principally towards Mahabaleshwar, Satara and Pune. The Par pass, 15 miles south-east of Mahad, leads towards Mahabaleshwar. Only half a mile north of it, the Fitzerald pass led in the direction of Satara and was backed by at least two passes. The passes further to the north, such as Verandah, Umbarda, Gupya, Ambenal, Shevtya, Kavaliya, Kumbha, etc. led in the direction of Pune. In addition, there is a sizeable number of minor openings or *khinds* and even passes, two each in the cases of Pen, Roha and Mahad. The latter passes were considered suitable for cart traffic by the Kolaba gazetteer, and the Pir pass near Chaul has been considered a highway of traffic during the heyday of Chaul as a port.

The Buddhist rock-cut cave complexes lay clustered around both Chaul and Mahad on the coastal side of the Western Ghats and around Satara on the side of the hinterland. The number of caves near Chaul is limited, and the only ones frequently mentioned are those of the Hinglaj spur. The Pali and Kol complexes are the two main rock-cut cave groups near Mahad. The group of 29 rock-cut caves at Pali, only 2 miles to the northwest of Mahad, gave the name Palipattana to Mahad in a Silahara copper-plate inscription of AD 1094. This offers a solid ground for identifying Mahad with 'Balipatana' or 'Palaipatmai'of the Classical sources. Cave 28 of this complex mentions, in an inscription engraved in its verandah, a rich merchant or *Sresthi* called Sangharakshita who has also been mentioned in an inscription in the Kol rock-cut cave complex, also near Mahad. The names of merchants also figure in the inscriptions of the Kuda group of caves, which overlooks the Rajapuri creek near Mahad. The Kuda caves seem to be more important than the other caves of the area, and the inscriptions found there range in date from the 1st-2nd century BC to the 5th-6th century AD. An important feature of the Kuda caves is that "the walls of almost all the caves were plastered with earth and rice-chaff, and several of them have remains of painting" (*GZB, Kolaba District*, 1883, p. 333). It is interesting that the term *Sathavaha* (*Sarthavaha*), which denotes a caravan or the leader of a caravan, occurs in a number of Kuda inscriptions (Luders' inscriptions 1062, 1065, and 1066). Another Kuda inscription (Luders number 1055) refers to an iron-monger or a trader in iron goods (*lohavaniyiya*) from *Karahakadaka* or Karad on the other side of the Western Ghats.

On the Satara side, the Buddhist rock-cut caves which may be said to be oriented towards the passes leading to the Mahad area on the other side of the Western Ghats seem to be centred at Tamkane (3 miles north-west of Patan at the entry to the Kumbharli pass), Wai (4 miles north of Wai) and Shirval (14 miles north of Wai). There is a group of 15 early Buddhist caves at Shirval. The Wai group has 8 caves and there are about 2 caves at Tamkane. These caves are not precisely dated but they are generally taken to belong to the early group of Buddhist rock-cut caves, which at its earliest dates from the 2nd century BC. At least one cave at Wai is supposed to contain sculptures of human figures.

The Ratnagiri sector of this part of the Konkan coast seems to be a particularly rich trading zone, although one cannot be sure of its early antiquity. The pre-modern records establish the significance of Bankot, Dabhol, Chiplun and Rajapur, but along with them one should also mention Kharepatan and Vijaydurg. Kharepatan finds mention in the Silahara inscriptions and the earliest inscriptional reference to Dabhol goes back to the same period. There is nothing positive regarding their early antiquity. An indirect, but nonetheless positive, evidence is supplied by the Karad group of Buddhist rock-cut caves, which the Satara district gazetteer, as we shall find later, puts in the early centuries AD. We would assume that by this period at least the trade going through the various passes to the Ratnagiri sector from the Satara side had come into its own.

Apart from the major ports of Bankot, Dabhol, Chiplun, Rajapur, Kharepatan and Vijaydurg, the following minor ports figure in the pre-modern records of the Ratnagiri sector: Mahapral, Kelshi, Ade, Anjarla, Harnai, Dapoli, Khed, Anjanvel, Guhagar, Boria or Adur, Jaygad, Sangameshwar, Ratnagiri, Jaytapur, Achra, Malvan and Vengurla. As we have earlier noted, a number of ports in this list have been identified with the ports mentioned by the *Periplus* in this sector. The identifications have to be considered tentative in all these cases, although in view of the general mercantile significance of the Ratnagiri part of the coast and the wide area it included in its orbit in the pre-modern historical records, we would accept the notion that there is a strong possibility of some of its ports finding a place in the *Periplus*.

The forts of Vijaydurg and Sindhudurg, which like the forts of Janjira and Alibag are excellent examples of massive forts built on rocks and encircled by water in high tide, lend grandeur to the coastline of Ratnagiri. At the height of the European trading in the 17th century, ships from as far as Japan and Batavia on the one hand and East Africa, the Red Sea and the Persian Gulf on the other were calling at the Ratnagiri coast which was connected with the hinterland by almost a maze of passes – Hatlot, Ambavli, North Tivra, Kumbharli, Mala, South Tivra, Kundi, Amba,

Anaskura, Kajirda, Bavda, Shevgad, Ghotga, Rangna or Prachitgad, Hanumant or Talkat, Amboli or Parpoli, and Ram, seventeen in all. There is occurrence of Buddhist rock-cut caves at Chiplun, Dabhol, Khed, Kol and Sangameshwar. On the Satara side, the important Buddhist rock-cut cave complex oriented in the direction of the Ratnagiri sector is the Karad group of caves, about 31 miles to the south of Satara. The occurrence of as many as 63 caves in this complex and the innumerable water cisterns and many other small excavations associated with them underlines the general significance of the Satara side of the Ratnagiri trading zone. Another major ancient place on this side is Kolhapur or the ancient Brahmapuri. Apart from being a major early historical site, Kolhapur is also known for its find of a hoard of ancient bronzes containing some Roman figures. Interestingly, as has been noted before (Khandalavala 1960, also, Chakrabarti 2005), these bronzes were possibly sent to Kolhapur for getting them melted down.

The political links of this second section of the Konkan coast are more or less identical with the links we have pointed out for the first section. Here places like Bijapur and thus northern Karnataka as a whole are within easy reach. The area between Satara and Belgaum lies at the heart of the network of links of this section, offering an easy access to different parts of Karnataka, including its bordering areas with Andhra.

In view of the crucial importance of the Satara, Solapur, Kolhapur, Belgaum and Dharwar sectors in mediating the routes from the Konkan coast to the various sections of its hinterland, it may be useful to discuss some broad features of their communication network at this point. The following routes are said to have been operative in the Satara district in 1826: the north-south Pune-Belgaum alignments which passed through Satara; the routes to the north-east from Satara to Sirur in Pune, and Ahmednagar; the routes to the east from Satara to Solapur; the routes to the south-west from Karad to Rajapur and Malvan, both in Ratnagiri; and the routes to the west from Satara to Dapoli. Of the two lines which linked Pune to Belgaum, the longer one went by the Bor pass through Koregaon while the shorter one passed by the Khamatki or Khandala or Harali pass through Satara, Karad and Islampur. The route to Sirur was shorter than the route to Ahmednagar, and both followed the Pune-Belgaum alignment by the Khamatki pass for a part of the way. The two routes from Satara to Solapur went through Pandharpur, a major pilgrim centre of the region but at some point they bifurcated and took different alignments to reach Solapur. The route to Rajapur went by the Ankusra pass while the route to Malvan went by the Phonda pass. The shorter route to Dapoli was by the Amboli pass and the longer one moved at some point through the Kumbharli pass (*GZB Satara* volume).

Among the important lines of movements which emanated from Solapur in the late 19th century, one went northeast to Tuljapur, and from Tuljapur the Rangareddi area of Andhra is easily approachable. One could also go to Hyderabad via Naldrug and Kalyani. Solapur was well connected with Bijapur in the south, and it had also easy links with Pandharpur and Pune.

In Kolhapur there were three major alignments in the 19th century: the Pune-Belgaum alignment which passes through Kolhapur, and the three alignments to the west coast across the Western Ghats: the Kolhapur-Amba pass route to Ratnagiri; the Kolhapur-Phonda pass route to Vijaydurg, Devgad and Malvan; and the Kolhapur-Parpoli pass route to Malvan and Vengurla. These three east-west alignments are linked in turn to a large slice of the country to the east of Kolhapur. For instance, for places like Athni, Gokak, Hukeri and Nipani in Belgaum, the Kolhapur-Parpoli alignment is said to be the most direct coast road. It is also important to note that from Belgaum, Badami, the capital of the Western Chalukyas, is within easy reach to the east.

Five main routes are said to have been centred in Belgaum in 1826. Two went north to Pune, with some difference in alignments. One went north-east to Kaladgi and Solapur. From Kaladgi, Bijapur lies within approachable distance to the north-northeast. One went southeast to Dharwar, from where there is a straight alignment in the east to Gadag, Hospet and Bellary. The fifth route from Belgaum went to Goa and Vengurla in Ratnagiri. This went by the Ram pass to reach Kudasi in Sawantvadi. At Kudasi it bifurcated, one going northwest to Vengurla and the other going southwest to Goa.

In relation to the interior of Karnataka reaching as far east as the Rayalseema area of Andhra and as far south as Hassan, Mysore and Bangalore, Dharwar occupies a nodal position. Apart from the Dharwar-Gadag-Hospet-Bellary orientation, Dharwar is linked to Chitaldurg and through it, to Hassan, Mysore and Bangalore.

Thus, on the eastern side of the Western Ghats, the north-south alignment of Satara, Kolhapur and Belgaum plays a crucial role in mediating the routes which linked the different sections of the Konkan coast to a vast region covering large sections of inner Maharashtra, the Gulbarga-Bijapur-Badami-Bellary section of Karnataka, and through them, Andhra, and at a further remove, Tamil Nadu. One can also add to this network Solapur in the east and Dharwar in the south. Viewed in the context of such wider links, the narrow coastal plain of Konkan and the associated openings of varying importance in the Western Ghats cease to be a closed world and become an integral part of the vast network of routes covering the Deccan and the southern peninsula.

I.5. Goa

The third segment of the Konkan coast from our point of view is Goa. Under the Kadambas in about AD 500, Goa seems to acquire a political identity of its own or at least becomes a part of the political growth in the Konkan itself under the aegis of the Kadamba dynasty. The earlier political configurations are not understood in detail, but one has to infer that the political forces which were earlier operative in the Maharashtra-Karnataka hinterland are also applicable in the case of Goa. Its early historic archaeological outline is not yet sharp and will require further work. Except Chandor there does not seem to be any major occupational site. As in other segments of the Konkan coast, there was a chain of pre-modern ports also in Goa. We have earlier listed them on the basis of Tom Pires' account: Devgarh, Banda, Old and New Goa, Liga, *Ancoll*, Pale, Sal River, Cape Ramas, *Chintacora*, and Anjediva. That was early in the 16th century, but by that time the Portuguese settlement of Goa had already become the strongest trading focus of the region. We have already cited Pires' description of the trading links of the Portuguese Goa, in which an important feature is Goa's role in importing horses "from all the kingdoms in Arabia Petrae, from Ormuz, from Persia and from the kingdom of Cambay". The horses were traded in the Deccanese and southern kingdoms, of which the principal one in Pires' time was the kingdom of Vijayanagara, the kingdom of 'Narasinga' in Pires.

To describe the links of Goa with this kingdom, Robert Sewell (1924 reprint: 210) cites the record of Filippo Sassetti, a Florentine merchant who died in Goa in 1588:

> The traffic was so large that it is impossible to imagine it; the place was immensely large; and it was inhabited by people rich, not with richness like ours, but with richness like that of the Crasii and the others of those old days.... And such merchandise ! Diamonds, rubies, pearls ... and besides all that, the horse trade. That alone produced a revenue in the city (Goa) of 120 to 150 thousand ducats, which now reaches only 6 thousand.

Sassetti wrote after Vijayanagar was destroyed by a confederacy of the Muslim kings of the Deccan, in which the leading role was taken by the Bahamani sultans of Bidar (Gulbarga area) in 1565.

One gets an idea of how people used to cross the Western Ghats from Goa in the account of the French missionary Abbe Carre (Fawcett

1947, vol. 1, pp. 221ff) who went from Goa to Bijapur. He went via Bicholim, and passed through a village now identified with Bamburde, which lies in the hills on the bank of a tributary of the Tilary. From there he went to Medin, a village at the foot of the Ramghat pass where the climb to the pass begins. While climbing up the range, he encountered various wild animals – "several raging tigers, which passed before, behind, and beside us, and a herd of about thirty wild boars". He found some houses and a temple on the hill-top. That was where the frontier of the Bijapur kingdom began. From now on the road passed through a flat country, although full of 'dangerous jungles, full of wild beasts'. The road to Bijapur from here onward had the following halting points: Chandgad on the bank of the Tamraparna River, 22 miles west of Belgaum, Nesari near the Ghataprabha, Jambulvadi, Halkarni, Khanapur, Hukeri, Raybagh, Athni, Aigale (on the bank of a tributary of the Krishna), Telingacin, Tikota and Bijapur.

One gets an idea of how goods were transported in this sector from the following experience of Abbe Carre. Since leaving Bicholim, he was astonished by the number of people on the road carrying heavy weights on their heads. Later, he learnt that "they dwelt on the coast near Goa, and gained their living by taking dried fish, coconuts, arracks, and other comeatibles, to sell in Bijapur". They were paid by loads, and the entire trip lasted 25 to 30 days.

I.6. North and South Kanara

The coastline of North and South Kanara, which falls between Karwar and Mangalore has a significant number of pre-modern ports, beginning with Karwar: Karwar, Bhatkal, Kumta, Honavar, Malpe, Hangarkatta, Kundapur, Baindur, Barkur, Basrur, Udayavara, Udupi, and Mangalore. The Satavahanas and later, the Kadambas, the Alupas and others down to the successors of the Vijayanagara kings provide the political focus of the region, with Banavasi near Sirsi being its first visible major early historic settlement. The antiquity of Mangalore can be traced, as we have seen, on the basis of the Geniza documents to the 11th century AD. It is likely to have an earlier beginning, but apparently there is no published early site in this area except Banavasi, which falls in North Kanara and lies more than 200 km north of Mangalore. The apparent absence of a properly identified early historic site in the South Kanara coast or its periphery is a serious archaeological problem. However, to some extent this may also be due to the lack of proper, timely and accessible publications. For instance, excavations have been supposed to have been recently conducted at

Barkur near Udupi, but one gathers that the emphasis was given on the excavations of a palace of the Vijayanagara period. C.B. Patil (2006) refers to some early historic remains in the area of Honavar and Udayavara but nothing has yet emerged in clear focus.

In the case of North Kanara, the Dharwar region possibly played a major role in maintaining links between the coast and the Karnataka hinterland. We have drawn attention to the significance of Dharwar-Bellary and Dharwar-Chitaldurg alignments. The Dharwar district gazetteer of 1884 describes the link roads of this area in some detail. The first is the Pune-Harihar alignment, Harihar lying on the way to Chitaldurg from Dharwar. The second alignment is Karwar-Bellary, of which the Dharwar-Bellary alignment is a part. The third alignment is Dharwar-Kumta which passes through Sirsi and the Devimani pass to reach Kumta. The fourth major alignment is Dharwar–Bijapur / Solapur alignment which follows the Hubli-Gadag-Solapur-Bijapur line. Regarding the passes by which the produce of Dharwar is carried to the coast, the gazetteer of 1884 states the following (p. 345):

> Of passes to the west coast the Arabil and Devimani passes are the most important. Cotton mostly goes by these passes to Bombay. The Arabil pass which runs to Karwar lies twelve miles south of Yellapur in Kanara and sixty-five miles south-east of Dharwar. The Devimani pass which runs to Kumta lies about twenty miles south of Sirsi in Kanara and ninety miles south-east of Dharwar....Besides these, the Tinai pass, about thirty miles north-west of Supa in Kanara and fifty miles west of Dharwar, runs into Goa through part of Belgaum and Kanara.... Within the limits of the district there are few important hill-passes. The only passes worthy of notice are the Sortur-Doni and Virapur passes in the Kapatgudd range.

Banavasi is located in the Sirsi area. It is clear from the gazetteer's description that it is conveniently located in an area which offers ready access from the interior to the coast. The point is that Sirsi / Banavasi is conveniently located for Kumta and Honavar and Bhatkal. Considering that Banavasi is the only early historic city site of the region, the antiquity of maritime activities in the Kumta-Honavar-Bhatkal section is likely to go back to the pre-Christian era.

The details of the linkages of South Kanara with its hinterland are not particularly clear, but an idea can be had from F. Scott's treatment of the British Indian military routes till the 1850s. The route from Bangalore to Honavar lay through Shimoga and the area of the Gersoppa falls. The route from Bangalore to Harihar lay through Tumkur and Chitaldurg. From Mangalore one went to Shimoga on the other side of the Western

Ghats by the Agumber pass. One went to Hassan from Mangalore by the Manjarabad ghat.

No segment of the Konkan coast can, thus, be called isolated. In fact, going through the list of myriad passes across the Western Ghats, one realizes that this coast was as close a part of its hinterland as any other coastal region of the country. Domingos Paes, a Portuguese writer who wrote on India in 1520-22, expressed the links between the kingdom of Narsymga (i.e., Vijayanagara) and the western coast in the following way:

> ... To travel towards the kingdom of Narsymga from the sea-coast, you have (first) to pass a range of hills (*serra*), the boundary of the said kingdom and of those territories which are by the sea. This *serra* runs along the whole of the coast of India, and has passes by which people enter the interior; for all the rest of the range is very rocky and is filled with thick forest. The said kingdom has many places on the coast of India; they are sea-ports with which we are at peace, and in some of them we have factories, namely Ankola, Mirgeo, Honor, Batecalla, Mangalor, Bracalor and Bacanor. And as soon as we are above this *serra* we have a plain country in which there are no more ranges of hills, but only a few mountains, and these small ones, for all the rest is like the plains of Ssantaram (in Portugal) only on the road from Batecala to a town called Zambuja, there are some ranges with forests; nevertheless the road is very even. From Batecala to this town of Zambur (modern Sandur, about 120 miles from the coast at Batecala) is forty leagues; the road has many streams of water by its side, and because of this so much merchandise flows to Batecala that every year there come five or six thousand pack-oxen (Sewell 1924 reprint, pp. 236-237).

We have noted that the Dharwar area is closely linked to the Banavasi area, and at the same time it also closely linked to the Bellary and Chitaldurg segments of Karnataka, where there are a few Mauryan inscriptions. In view of these linkages and also because of the richness of the coastal trade, it may be logical to infer that the Konkan coast up to the border of South Kanara was within the control of the Mauryas. The Satavahana control of the Banavasi area is not at all a matter of surprise from this point of view. Neither is the fact that a trader from Banavasi would endow such a richly sculptured architectural wonder of the Karle cave at the other end of the Konkan coast.

The archaeological data from the Konkan coast cannot be called rich, and not much of it is based on excavations either. We have tried to offer some insight into the ancient picture by drawing extensively on the pre-modern sources of various kinds.

II. TAMIL NADU AND KERALA

The dimension of our problem changes when we move from the Konkan coast to Tamil Nadu and Kerala. In the Konkan coast our first problem was to understand the linkages between its chain of generally pre-modern ports and their linkages with the Maharashtra and Karnataka hinterlands across the Western Ghats. Our second problem was to understand the arterial lines which linked the major sections of these hinterlands. These problems of routes had to be approached differently in the case of Tamil Nadu and Kerala mainly because of their different geographical characters. First, because of the presence of the Palghat gap, Tamil Nadu and Kerala have been closely linked historically. There is a large open corridor between them, and there are also some less prominent but nonetheless important gaps south of this corridor. One can, of course, easily continue to move along the Kerala coast which, although named differently, is a continuation of the Konkan coast. However, here we do not have the series of passes which are present at regular intervals in the Western Ghats. Apart from the Palghat gap, all the passes linked to the Kerala coast led either to the Mysore plateau or the southern section of Tamil Nadu. Besides, one is not quite sure if the north-south movement along the coast was the most important line of movement in Kerala. Boat traffic in the backwaters and navigation along the coast were possibly equally important. In the case of Tamil Nadu, there are clear entry points in the north, which are linked to the Mysore plateau and the Rayalseema part of Andhra. There is a narrow coastal strip leading up to Nellore from Pulicat, but one is not sure if there was a major line of movement in the ancient context. The entry points across the Eastern Ghats or its outliers are, in any case, historically more visible. The configuration of uplands in the interior of Tamil Nadu and the Palghat gap have greatly influenced its internal lines of movements. Certain major lines can easily be delineated in this context.

In Tamil Nadu and Kerala one cannot also ignore the historical factors behind the nature of their routes. Chronology is important. If the early historical archaeological features are found to lie along certain routes in these areas, one gets an idea of the time when these routes developed. What can be the relevant early historical chronology and if the currently accepted chronology needs revision, what should be the arguments in favour of this revision? The Coromandel coast and the Malabar coast both possess a chain of pre-modern ports, some of which are indisputably ancient. Their locations should indicate the specific parts of the hinterlands they were primarily connected with. How many of them indicate continuity from the ancient and early mediaeval contexts, and how many of them have to be considered the products of comparatively recent but generally pre-modern trade?

In fact, in the case of Tamil Nadu and Kerala, it is difficult to get away from the historical factors which played a role in shaping their communication framework. As J. Deloche (1993, p. 74) puts it, "The meshes of the network have been made and re-made according to the evolution of urban centres." Here the passes do not provide the fixed points as they do in the case of the Konkan coast and its hinterland. Deloche (1993, pp. 74-81) tries to offer an idea of the relative importance of the Tamil Nadu routes. For instance, he points out that the Aramboli gap at Nagercoil in southern Kerala could be more important in the early context than the Palghat gap, because in the ancient Tamil literature it is supposedly more frequently mentioned than the Palghat pass. The Shencottah gap is considered by him probably impassable in the ancient context. We are hesitant to ascribe much importance to such conclusions derived from literary references, but he is undoubtedly right when he comments that "the information provided by the Cola inscriptions concerning the passageways is vague, and scarcely more than the main lines of the Vijayanagara network can be adumbrated". The important point to remember is that the form and content of the ancient Indian inscriptions of any period do not permit references to anything except the obligatory remembrance of deities, royal genealogy and glories, the names and ancestry of the donors, and a description of the donation itself. How many battlefields the ancient Indian inscriptions have mentioned and helped to identify in India?

Thus, the way in which we framed our discussions on the routes from the Konkan coast to the interior cannot be replicated in the case of Tamil Nadu and Kerala. Here, we begin by pointing out the basic geographical frame of entries and linkages and then focus on what was likely to be the broad network of routes in the early historic period. We argue for a revision of the generally accepted early historical chronology of the region and point out that its route-network took shape by c. 500 BC and that the Pandyan kingdom was possibly the earliest historical state to emerge in Tamil Nadu. We also examine what the route-network was like in the early centuries AD and later. The political history of the various region-specific dynasties of Tamil Nadu and Kerala shows how they were interacting and how through their movements in search of poltical conquests, they were not merely opening up the whole of this region but also were venturing in the direction of Karnataka and Andhra, bringing the latter closely within their political orbit. Similarly, when one takes into consideration the distribution of pre-modern ports along the Coromandel and Malabar coasts along with the details, however few, of the intensity and scale of the commercial activities of the period in this wide region, one realizes that its route-network of the early mediaeval and later periods must have been intimately linked both to the ports and the commerce conducted through them.

The importance of the passes linking the Mysore plateau with Tamil Nadu cannot be minimised in the Tamil Nadu history. The relevant district gazetteers have repeatedly emphasized the importance of this section in the 18th century wars between Haider Ali and Tipu and the East India Company. The defensive positions – the *petas* lying on the saddle between two fortified hill strongholds – were scattered all through this hilly section and underlines the intensity of military operations conducted across it. That the Anchetti pass route to Salem and Dharmapuri could lead straight to the Kaveri valley is an important indicator of the ease with which the links were maintained between the Mysore plateau and Tamil Nadu. The links could be maintained equally closely between Tamil Nadu and Andhra. Among the various passes, we have drawn attention to the line which comes from the Tirupati-Kalahasti area and enters Tamil Nadu through Chittoor. The most important archaeological landmark along this route in the Andhra section of the route, which is close to Tamil Nadu, is the Gudimallam Siva of the 3rd century BC. Regarding this Siva, I find a problem very baffling. The *Sivalinga* here lay within a railing enclosure which is identical with the type of railing enclosure that one sees around the stump of the Asokan pillar at Sarnath. Why on earth should there be such a railing enclosure around a *Sivalinga* at one of the entry points to Tamil Nadu. At Sarnath, it was put up by Asoka. By whose order was it put up at Gudimallam? Besides, such railings have so far been found only at Buddhist religious sites. Why this type of railing occurs at Gudimallam, a place which apparently does not have any Buddhist association? Or, is it possible that this railing evokes in some way the early spread of Buddhism in Tamil Nadu? Whatever the answer is, the Gudimallam Siva is one of the most perplexing archaeological relics of the sub-continent. Indirectly, it may also hint at the Mauryan incorporation of the North Arcot segment of Tamil Nadu, which does not seem to have been a part of the Satiyaputra kingdom which incorporated basically South Arcot and Dharampuri.

In the Dharampuri-Salem-Erode-Coimbatore stretch there is a series of uplands, and through this stretch one can go either through the Palghat opening to the Kerala coast near Trichur and Ponnani or to the eastern coast near Tirukkoyilur. One can also go to the central Kaveri valley around

Karur and move easily to Trichinopoly and beyond. Trichinopoly and other related sectors have also easy access to the Palghat gap by Dindigul-Pollachi or Dharapuram. In the Tamil Nadu zone, which falls at the mouth of the entry from Andhra, the routes, especially to the coast and the Trichinopoly-Tanjore-Madurai sector, are wide open.

Through the Wynad plateau, the Mysore area had links with the Kerala coast. These links also encompassed the hilly link from the Nilgiris in the direction of Kerala. South of the Palghat gap, a regular chain of passes including the Bodinaikannur pass, Shencottah gap and Aramboli gap makes links possible between the Madurai-Tinnevelly sector of Tamil Nadu and the southern segment of Kerala below Quilon.

Our argument that the beginning of early history in the region can be taken back to c. 500 BC is based on a number of considerations, the most important of which, apart from a re-consideration of the internal archaeological evidence of Tamil Nadu, is the mid-5th century BC date of the sherds inscribed in Tamil-Brahmi at the Sri Lankan site of Anuradhapura. In view of this major discovery, the general tendency to date the host of similarly inscribed sherds and inscriptions at various Tamil Nadu sites not earlier than the 3rd century BC does not make any sense at all, because the script found on the Anuradhapura sherds and the script found on the Tamil Nadu sherds and inscriptions are identical. The internal Tamil Nadu evidence cannot also be brushed aside: the references to the Pandya kingdom in Megasthenes' account of Mauryan India and the Arthasastra's reference to the pearl jewellery which must have been fashioned from the pearls derived from the Gulf of Mannar because this is the only area in the sub-continent where the tradition of pearl-fishery has ever been known; the occurrence of the pre-4th century BC Magadhan type silver punch-marked coins, which came down from a much earlier period than the date suggested by the date of their being hoarded with later coins, in Kerala and Tamil Nadu; the date of the occurrence of NBP at Korkai and Alagankulam; and finally, the probable date of the 5th century BC for the inscribed sherds at Kodumanal. Considering the various factors, such as the presence of the early NBP at the two Pandyan territory sites of Alagunkulam and Korkai, the presence of the pre-4th century BC Magadhan type silver punch-marked coins in the Madurai area, and the references to the Pandyan area in Megasthenes and Kautilya we have argued that the Pandyan kingdom was possibly the first historical state to emerge in Tamil Nadu. We also think it possible that this kingdom, because of the intrinsic importance of the pearl fishery of the Gulf of Mannar and its early date as evidenced by the find of broken oyster shells in association with NBP at Korkai, had maritime links with north India.

We have pointed out that such links with north India antedate the beginning of early history in the region, the most important evidence in this regard being the find of the antennae-swords of the Gangetic valley copper hoards at Vellore and in the Ramanathapuram district of Tamil Nadu and the Idukki area in southern Kerala.

A brief review of the political events of the Pandya, Chola, Pallava and Chera territories demonstrates both a see-saw struggle for power between them and occasionally successful thrusts towards the Mysore plateau, the Deccan, the Andhra coast and beyond, Sri Lanka, the islands in the Indian Ocean and the Bay of Bengal, and the Malayan peninsula. There is little doubt that through this long-drawn process of political interaction, the internal routes of Tamil Nadu and Kerala were being meshed into the wider route network of the northern regions. Among other things, the fact that the Chola king Rajendra II advanced as far as Kolhapur shows that the arterial line of Dharwar-Belgaum-Kolhapur-Satara-Pune was very much within the comprehension of the Cholas. This is just an example of how the routes of Kerala and Tamil Nadu were not isolated in themselves but were operative in the frame of a much wider area. Secondly, a major part of these routes must have been directed towards maintaining easy approaches to the innumerable pre-modern ports that we have listed. We do not for a moment claim that all these ports date from the ancient or even the early mediaeval context, but the point is that all the four ancient territories of Tamil Nadu and Kerala had maritime outlets in their own areas. Alagankulam, Korkai and Tondi were the ancient ports of the Pandya territory but the locations of other pre-modern ports in the same area indicates that theoretically there could be more landing places on the coast of the Pandya territory even in the ancient context. In fact, this can be true of any of the other three territories.

On the basis of Champakalakshmi's distribution maps of the historic settlements of Tamil Nadu, we have argued for a continuity of the Tamil Nadu route network from the early historic period to the later contexts up to c. AD 1300. Two communication lines have always been important: the Coimbatur-Salem-Dharmapuri axis, with its own approach to the Kerala coast, and the axis from Kanchipuram-Madras sector to the areas down south up to Madurai and Tinnevelly. Their relative importance might have varied from period to period, depending on the political exigencies and the needs of the coastal and inland trade. Deloche (1993, p. 76) illustrates a great number of Tamil Nadu and Kerala routes in the context of the second half of the 18th century. The mid-19th century enumeration of these routes by Francis Scott (1853) does not significantly differ from Deloche's picture. In fact, the basic frame of it may be said to have been rooted in the early historic context itself.

III. ANDHRA

Andhra is largely encircled on the west and the north by Karnataka and Maharashtra, and the passages from both these directions vary from easy to relatively easy. Unless one moves down the coast to the Pulicat area below Nellore, one has to approach Tamil Nadu from Andhra through Chittoor which also offers easy access to the Mysore-Bangalore area of Karnataka. The whole section from Bidar-Gulbarga to Chitaldurg in Karnataka has open border with the Nizamabad – Rangareddi – Mahbubnagar – Kurnool – Anantapur part of Andhra. The Aurangabad-Daulatabad area of Maharashtra lies to the northwest of Nizamabad. The Vidarbha or Berar section of Maharashtra which extends eastward up to Nagpur, Bhandara and Chandrapur lies basically to the northwest and north of the Andhra districts of Adilabad and Karimnagar. Along the eastern edge of the Bastar hills, a road runs through the Koraput-Kalahandi area of southwest Orissa to the Raipur segment of Chhattisgarh or the ancient South Kosala or Mahakosala. The Orissan coast is a straight continuation of the Srikakulam coast area in the easternmost coastal stretch of Andhra. Movement to, and from, Andhra was not apparently difficult at any period of its history.

Within Andhra itself the hills have occasionally intervened in the line of movements. The Eastern Ghats form a hilly line between Sri Sailam and Nagarjunakonda along the Krishna. The Nallamalais and Erramalais, both parts of the Eastern Ghats, form barriers between the coast and the districts of Kurnool and Anantapur. There are also hill ranges between the Nellore coast and the districts of Cuddapah and Chittoor. It is only in this section that the relevant district gazetteers refer to passes. However, none of them was considered difficult and most of them were in any case minor and important only in the local grain trade and movements like that. In the southward movement to Tamil Nadu, and the area of Kolar, Bangalore and Mysore, the Tirupati gap provided an easy passage, presided over by Vishnu at Tirupati and Siva at Gudimallam. The Andhra coastline in the Visakhapatnam section is fringed by the hills, occasionally sending large boulders and bedrock to the sea, but there is no difficulty in moving along this part of the coast if one follows the foot of the hills. Hills and rocks occur sporadically all over Andhra except in the two deltas of the

Krishna and the Godavari. In many cases they have provided the locations of Buddhist monastic sites which widely dot the State's landscape. Among the less important rivers, the name of Vamsadhara further up the coast from Srikakulam comes readily to mind, if for no other reason except that the view of its delta from the top of the hillock of the Buddhist site of Salihundam is not something which one easily forgets.

From the northern parts of India, Andhra was relatively easy to move to. From the Aurangabad area in Maharashtra or from Paithan, a Satavahana capital city, one followed the alignments which were traditionally followed to reach the Nizamabad area, and to reach Aurangabad or Paithan from the Ganga valley there was an easy route coming from the side of Burhanpur on the northern bank of the Tapti. From the Ganga valley one could also come by Vidarbha, entering the Adilabad-Karimnagar section through the occasionally forested patches of Chandrapur. From the Ganga valley, the passage along the Orissa-Kalinga coast is not at all difficult, and finally, one could opt to travel through South Kosala or Chhattisgarh to reach the area of modern Vizianagram and then follow the coastline to the Konasamudram delta of the Godavari.

There is absolutely no reason to believe that the north Indian coins (silver punch-marked) and pottery (NBP) found at the base of the Andhra sites of Amaravati and Vaddamanu should be late in comparison with their dates in North India even by a hundred years. We would claim that the NBP and punch-marked coins were carried by way of trade to Andhra soon after their beginning in the Ganga plain. The date of the NBP is currently held to be c. 800 BC in the central section of the Ganga valley. Even assuming that the NBP which came to Andhra came from a different section of the Ganga plain where the beginning of the NBP might be later than its beginning in the section of Ayodhya-Allahabad, it is almost impossible to put the date of the Andhra NBP later than c. 600 BC. The inscribed and fragmentary *stupa* railing of the 3rd century BC from Amaravati, which shows the existence of *Mahastupa* before the Mauryan period, also suggests the probability of Buddhism being carried to Andhra during or a little after the death of the Buddha.

George Buhler's analysis of the Bhottiprolu relic inscriptions (Buhler 1894) is a further pointer in this direction. There are ten inscriptions in all on the three relic-caskets from Bhottiprolu. Nine of them are incised partly on the circular tops of the relic caskets and partly on the rims of the lower stones. Inscription 10 is scratched on a small hexagonal piece of crystal and was considered "difficult to read on account of the shallowness of the strokes". Buhler dated them not later than 200 BC, but thought that they might be 'somewhat earlier'. According to Buhler, these inscriptions prove, among others, that during the third century BC there were 'several well-marked varieties of the Southern Maurya alphabet' and that the Bhottiprolu inscriptions "now show a system of writing, which in some respects is radically different and which may be reasonably supposed to have arisen in Asoka's times or even earlier". According to him, "they furnish a very great help to those who, like myself, believe the art of writing to have been practised in India for many centuries before the accession of Chandragupta Maurya to the throne of Pataliputra".

From the present point of view, more important is his assertion that two of the caskets were intended for relics of the Buddha. His 'Inscription I' reads "a box of crystal in order to deposit some relics of Buddha". Inscription IV mentions *Budhasa sarirani*. On the whole, it is virtually impossible to deny that Buddhism came to Andhra soon after the death of the Buddha.

The pre-modern ports that we have been chasing all along the Konkan, Malabar and Coromandel coasts does not fade away after hitting the Andhra coastline above Pulicat. There were a few of them in the Nellore segment alone, and by the time one reaches the Krishna delta, the number increases significantly, encompassing ports mentioned in the Classical sources. Whether the ports in the Vengi area played the most important role in sending ships to Southeast Asia can be debated, but they were likely to have played a major enough role. That a donor to the Guntupalle rock-cut complex of the 3rd-2nd century BC and later should style himself a 'great sailor' or *Mahanavika* is a positive indicator of the maritime importance of this area.

The distribution of early historic urban centres in Andhra gives a clear idea of its major routes in the ancient context. Two fortified city sites – Kotilingala and Dhulicotta – are in the Karimnagar-Adilabad section and oriented towards Vidarbha by Chandrapur or Chanda. Southward, this orientation points to the Warangal area and then to the Krishna valley and the delta. This can also lead through Khammam to West Godavari and thus the Godavari delta. The Vidarbha section of this route has still some uncertainty regarding the details. For instance, after the Godavari was crossed at or near Kotilingala, the next major site in the Vidarbha area is Pauni where the Wainganga is crossed to reach the Balaghat area and move towards Jabalpur or ancient Tripuri, from where there is a straight route through Rewa to the area of ancient Kausambi on the bank of the Yamuna. There is some problem about the location of Adam which lies somewhat to the west of Karimnagar-Chanda-Pauni alignment. And yet, this does not lie on the Adilabad-Nagpur axis which is shown on modern maps and also on Deloche's map of the 'ancient Gondvana' routes in the second half of the 18th century. It is possible that Adam lies on the route which comes from the direction of Bhandara in the east and goes toward the Ajanta-Aurangabad sector. On the other hand, there could be a connection with the Nagpur area from Adilabad via Adam. As we have not done field-study of the Hyderabad-Nirmal-Adilabad-Nagpur axis, we are somewhat uncertain about this. As far as we are aware, no early historic site lies on this axis, with Adam falling to its east, just as Pauni lies a little to the east of the modern Chanda-Nagpur alignment. In fact, Pauni lies straight on the Chanda-Bhandara alignment, which should also lead in the direction of Jabalpur. It is possible that the ancient alignments in this sector do not overlie the 18th century or later alignments. There could be two alignments, one certainly through Pauni, and the other possibly through Adam. It is further possible that the ancient 'Asika/Asmaka' *janapada* did not lie wholly in the Godavari section of northern Andhra but included some parts of the area to the south of Nagpur as well. If the reading of 'Asika' on a terracotta sealing from Adam is beyond dispute, that should be the case. In the Nizamabad section, the city-site of Bodhan can give access in a number of directions: towards the Krishna valley and the delta through the area of Hyderabad and then to Nagarjunakonda; towards Ter which is located in the Osmanabad area (west-southwest of Latur); towards Yeotmal in the north; and finally, towards Aurangabad/ Daulatabad. Regarding the position of Kondapur in the southern part of Medak (closer to Sangareddi than to Medak), one can see that it lies at a kind of entry point to the modern Hyderabad area and thus the Nagarjunakonda area. On the other hand, the Mauryan city-site of Sannati lies to its southeast in the Gulbarga area (not far from Yadgir), and the Raichur-Adoni-Guntakal-Anantapur section lies almost in a straight line from Sadasivpet near which Kondapur is located. Interestingly, the latter axis can lead one straight up to the entry points of the Mysore plateau and Tamil Nadu in this section.

The location of the city-sites in the Krishna valley and delta is not problematic in the sense that they formed the terminal points of the routes which entered Andhra from various directions. Nagarjunakonda was selected for its defensive position at a point where the Krishna comes out of the hills and flows through an open valley to the delta. Amaravati/ Dhenukataka lies in the valley but at the head of the delta. The position of Vengi is the same in relation to the Godavari delta. The route, which

Deloche (1993) has drawn for the section from Hyderabad to Puri, passes through the head of both the Krishna and Godavari deltas, although it hugs the coast from time to time. In the ancient context the route must have come very close to the coast because one cannot otherwise explain the location of Buddhist sites like Bavikonda and Thotlakonda near Visakhapatnam. Peddavegi or ancient Vengi lies to the north of Elluru located at the head of the deltaic region.

The location of Dantapuri east of Srikakulam needs some special consideration. This was the capital of ancient Kalinga and must have borne the brunt of the Mauryan attack because it was the capital. This lies in a coastal tract which gives access to the Baitarani-Mahanadi deltaic area and the upper Mahanadi stretch of Orissa. In addition, the Vijianagram-Srikakulam area where the site is located, receives a route coming from the modern Raipur sector of Chhattisgarh or ancient South Kosala through the Koraput-Kalahandi-Jeypore section of Orissa. Samudragupta, who swept down the Andhra coast in the 4th century AD, came from Pataliputra following this route. Following this historical parallel, it is possible that Asoka, who also came from Pataliputra, came by this route to conquer Kalinga. The Mauryan army would have struck the Andhra coast in the area of modern Vizianagram and turned east along the coast for the subjugation of Dantapuri. As the battle for Delhi used to be fought at Panipat, which lies at some distance to the west of Delhi, similarly, it is logical to infer that the battle of Kalinga took place in a stretch between Vizianagram and the site of Dantapuri. Interestingly, there is a place called *Ranasthalam* ('battle-field') in this stretch. One does not know if the term carries the folk memory of the Mauryan battle for Kalinga fought many centuries ago, but a convenient example of such retentions of folk memory in Andhra is the term *Dipaladinne* ('mound of lamps') for the *Mahastupa* of Amaravati. *Ranasthalam* lies in an area where the battle for Kalinga is likely to have been fought.

In the Kurnool area, at the other end of Andhra, the location of Satanikota is problematic, unless one assumes that this Satavahana period fort was built at an important Tungabhadra crossing. The general importance of the area can be guessed from the locations of Rajula, Mandagiri and Erragudi in the southwestern section of the Kurnool district. If one assumes that the modern Raichur-Adoni-Pattikonda alignment is a part of an ancient alignment, it is possible to think that this led to the entry points of the south in the Gulbarga-Anantapur-Cuddapah-Chittoor section on the one hand and also led to the Kopbal area near Bellary on the other. The Kopbal area is important for its cluster of four Asokan

Minor Rock Edict sites – two around the modern Kopbal (Jatinga Rameshwar and Palkigundu), Udegolam and Nittoor. The Chitaldurg section where the Rock Edict site of Brahmagiri and a Minor Rock Edict site are located lies to the south of the Kopbal area.

Regarding the distribution of Buddhist monastic sites in Andhra, those who are not located in the immediate periphery of the settlement sites usually mark the alignment of routes. For instance, the site of Nelakondapalli lies near the highway between Khammam and Bezwada, the latter giving access to a number of areas including the Krishna valley and delta. We have argued that there is a possibility that Guntupalle located 65 km to the north of Ellur could be linked with Khammam and through that, with the Karimnagar-Pauni alignment.

IV. SOME ARTERIAL LINES

As we have seen, there are many details regarding the ancient route network of the Konkan coast and its Maharashtra and Karnataka hinterland, Tamil Nadu and Kerala, and Andhra, which are not particularly clear and would require more field-research. However, there are certain arterial lines which were operative through this vast region, and here we would try to dwell on them.

The Konkan coast which begins south of Daman and continues for about 900 km to Mangalore at the north end of the Malabar coast has a number of focal points of trade, although all along its length it possesses a great number of major and minor ports. The Sopara-Thana-Kalyan area was the focal point in the ancient context, leading, across the Western Ghats, to Nasik in the north and Junnar in the south. There was another focal point, although somewhat less in significance, in the area of Dahanu and Sanjan, which was linked to Nasik. There were two major focal points in the second segment from Alibag-Chaul to Ratnagiri-Vengurla. The first of these was Chaul and from here one could reach equally easily Junnar and Pune. The second focal point was Ratnagiri-Vengurla, from where a large slice of the Maharashtra hinterland was open, and that includes Satara, Karad, Kolhapur and Belgaum. Goa, which forms a segment by itself is linked to Belgaum in the north and Dharwar in the south. The ports of the fourth segment between Karwar and Mangalore, i.e., North and South Kanara, have hinterlands stretching from Dharwar in the north and Hassan and Coorg in the south.

If Konkan is a long stretch of coast, it has also a long stretch of hinterland. It is a long distance from Nasik to Hasan, and the link-ups of the different major sectors of this long alignment are also different. Nasik at the mouth of the Thal pass, is ideally placed to approach Gujarat,

Madhya Pradesh across the Tapti, and the Aurangabad-Bhokardan-Paithan section of Maharashtra. The last section has clear link-up with places like Bodhan in the Nizamabad area of Andhra. Junnar at the mouth of the Nana and Malsej Ghats is suitable for link-up with Paithan and the general hinterland of Ahmednagar-Pune. Pune sits at the head of the Pune-Satara-Kolhapur-Belgaum alignment. From the Pune area one can also go southeast to a large part of Maharashtra (cf. Solapur, Osmanabad) and parts of Karnataka (cf. Gulbarga) and Andhra (through Osmanabad). The major option at Kolhapur as a hinterland point is to move in the direction of Bijapur and the adjacent areas. More extensive options are open at Belgaum and Dharwar. The whole of Karnataka is open from these two places: the Raichur doab or the doab between the Tungabhadra and the Krishna, the doab between the Krishna and the Bhima, and the Bellary and Chitaldurg sectors. The Rayalseema section of Andhra adjoins the Bellary sector in the east. Finally, Hassan leads to the Mysore, Bangalore and Kolar sectors which border both Tamil Nadu and Andhra. Thus, in the total stretch of hinterland on the eastern side of the Western Ghats, one can envisage a number of major lines. The base-line was the alignment from Nasik and Junnar to Belgaum and Dharwar via Satara, Karad and Kolhapur. As we have seen, a number of lines radiated from this line to the east and the southeast. For instance, the line which radiated from the Nasik area and went eventually to the Andhra coast through Ter and Kondapur and Nagarjunakonda was certainly a major avenue of links. The Dharwar-Bellary alignment was also an important one, because from this alignment one could proceed across the Nandikanama pass to the Andhra coast or turn south towards Tamil Nadu.

Between Gulbarga and Badami, Karnataka has had a number of centres of political power: Sannati of the Mauryan-Satavahana times, Badami of the Western Chalukyas, Malkhed of the Rashtrakutas, Bidar of the Bahmani sultans, Bijapur of the Adil Sahi sultans and finally, Hampi of the Vijayanagara kings. Along with these, one has to mention the Hoyasalas with their power centre at Belur-Halebid near Hasan, and the Western Gangas with their power centre at Talakkad. The arterial lines that we have mentioned above are likely to have served the purpose of knitting this large sector together.

In Tamil Nadu, there were two major alignments, one of which came through Chittoor and ran north-south, with loops, to Madurai, Tinnevelly and Cape Comorin. The other line was the Dharmapuri-Salem-Coimbatore axis which reached the regions in the far south and the Kerala coast. With variations, these two lines form the spine of the route network of the ancient Tamil Nadu. The major opening in the Kerala coast was the Palghat gap, with subsidiary openings, as we have seen, both in the north and the south.

The line which links the different parts of the Andhra coast from Nellore to Srikakulam is in a sense the base-line of the Andhra routes, and it is joined by a host of routes which come from South Kosala or Mahakosala, Vidarbha, Nasik, Aurangabad, and the Rayalseema districts. The significance of the route which came from Nasik and touched the Andhra coast cannot be minimised. Its importance in the light of the testimony of the *Periplus* was emphasised by J.F. Fleet (1901) in connection with his identification of Ter, and we drew attention to this while discussing the routes which came from the Ganga plain to the Deccan (Chakrabarti 2005). The existence of this arterial line linking two focal points of India's ancient maritime trade is suggested not merely by the *Periplus* but also by the repeated mentions of Dhenukataka or Amaravati in the inscriptions of Karle and Kanheri. Inscription 1020 of Luders' list records the donation of a cave and a water-cistern by the nun Sarpa who was the "daughter of the lay-worshipper Kulapiya Dhamanaka, the *Dhenukakatiya*". At Karle, Inscription 1089 of Luders' list mentions the perfumer Simhadatta from Dhenukakata. Inscription 1092 refers to 'the son of Venuvasa, a Dhenukakataka'. In Inscription 1093 the 'Yavana Sihadhaya' is mentioned as being from Dhenukakata. Inscription 1096 records the "gift of Dhamma-Yavana from Dhenukakata". This linking up of the Krishna delta with the monastic sites like Karle and Kanheri at the approach to the ports of Sopara and Elephanta on the west coast gives this route a significance of its own in the early historic period.

V. SOME ASPECTS RELATED TO THE MAURYAN PRESENCE IN THE SOUTHERN PENINSULA

The interconnections between the different areas of Konkan, the Deccan and the southern peninsula will remain incomplete if we do not raise some problems related to the Mauryan presence in this region. Can the Konkan coast up to Mangalore be considered a part of the Mauryan domain? Does the location of major cities like Suvarnagiri and Isila, which are mentioned in the Asokan edicts throw any light on the network of communications during the Mauryan times? The southern kingdom which was closest to the border of the Mauryan empire was Satiyaputra. Does its location in South Arcot and Dharampuri leave any scope for the Mauryan control to touch some parts of Tamil Nadu? We have already drawn attention to the possible route of the Mauryan invasion of Kalinga and also suggested a place where the battle of Kalinga was likely to have been fought. Here we discuss the problems of identifications of Suvarnagiri and Isila and the southern limits of the Mauryan empire.

V.1. The Identifications of Suvarnagiri and Isila

These two places are mentioned in the Brahmagiri and Siddapur versions of Minor Rock Edict I:

"From Suvarnagiri, at the word of the prince (*aryaputra*) and of the *Mahamatras* at Isila must be wished good health and be told this" (Hultzsch 1925, p. 177).

Hultzsch added the following note:

"This place (Suvarnagiri) seems to have been the capital of the province administered by the *Aryaputras* and his *Mahamatras*. Buhler compared the second separate edict at Dhauli, according to which, a *Kumara* and his *Mahamatras* resided at Tosali. The separate edicts of Dhauli and Jaugada were addressed by the king to the local authorities themselves, while in the Mysore edicts the king commands the authorities of the Suvarnagiri province to communicate his orders to their subordinates at Isila. In Fleet's opinion the Mysore edicts were issued from Suvarnagiri by Asoka himself; and he identified the place with one of the hills, still known as Sonagiri, near Rajagriha in Bihar. H. Krishna Sastri connects Suvarnagiri, i.e. the gold mountain, with the country around Maski, which abounds in gold-workings. Perhaps it may be identified with the synonym Kanakagiri, south of Maski and north of the ruins of Vijayanagara" (Hultzsch 1925, p. 177, note 5).

In 1894-95, G. Buhler suggested that the extent of Asoka's possessions certainly 'included more than the northern extremity of Mysore' and that Suvarnagiri should be considered 'the headquarters of the viceroy of the Dekhan'. "If it still exists, it will now go by a name like Songir or Songadh, Sondurg, Suvarnadurg, or the like" (Buhler 1894-95, p. 137).

J.F. Fleet who identified (Fleet 1909) Suvarnagiri with Sonagiri of Rajagriha, thought that "Isila was evidently an ancient town situated somewhere in the locality where the records are, and it was, no doubt, a subdivisional town of the Vanavasi kingdom: its name has apparently now disappeared".

The opinion that the occupational site represented by the level ground near the site of Brahmagiri inscribed boulder was ancient Isila gained ground after Mortimer Wheeler's excavation of the site in 1947 (Wheeler 1948, p. 185). N.P. Chakravarti (1948) wrote that "Isila must be identified with the site of the ancient town at the foot of Brahmagiri near Siddapur" and that Suvarnagiri, although unidentified, was the headquarters of the southernmost province of Asoka's empire. Regarding Isila, we here draw attention to two points. An Amaravati inscription (Inscription 1248 of Luders' list) of the time of the Satavahana king Vasishthiputra Pulumavi refers to a householder called Isila (Sanskrit Rishila). Thus, Isila can both be a personal name and a place name. More importantly, our observation is that the level field available near the edict-carrying boulder at Brahmagiri was too constricted to be considered a city-site, which Asoka's Isila apparently was. In fact, the other site explored by Wheeler along with Brahmagiri, i.e., Chandravali, has a much better claim to be considered a city-site: "The main body of the ancient town was some 800 yards long in that direction, and the configuration of the valley suggests that it may have had an approximately similar width" (Wheeler 1948, p. 270). Chandravalli lay much nearer modern Chitaldurg than Brahmagiri. Location-wise, Chitaldurg has an easier access to Bellary, Dharwar, Shimoga and Hassan than the Siddapur area, although the latter is in the modern Chitaldurg district. We would say that if Isila was an important enough place to have Mauryan *Mahamatras* or judicial officers in this part of Karnataka, its likely jurisdiction possibly included a chunk of the Bellary-Dharwar-Shimoga-Hassan sector of Karnataka. From this point of view, Chandravalli enjoys the advantage of a better location. We would place Mauryan Isila at the site of Chandravalli.

If Suvarnagiri was the centre of the Mauryan administration of the south and important enough to have a prince as the governor, there can be only one contemporary site which displays that level of significance. The site is Sannati, a large fortified site with the remains of two *stupas* outside its fortification. One of these *stupas* is represented by the excavated remains of Kanganahalli which have yielded exquisite sculptures of the Amaravati style. In the local Chandralamba temple, inscribed stone slabs containing Rock Edicts XII and XIV and the two separate edicts of Dhauli and Jaugada were found, and I.K. Sarma and J.V. Rao (1993) have listed a total of about 83 inscriptions from this indisputably large and fortified city-site, including those of the Satavahana rulers. Although the modern place name 'Jonnagiri' near the site of the Erragudi edicts sounds like Suvarnagiri, there is nothing except this similarity to justify its identification as Suvarnagiri of the edicts. There are no visible occupational debris in the sweep of the cultivated fields below the Erragudi hill, and although only a thorough exploration of the area can settle the issue, the pre-eminence of Sannati as a site is so visible and its location is so suitable to control the southern possessions of the Mauryas that we have no hesitation to identify Sannati as Suvarnagiri.

V.2. The Southern Limits of the Asokan Control

The relevant edict sites are the following: Sannati (near Yadgir in Gulbarga), Maski (in Lingsugur), Gavimath and Palkigundi (both in the outskirts of Kopbal), Nittur and Udegolam (between Bellary and Kopbal), Brahmagiri, Siddapur and Jatinga Rameshwar (all three around Siddapur), and Rajula Mandagiri and Erragudi (both near Patikonda). Sannati is linked on its northwest to Ter, and on the northeast to Kondapur. In the south this seems to be aligned towards the Adoni-Pattikonda sector of Kurnul, and from this sector the Bellary-Kopbal segment is easily approachable. From Sannati, it was also possible to move in the direction of Alampur on the Tungabhadra, cross the river in that section and proceed towards the Nandyal valley from where there is a straight route through the Nandikanama pass to the Andhra coast. From the Nandiyal valley again, one could move in the direction of Cuddapah and Chittoor from where a route led to the modern Tamil Nadu sector. It thus appears that Sannati or, as we have argued, ancient Suvarnagiri occupied a nodal position in the network of communication between the Deccan and the south. Through Ter it could approach the line of communication to Paithan on the one hand and the Solapur-Pune area on the other. It could approach the Andhra coast either through Kondapur and the Krishna valley or through Nandiyal and Nandikanama. The Tamil Nadu sector could be approached through Cuddapah and Chittoor. The Bellary-Kopbal-Maski area was within its easy distance, and once in Bellary, Chitaldurg and the area around it was easily approachable. From Sannati, one could reach the Kopbal-Bellary segment also via Maski. The cluster of four edict-bearing sites – Gavimath, Palkigundu, Nittur and Udegolam – in the Bellary-Kopbal segment is decidedly interesting. To argue that these fall in and around the gold-mining area of Hatti does not possibly explain everything about their location in an area which, many centuries later, was also the heartland of the Vijayanagara kingdom. Apparently, this area had enjoyed, even during the Mauryan times, a geo-political importance of which we are not yet aware. The Siddapur cluster of edicts was, as we have already noted, in an area which gave access not merely to the Hassan sector of modern Karnataka but also its Hubli-Dharwar area.

On the whole, looking closely at the distribution of the Asokan edicts between Sannati and Siddapur-Brahmagiri-Jatinga Rameshwar, one may realize certain points about the Mauryan control of this part of the Deccan. First, there is no doubt that the Mauryans had under their control the coastal North Canara and possibly South Kanara as well up to Mangalore. With the Mauryan controlling points around Chitaldurg and Kopbal-

Bellary, this is a logical conclusion, especially in view of the fact that the later dynasties who were ensconced in this zone had no difficulty in extending their supremacy to the Konkan coast of North and South Kanara. What is further intriguing is that through Sannati and Ter a long line of trade ran from the Krishna delta to the northern part of the Konkan coast and beyond. Fleet pointed this out in the context of the *Periplus*' testimony in the 1st century AD, and that his supposition was entirely right is also proved by the occurrence of the name of Dhenukataka or ancient Amaravati of the Krishna valley in a number of Karle and Kanheri inscriptions. We have cited these references above. It appears from our understanding of the location of Sannati that this line of communication also ran during the Mauryan period.

The question of the southernmost limits of the Mauryan empire cropped up in our mind because of a specific feature of the 3rd century BC Siva of Gudimallam. This site lies near Kalahasti and Tirupati, both connected with the southern route to Vellore and Arkkonam through Chittoor. The point which we find baffling is that there is a three-bar railing around the Gudimallam *linga*, certainly the only example of such a railing around a *Sivalinga*. This railing is exactly like the railing which one can see around the stump of the Asokan pillar at Sarnath. I.K. Sarma has shown stratigraphically that the Gudimallam Siva was put in its position in the third century BC. Even on the analogy of its railing enclosure with the railing enclosure of Sarnath, this dating could be argued for this Shiva. The point is that this type of railing does not occur anywhere else further south. In fact, on the basis of the Sarnath analogy, one may say that this marks the presence of the Mauryas as far as the Chittoor segment of Andhra. What also sets our mind ticking is its location at one of the northern gateways of Tamil Nadu. Did the Mauryan empire include a part of the northernmost segment of Tamil Nadu? The Satiyaputra kingdom of Tamil Nadu during the Asokan period included South Arcot where the Jambai inscription of Athiyaman has been found near Tirukkoyilur, and Dharampuri where his capital Tagadur has been placed. The point is that we do not yet know if North Arcot and the Kanchipuram-Chingleput segment were within the Satiyaputra kingdom. The problem cannot yet be settled, but in view of the 'Mauryan railing' around Gudimallam Siva and the possibility that North Arcot and Chingleput could be outside the Satiyaputra kingdom, a case can logically be made of the possibility of the Mauryan control of Tamil Nadu up to Kanchipuram and Chingleput. It appears that the whole of the Mysore plateau was within the Mauryan empire.

The details of the ancient route network of the vast region that we have considered in this volume will need, as we have repeatedly emphasized, many more years of ground research, but hopefully, a basic outline of its geographical and historical complexities has been put forward in this volume.

The Summary of Arguments

1. THE KONKAN COAST AND ITS HINTERLANDS

(1.1)

PRE-MODERN PORTS Umbergaon> Sanjan sector	PASSES		CAVES
Maroli			14 rock-cut
Nargol			cells under
Umbergaon			the walls
SANJAN	Shir	>Vaitarna valley	of
Dheri	Tal	> Ulhas valley	Indragad
Gholbad	Malsej	>Kalyan	fort, north
Dahanu	Nana	>Kalyan	of
Tarapur	Bhimshankar	>Elephanta	Umbergaon
Savta	Kusur	Elephanta	-
Navapur	Bor	Elephanta	Halkhurd
Satpatti			Dahanu
Kelve-Mahim			Jamburg
Alibag			(Bor pass)
Agashi			Kanheri

PRE-MODERN PORTS Umbergaon> Sanjan sector	PASSES		CAVES
SOPARA			Kondivti
BASSEIN			Jogeshwari
THANA			Mandapeshwar
KALYAN			Magathana
Bhiwndi			Elephanta
Versova			
Utan			
Bandra			
Panvel			
ELEPHANTA			
Alibag-Mahad			
Sector			
Mandva	Pimpri		
Avas	Tamhana		
Revas	Nisni		
Dharamtar	*Linga*		
Alibag	Kumbha		Chaul
Pen	Kavaliya	>Pune	Kuda
CHAUL	Shevtya	>Pune	Mahad
Nagothna	Madhya	>Pune	
Roha	Ambenal	>Pune	
Mandad	Gopya	>Pune	
Murud	Umbarda	>Pune	
Mhasla	Veranda	>Pune	
Janjira	Kamtha		
Danda-Rajpur	Dhavla	>Vai/Satara	
Dasgaon	Fitzerald		
Mahad	Pir	>Satara	
		Mahabaleshwar	

(1.2)

RATNAGIRI SECTOR

PRE-MODERN PORTS	PASSES ALIGNMENTS	CAVES
Bankot	Hatlot >Khed	on the western
Mahapral	Ambavli > Satara	side of the
Kelshi	North	Western Ghats:
Ade	Tivra > Satara	Chiplun
Anjalla	Kumbhali > Karhad>Satara>Solapur	Dabhol
Harnai	Mala > Satara	Khed
Dapoli	South	Kol
Dabhol	Tivra > Miraj	Sangameshwar
Anjanvel	Kundi	
Chiplun	Amba > Kolhapur > Miraj	on the eastern
Guhagar	Anaskura > Karad	side of the
Adur	Kajirda > Kolhapur	Western Ghats:
Jaygad	Bavda > Kolhapur	Shirval
Sangameshwar	Shergad >Kolhapur	Wai / Vai
Ratnagiri	Phonda > Kolhapur	Kundal
Rajapur	Ghotga > Kolhapur	Tamkane
Jaytapur	Rangna > Kolhapur	
Vijayadurg	Hanumant > Kolhapur	
Kharepatan	Amboli > Kolhapur	
Achra	Ram > Goa> Dharwar	
Malvan		
Nivti		
Vengurla		

GOA TO MANGALORE

PRE-MODERN PORTS	PASSES	HINTERLAND	ANCIENT SITES
Goa	Kele		
Mapusa	Tinai		
Margao	Ramghat		
Karwar	Gopshitta		
Bhatkal	Kaiga		
Kumta	Anshi	Belgaum	Vadgaon-Madhopur
Honavar	Arebail	Dharwar	
Barkur	Devimane	Harihar	Banavasi
Malpe/Udupi	Gersoppa	Shimoga	
Kundapur	Hogevadi	Hassan	
Basrur	Gundilkatta	Chitradurg	
Udayavara	Kuveshi		
Mangalore	Digi		
	Kundal		
	Dhokarpa		
	Ganeshgudi		
	Vaddi		
	Nilkund		
	Dodmane		
	Gersoppa		

(1.3) ALIGNMENTS IN THE HINTERLANDS

1. The ports and passes in the Umbergaon to Mahad sector lead to the following major ancient places in the immediate hinterland.

NASIK with linkages to coastal Gujarat, Burhanpur on the Tapti for Malwa, Vidarbha via Aurangabad and Jalgaon, Paithan via Nevasa, and Junnar to the south.

JUNNAR with linkages to Paithan via Nevasa, and Pune to the south.

PUNE with two major linkages, one towards Gulbarga via Solapur and the other towards Satara, Karad, Kolhapur, and Belgaum.

2. The ports and passes in the Ratnagiri sector lead to (from the north to the south) Satara, Karad, Kolhapur and Belgaum. From this north-south line, the entire Gulbarga, Raichur and Bellary sections to the east are open.

3. The ports and passes from Goa to Mangalore lead to Belgaum, Dharwar, Shimoga, Chitradurg and Hassan, linking basically the whole of Karnataka and the Bellary segment of Andhra to the coast.

2. THE BASIC STRUCTURE OF THE CHAPTER ON TAMIL NADU AND KERALA

1. The chapter begins with the enumeration of the major routes from the Mysore plateau and Andhra to Tamil Nadu and from Tamil Nadu and the Mysore plateau to Kerala.

The routes between the Mysore plateau and Tamil Nadu can be seen in two sections on the Tamil Nadu side: the Dharampuri-Salem sector, and the Coimbatore-Erode sector. In the Dharampuri-Salem stretch there are four major passes: (1) the Budikota pass between Krishnagiri in Tamil Nadu and Budipeta in the Bowringpet area of Kolar in Karnataka; (2) the Sulagiri pass between Sulagiri in Tamil Nadu and Hosur in Karnataka; (3) the Anchetti pass between Denkanikonda and Pennagoram, leading to the Toppur river valley in Karnataka; (4) and the Palakodu-Rayakota pass, lying entirely in the Krishnagiri area of Tamil Nadu.

In the Coimbatore-Erode section there are three passes: the Talamalai, Gazzalhatti and Hasanur passes, with the Gazzalhatti lying close to the Moyar valley. The Dharampuri-Salem passes easily lead to the alignments from this area to the coast, especially the section between Porto Novo in the south and Pondicherry in the north. They can also join up with the alignments emerging from the passes to the Coimbatore-Erode area.

The alignments which are based on the line between Coimbatore and Erode lead to Karur and Trichinopoly (ancient Uraiyur) on the one hand and the Palghat gap on the other. From Karur it is also possible to penetrate deeper into southern Tamil Nadu – the Madurai-Dindigul-Pollachi alignment towards Palghat, for instance.

The routes from Andhra to Tamil Nadu pass through the numerous openings in the Chittoor, Cuddapah and Anantapur sections of Andhra, opening into the North Arcot, Chingleput, Chennai and Dharampuri areas of Tamil Nadu, including the coast from Pondicherry upward.

2. Kerala can be approached from the inland side in two ways: (1) through the Palghat gap, the Aramboli gap near Nagercoil, and the many narrow openings, among which the Cumbam valley is a convenient example, and

(2) through Wynad from the Mysore plateau to the Cannanore-Calicut stretch of the Kerala coast.

3. Once beyond the issue of routes, the chapter dwells on the geographical and political territories of the Satiyaputras, Cheras, Cholas and Pandyas, and argues, on the basis of a wide body of evidence including the testimony of Megasthenes and Kautilya, that these territorial units had emerged into the historical period by the mid-first millennium BC. This date is also corroborated, according to our analysis, by early inscriptions found in caves, inscribed sherds and punch-marked coins in Tamil Nadu and Kerala, which also throw light on the alignments of early historic routes of the region. The chronology of these inscriptions has been argued to be as early as the inscriptions found in the Anuradhapura excavations in Sri Lanka (i.e., the mid-first millennium BC) and the punch-marked coins have been supposed to have been put in hoards much later than the original date of their circulation. The geographical implications of these occurrences have been discussed in each case. An important point which emerges is that the Pandyan territory was likely to be the earliest early historic area of Tamil Nadu, a point made plausible by the antiquity of pearl-fishery in the Gulf of Mannar and the occurrence of NBP at Alagankulam and Korkai.

In the next section, the archaeological background of the early historical development in Tamil Nadu and Kerala has been briefly examined, pointing out a continuity of sequence between the Iron Age settlements and burials which date from the second millennium BC and the beginning of the early historic period.

4. The next emphasis of our discussion is on the excavated coastal and inland sites of Tamil Nadu and Kerala with reference to their dynastic and maritime contexts. The Pandyan power interacted with the Cholas, Cheras and the Tondaiman or Pallava territory, and through the Pallava territory, with the Western Chalukyas and Rashtrakutas of south Deccan, and the Hoyasalas of the Mysore plateau. The contact with Sri Lanka was a feature common to all the South Indian power groups. In the case of the Pandyas, we examine the geographical linkages of Madura. In Kerala, they led to Kottayam through Bodinayakkarur, to Alwaye through Periyakulam, and to Quilon through the Shencottah gap. In Tamil Nadu, Madura was well-linked with several areas including Uraiyur. The major excavated sites of the Pandya territory are Alagankulam and Korkai, and according to our analysis, the beginning of their early historic period falls in the first half of the first millennium BC. We also argued that the presence

of the NBP at these two sites was possibly due to maritime contact with Gangetic India.

The maritime contacts of the Cholas with Southeast Asia, Sri Lanka, the Maldives, the Laccadives and the Nicobar group of islands are well-known, but in the peninsula their main thrust of power was towards south Deccan and the Andhra coast. From south Deccan they once moved up to Kolhapur, and from the Andhra coast they dominated Orissa and ventured up to the Ganges in Bengal. The major excavated inland site of the Chola territory was its early capital Uraiyur and the major excavated coastal site is Kaveripattinam.

Till the 9th century AD, the Pallavas of the Tondaiman territory were a major force, interacting with south Deccan, Andhra, the Mysore plateau and the area further south. In the subsequent periods, the Pallava territory was a corridor of movement from the deep south to the areas lying to the north. Three major ancient places occur in this territory: Kanchipuram whose port site was Vasavasamudram (near Sadras), Mahabalipuram and Mylapuram.

5. The early ports of the Coromandel coast had a large number of successors in the mediaeval and still later contexts. S.J. Stephen's list of mediaeval ports on the Coromandel coast, beginning with those in the Tamraparni mouth, included Virapandiyanpattinam, Kayal, Tuticorin (Tamraparni); Kilakkarai (Vaigai), Nagapattinam, Nagore, Thirumalairayanpattinam (Kaveri); Cuddalore, Devanampattinam, Kunimedu, Marakkanam, Sadurangapattinam (Ponnaiyar), and Pulicat. The list partly overlaps with S. Arasaratnam's list of 17th century ports. Whether in the ancient context the coastal ports were linked to the productive centres of weaving, etc. on the model of the links between the coast and the inland weaving centres of the mediaeval and pre-modern periods cannot be ascertained, but the possibility is very much there, and one can expect the various routes of communication between the coast and the interior in the ancient context as well.

6. In the Chera territory, Karur and Muziris or Pattanam at the mouth of the Periyar River are the main sites, although one cannot be sure that Karur was the only capital of the Cheras. The maritime significance of Kerala is amply highlighted by later inscriptions, including those of Sthanu Ravi (9th century) and Vira Raghava (13th century). Two lists of coastal ports of Kerala are significant: the list given by the *Periplus* (Naoura or Cannanore, Tundis or Tanor, Muziris or Pattanam, Nelkunda or Kottayam, Bakare or Vakkarai, Balita or Trivandrum and Komar or Cape Comorin), and the list given by Tome Pires (Manjeswaram, Mayporum,

Kumbla, Kattakulam, Nileshveram, Hyeri, Baliapatam, Cannanore, Durmapatan, Madayid, Chombakulu, Puthupattanam, Tricodi, Bairacono, Kollam, Kapatta, Calicut, Chaliyam, Parappanangadi, Tanor, Ponnanai, Velankode, Chetwayi, Kranganur, Cochin, Kayankulam, Quilon, Vilinjam and Comorin).

7. In the case of Tamil Nadu, the question of the general alignments of routes has also been highlighted by R. Champakalakshmi's series of maps detailing the history of urban processes in Tamil Nadu between the early historic period and c. 13th century AD.

3. THE BASIC STRUCTURE OF THE CHAPTER ON ANDHRA

1. The section on the elements of geography underline Andhra's different geographical linkages: the Kanchipuram sector of Tamil Nadu, the Bellary-Gulbarga-Bidar-Bijapur section of Karnataka, and through this section of Karnataka, the part of Maharashtra which lies immediately to the east of the Western Ghats, the Aurangabad-Daulatabad area of Maharashtra through Nanded, the eastern or the Vidarbha part of Maharashtra through Karimnagar and Adilabad, the southwestern Orissa and Chhattisgarh from Vizianagram and, finally, the whole of the coastal sweep of eastern India up to the Bhagirathi from Srikakulam. All these areas have played direct or indirect roles in Andhra's political history. The Andhra coast was the terminal point of the routes which came from the direction of the Ganga plain through Vidarbha and South Kosala and came from the upper Godavari valley site of Paithan via Nanded.

2. G. Jouveau-Dubreuil considered Vengi 'a great meeting place of roads' and five 'great routes' – the roads to Kalinga, Dravida, Karnataka and Maharashtra – supposedly converged upon that place. We have argued that Vengi might not have been the only focal point of Andhra's communication network but it was certainly one of its major points.

3. The beginning of the early historic period in Andhra has been assessed in terms of the pre-Mauryan date of the spread of Buddhism to Andhra and the pre-Mauryan antiquity of the Amaravati *stupa*. The pre-Mauryan date of the spread of Buddhism is indicated by the early date of the NBP at Vaddamanu and Amaravati, the existence of a pre-Asokan *stupa* at Amaravati as indicated by the representation of a simple *stupa* structure on a Mauryan period relief fragment from the site, and by the location of the ancient Asmaka territory (mentioned in the Suttanipata) in the Kotilingala and Bodhan sections of northern Andhra. The Mauryan period relief fragment from Amaravati unequivocally suggests the existence of a

pre-Asokan *stupa* at the site, and the inscribed relic caskets from Bhottiprolu date, equally unequivocally, from at least the Maurya period. The collective evidence, when considered in the light of the hypothesis that the NBP in Andhra is not much later than the NBP of the Gangetic valley, suggests that the beginning of the early historic period in Andhra cannot be later than c. 500 BC.

4. This section briefly comments on the political history of Andhra, emphasizing that the lines of the political boundaries of Andhra had been interacting and fluid.

5. Concerned with the distribution of historical sites, inclusive of the Buddhist monastic sites, this section offers an area-wise inventory of at least the major reported sites, some of which have been excavated. The excavated data have been incorporated in the main text. The varying density of early historic site distribution has been clearly highlighted.

6. In addition to Ptolemy's mid-second century AD references to the ports of Manarphe, Kottis (Kottapatnam), Maisolia (Masulipatam), Kontakassyla (Ghantasala), Kaddoura (Koduru) and Allosygne (near Kakinada), Milburn in the 18th century offers a list of ports north of Pulicat: Armagon or Duvaspattam, Motapilly (near Chhinnaganjam), Nizamapatnam, Pettapollee, Masulipatam, Yunan (on the Coringa bay), Jaggernautpuram, Visakhapatnam, Bimlipatnam and Kalingapatnam. A number of other ports have been listed in the Nelloresection of the coast.

6. On the basis of the evidence discussed in the foregoing sections, this section examines the basic route alignments of Andhra, section by section beginning with the lines coming from the side of Vidarbha. The link-up with the Aurangabad area of Maharashtra is also obvious, and equally importantly, one has to draw attention to the trunk line coming from the general direction of Paithan and Gulbarga and proceeding in the direction of Bellary and further south in Karnataka and eventually to Tamil Nadu through the area of Chittoor. From the Godavari valley, the routes go to both Vidarbha and South Kosala.

The routes which move in the direction of the Deccan from the Ganga-Yamuna plain do not end in the Deccan itself but throw further lines connecting virtually the whole of peninsular India from north Konkan to Cape Comorin, with many variations of their own.

Bibliography

Abraham, Meera. 1988. *Two Mediaeval Merchant Guilds of South India*. Delhi: Manohar Publications.

Arasaratnam, S. 1986. *Merchants, Companies and Commerce on the Coromandel Coast*. Delhi: Oxford University Press.

Arunachalam, T., B. Sukumar and R. Sukumar. 2006. Reconstruction of the ancient port Korkai in Tuttukudi district of Tamil Nadu. *Current Science* 91(3): 278-280.

Babu, B.S.R. 1999. *Material Culture of Deccan (with Special Reference to Satavahana-Ikshvaku Period)*. Delhi: Agam Kala Prakashan.

Buhler, G. 1894. The Bhottiprolu inscriptions. *Epigraphia Indica* 2, pp. 323-329.

———. 1894-95. The Siddapur edicts of Asoka. *Epigraphia Indica* 3, pp. 134-142.

Chakrabarti, Dilip K. 1997. *The Archaeology of the Ancient Indian Cities*. Delhi: Oxford University Press (paperback).

———. 2005. *The Archaeology of the Deccan Routes. The Routes which Linked the Ganga Plain with the Deccan*. Delhi: Munshiram Manoharlal.

———. 2006. *The Oxford Companion to Indian Archaeology. The Archaeological Foundations of Ancient India. Stone Age to AD 13th Century*. Delhi: Oxford University Press.

Chakrabarti, Dilip K. and Nayanjot Lahiri. 1996. *Copper and Its Alloys in Ancient India*. Delhi: Munshiram Manoharlal.

Chakravarti, N.P. 1948. The minor rock-edicts of Asoka and some connected problems. *Ancient India* 4, pp. 15-25.

Chakravarti, Ranabir. 1986. Merchants of Konkan. *The Indian Economic and Social History Review* (hereafter cited as *IESHR*). Vol. 23, pp. 207-215.

———. 1990. Monarchs, merchants and a 'matha' in northern Konkan (c. AD 900-1053). *IESHR*, Vol. 27, pp. 189-208.

———. 1992. Horse trade and piracy at Tana (Thana, Maharashtra, India): Gleanings from Marco Polo. *Journal of the Economic and Social History of the Orient* 34, pp. 159-182.

______. 1996. The export of Sindani indigo from India to the 'west' in the eleventh century. *The Indian Historical Review* 18(1-2): 18-30.

______. 2000. Nakhudas and Nauvittakas: Ship-owning merchants in the west coast of India (c. AD 1000-1500). *Journal of the Economic and Social History of the Orient* 43, pp. 34- 64.

Champakalakshmi, R. 1996. *Trade, Ideology and Urbanization: South India 300 BC to AD 1300*. Delhi: Oxford University Press.

Chhabra, B.C. and G.S. Gai (eds.). 1981. *Inscriptions of the Early Gupta Kings, Corpus Inscriptionum Indicarum*. Vol. III. Delhi: Archaeological Survey of India.

Cortesao, A. 1944. *The Suma Oriental of Tome Pires*. London: The Hakluyt Society.

Cox, A.F. 1881. *A Manual of North Arcot*. Madras: Government Press.

Crooke, W. 1925. *Travels in India by Jean-Baptiste Tavernier*. Vol. I. London: Oxford University Press.

Deotare, B. *et al.* 2007. Discovery of structural stupa at Bhon, district Buldana, Maharashtra. *Puratattva*, no. 37, pp. 176-185.

Deshpande, C.D. 1971. *Geography of Maharashtra*. Delhi: National Book Trust.

Digby, S. 1980. The maritime trade of India. In, T.C. Raychaudhuri and I. Habib (eds.). *The Cambridge Economic History of India, c.1200-c.1750*. Vol. I. Delhi: Orient Longman, pp. 125-182.

Elliot, H.M. and J. Dowson. 1897. *The History of India as Told by Its Own Historians. The Mohammadan Period*. Vol. 1. London: Trubner and Co.

Falk, H. 2006. *Asokan Sites and Artefacts*. Mainz: Von Zabern.

Fawcett, C. 1947. *The Travels of Abbe Carre in India and the Near East, 1672-1674*. Vol. 1. London: The Hakluyt Society.

Fleet, J.F. 1894-95. Chiplun copper plate grant of Pulakesin II. *Epigraphia Indica* 3, pp. 30-33.

______. 1901. Tagara, Ter. *The Journal of the Royal Asiatic Society of Great Britain and Ireland*, pp. 537-552.

______. 1909. The last words of Asoka. *The Journal of the Royal Asiatic Society of Great Britain and Ireland*, pp. 980-1016.

Fogelin, L. 2006. *Archaeology of Early Buddhism*. New York: Altamira Press.

Gaur, A.S. *et al.* 2007. New evidence on the maritime activity at Dabhol on the Maharashtra coast. *Puratattva*, no. 37, pp. 186-192.

Ghate, Savita. 2007. Geomorphic and environmental changes around Sopara: An early historic port site in north Konkan, Maharashtra: A review. *Man and Environment* 32(1): 74-88.

Ghosh, A. 1989. *Encyclopaedia of Indian Archaeology*. Vol. II. Delhi: Munshiram Manoharlal.

______. (ed.). 1989. *Encyclopaedia of Indian Archaeology*. Vol. 2. Delhi: Munshiram Manoharlal.

Ghosh, N.C. 1986. *Excavations at Satanikota, 1977-80*. Delhi: Archaeological Survey of India.

Gogte, V.D. *et al.* 2006. The ancient port of Chaul. *Journal of Indian Ocean Archaeology*, no. 3, pp. 62-80.

______. 2004. Discovery of an ancient port: Palaepatmai of the Periplus on the west coast of India. *Journal of Indian Ocean Archaeology,* no. 1, pp. 124-132.

Goitein, S.D. and M.A. Friedman. 2008. *India Traders of the Middle Ages, Documents from the Cairo Geniza ('India Book').* Leiden: Brill.

Gokhale, Sobhana. 1991. *Kanheri Inscriptions*. Pune: Deccan College.

______. 2004. Coins found in the excavations at Sanjan-2002. *Journal of Indian Ocean Archaeology,* no. 2, pp. 107-112.

Gune, V.T. (ed.). 1979. *Gazetteer of the Union Territory of Goa, Daman and Diu*. Panaji: Govt. Printing Press.

Gupta, P. 1973. *Geography in Ancient Indian Inscriptions*. Delhi: D.K. Publishing House.

Gupta, S.P. *et al.* 2001-2002. A preliminary report on the excavations at Sanjan (2002). *Puratattva,* no. 32, pp. 182-198.

______. *et al.* 2004. On the footsteps of Zorastrian Parsis in India: Excavations at Sanjan on the west coast. 2003. *Journal of Indian Ocean Archaeology,* no. 2, pp. 93-106.

Hemalatha, B. 1991. *Life in Mediaeval Northern Andhra*. Delhi: Navrang.

Hodivala, S.H. 1920. *Studies in Parsi History*. Bombay: The author, pp. 82-117.

Howell, J. and A.K. Sinha. 1994. Preliminary report on the explorations around Sopara, Surat and Bharuch. *South Asian Studies* 10, pp. 189-199.

Hultzsch, E. 1900-01. Mayidavolu plates of Sivaskandavarman. *Epigraphia Indica* 6, pp. 84-89.

______. 1925. *Inscriptions of Asoka, Corpus Inscriptionum Indicarum.* Vol. I. Oxford: Government of India.

Huntingford, G. 1980. *The Periplus of the Erythraean Sea*. London: The Hakluyt Society.

Indraji, B.L. 1881-82. Sopara. *The Journal of the Bombay Branch of the Royal Asiatic Society* 15, pp. 273-328.

Jadhav, S. 2006. A preliminary report of excavation at the Satavahana site of Junnar, district Pune, Maharashtra. *Man and Environment* 31(1): 108-113.

Joglekar, P.P. *et al.* 2003-2004. A preliminary report on the early historic site at Shirwal in Satara district, Maharashtra. *Puratattva,* no. 34, pp. 127-137.

Jouveau-Dubreuil, G. 1920. *Ancient History of the Deccan*. Pondicherry.

______. 1981 (reprint of the 1927 edition). Foreword. In, Subramanian 1981, pp. v-x.

Kamath, S. (ed.). 1985. *Uttara Kannada District Gazetteer*. Mysore: Govt. of Karnataka.

Khandalavala, Karl. 1960. Brahmapuri. *Lalitkala* 7, pp. 29-75.

Kielhorn, F. 1894-95. Kharepatan plates of Rattaraja; Saka-Sambat 930. *Epigraphia Indica,* Vol. 3, pp. 292-304.

Lal, B.B. 1949. Sisupalgarh 1948: An early historical fort in eastern India. *Ancient India* 5, pp. 62-105.

Logan, W. 1887. *Malabar Manual*. Madras: Government Press.

Luders, H. 1912. *A List of Brahmi Inscriptions from the Earliest Times to about AD 400 with the Exception of those of Asoka, Appendix to Epigraphia Indica.* Vol. 10. Calcutta: Government of India.

Mahedevan, I. 2003. *Early Tamil Epigraphy. From the Earliest Times to the Sixth Century AD*. Chennai: Crea-A.

Mangalam, S.J. 1986. *Historical Geography and Toponomy of Andhra Pradesh*. Delhi: Sundeep Prakashan.

Mathew, K.S. (ed.). 1995. *Mariners, Merchants and Oceans: Studies in Maritime History*. Delhi: Manohar.

McCrindle, J.W. 1926. *Ancient India as Described by Megasthenes and Arrian*. Calcutta: Thacker, Spink.

Milburn, W. 1813. *Oriental Commerce*. Vol. II. London: Black, Parry, and Co.

Mitchiner, M. 1995. *Coin Circulation in Southernmost India*. Anjaneri: Indian Institute of Research in Numismatic Studies.

Nagaraju, S. 1981. *Buddhist Architecture of Western India, c. 250 BC-AD 300*. Delhi: Agam Kala Prakashan.

Nagaswamy, R. 1995. *Roman Karur*. Chennai: Brahadish Publications.

Parthasarathy, T.A. 2003 (reprint of 1884 edition). *South Kanara by Sturrock*. Mysore: Government of Karnataka.

Patil, C.B. 2006. Man-land relationships in ancient coastal Karnataka. *Man and Environment* 31(1): 40-47.

Prasad, E.S.M. 1997. *Studies in the Natural, Historical and Cultural Geography and Ethnography of the Coastal Andhra (Based on the Inscriptions from the Earliest to 1325 AD)*. Delhi: Bharatiya Book Corporation.

Rajagopal, M.V. 1977. *Andhra Pradesh District Gazetteers, Guntur*. Hyderabad: Government of Andhra Pradesh.

Rajan, K. 1997. *Archaeological Gazetteer of Tamil Nadu*. Thanjavur: Manoo Patthippakam.

Rajan, K., N. Athiyaman and P. Jayakumar. 2004. Excavation at Mayiladumparai. *Man and Environment* 29(2): 74-89.

Ramesan, N. (ed.). 1979. *Andhra Pradesh District Gazetteers, Chittoor*. Hyderabad: Government of Andhra Pradesh.

Rao, Hanumantha *et al.* 1998. *Buddhist Inscriptions of Andhradesa*. Secunderabad: Ananda Buddha Vihar Trust.

Rao, K.P. 1999. Ports of the Satavahana period. In, A.M. Sastri (ed.). *The Age of the Satavahanas*. Delhi: Aryan Books, pp. 445-459.

Raychaudhuri, H.C. 1960. The geography of the Deccan. In, G. Yazdani (ed.). *Early History of the Deccan*. Vol. 1. Oxford: Oxford University Press, pp. 1-65.

Richards, F.J. 1918. *Salem District Gazetteer*. Vol. I. Madras: Government Press.

Sankaranarayana, B. (ed.). 1967. *Andhra Pradesh District Gazetteers, Cuddapah*. Hyderabad: Government of Andhra Pradesh.

———. 1970. *Andhra Pradesh District Gazetteers, Anantapur*. Hyderabad: Government of Andhra Pradesh.

Sarma, I.K. 1988. *Studies in Early Buddhist Monuments and Brahmi Inscriptions of Andhradesa*. Nagpur: Dattsons.

———. 1994. *Parasuramesvara Temple at Gudimallam (a Probe into Its Origins)*. Nagpur: Dattsons.

Sarma, I.K. and J.V. Rao. 1993. *Early Brahmi Inscriptions from Sannati*. Delhi: Harman Publishing House.

Sastri, K.A.N. 1935. *The Cholas*. Madras: University of Madras.

Sastry, V.V. Krishna. 1983. *The Proto- and Early Historical Cultures of Andhra Pradesh*. Hyderabad: Government of Andhra Pradesh.

Scott, F.H. 1853. *Routes in the Peninsula of India Comprising the Whole of the Madras Presidency and Portions of the Adjacent Territories of Bengal and Bihar*. Madras: Messers Pharoah and Co.

Sen, S.P. (ed.). 1949. *Indian Travels of Thevenot and Careri*. New Delhi: Indian Records Series.

Senart, E. 1905-06. The inscriptions in the caves at Nasik. *Epigraphia Indica*. Vol. 8, pp. 59-96.

Sewell, Robert. 1924. *A Forgotten Empire: Vijayanagar*. London: Allen and Unwin.

Shamasastry, R. 1923. *Kautilya's Arthasastra*. Mysore: Wesleyan Mission Press.

Shinde, V. *et al.* 2002-2003. New light on the history of Pune city: Results of an archaeological rescue excavation. *Puratattva*, no. 33, pp. 52-62.

______. *et al.* 2003-2004. A Satavahana period shrine of Laxmi-Parvati at Siddhapur, district Solapur, Maharashtra. *Man and Environment* 29(2): 117.

Shinde, V., S. Gupta and D. Rajgor. 2002. An archaeological reconnaissance of the Konkan coast from Bharuch to Janjira. *Man and Environment* 27(1): 73-82.

Sircar, D.C. 1962a. Rashtrakuta charters from Chinchani. *Epigraphia Indica*, Vol. 32, pp. 45-60.

______. 1962b. Three grants from Chinchani. *Epigraphia Indica*. Vol. 32, pp. 61-74.

______. 1963. Nagarjunakonda inscription of the time of Abhira Vasushena, year 30. *Epigraphia Indica*, Vol. 34, pp. 196-204.

______. 1983. *Select Inscriptions*. Vol. II. Delhi: Motilal Banarsidass.

______. 1979/2000. *Asokan Studies*. Calcutta: Indian Museum.

Soundararajan, K.V. (ed.). 2006. *Nagarjunakonda (1954-60): The Historical Period*. Vol. II. Delhi: Archaeological Survey of India.

Sreenivasachar, P. 1940. *A Corpus of Inscriptions in the Telingana Districts of H.E.H. The Nizam's Dominions*. Part II. Hyderabad. L H.E.H. The Nizam's Government.

______. 1956. *A Corpus of Inscriptions in the Telingana Districts of H.E.H. The Nizam's Dominions*. Part III. Hyderabad: Government of Andhra Pradesh.

Sridhar, T.S. 2005. *Alagankulam: Ancient Roman port city of Tamil Nadu*. Chennai: Department of Archaeology, Government of Tamil Nadu.

Stephen, S.J. 1998. *Portuguese in the Tamil Coast: Historical Explorations in Commerce and Culture (1507-1749)*. Pondicherry: Navajothi.

Sturrock, J. 1894. *Madras District Manuals, South Kanara*. Madras: Govt. Printing Press.

Subrahmanyam, B. 1999. *Buddhist Relic Caskets in Andhradesa*. Secunderabad: Ananda Buddha Vihara Trust.

Subramanian, K.S. 1981 (reprint of the 1927 edition). *Buddhist Remains in South India and Early Andhra History, 225 AD to 610 AD*. Delhi: Cosmo Publications.

Suresh, S. 2007. *Arikamedu: Its Place in the Ancient Rome-India Contacts*. Delhi: Embassy of Italy.

Taddei, M. 2000. A note on some luxury artefacts imported from Andhra into Gandhara. *Silk Road Art and Archaeology* 6, pp. 5-7.

Tripathi, A. 2004. Onshore and offshore exploration in Elephanta island: Evidence of Indo-Mediterranean trade. *Journal of Indian Ocean Archaeology*, no. 1, pp. 116-123.

Upadhyay, B.S. 1991. *Buddha-kalin Bharatiya Bhugol* (in Hindi). Allahabad: Hindi Sahitya Sammelan.

Venkayya, V. 1911. Five Bana inscriptions from Gudimallam. *Epigraphia Indica* 11, pp. 222-240.

Vogel, J.Ph. 1929-30. Prakrit inscriptions from a Buddhist site at Nagarjunakonda. *Epigraphia Indica* 20, pp. 1-36.

Wheeler, R.E.M. 1948. Brahmagiri and Chandravalli 1947. *Ancient India* 4, pp. 180-310.

Yule, H. 1903. *Hobson-Jobson*. London: J. Murray.

Index